TRADITIONAL TEXTILES OF THE ANDES

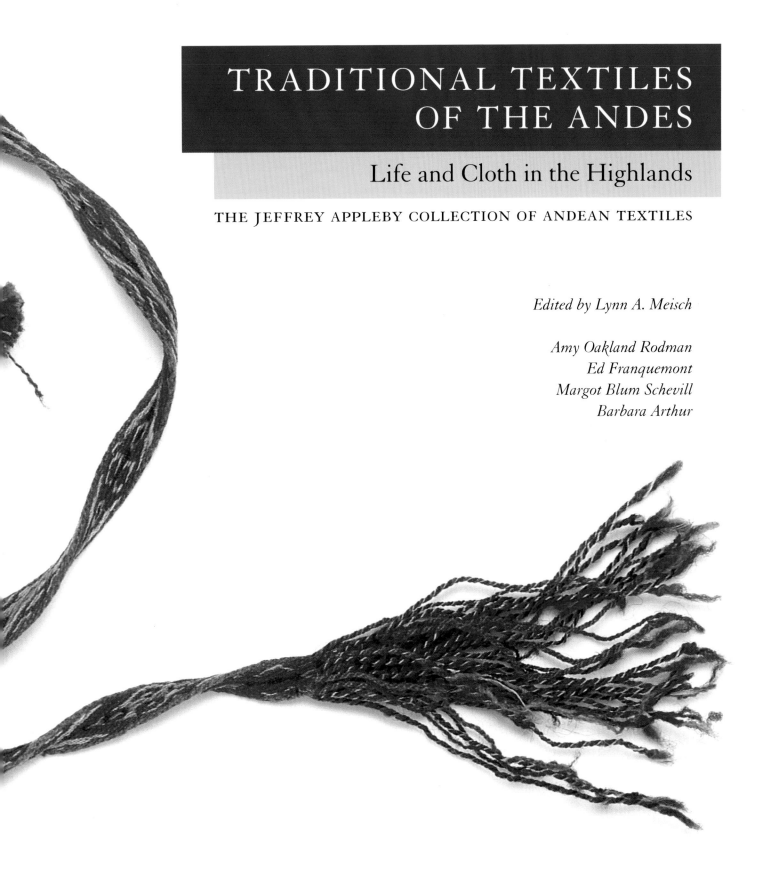

TRADITIONAL TEXTILES OF THE ANDES

Life and Cloth in the Highlands

THE JEFFREY APPLEBY COLLECTION OF ANDEAN TEXTILES

Edited by Lynn A. Meisch

Amy Oakland Rodman
Ed Franquemont
Margot Blum Schevill
Barbara Arthur

THAMES AND HUDSON
FINE ARTS MUSEUMS OF SAN FRANCISCO

This book has been published in conjunction with the exhibition *To Honor the Ancestors: Life and Cloth in the Andes.*

Fine Arts Museums of San Francisco
M. H. de Young Memorial Museum
21 June–19 October 1997

Published with the assistance of the Andrew W. Mellon Foundation Endowment for Publications and additional support from Jeffrey Appleby.

First published in the United States of America in paperback in 1997 by Thames and Hudson Inc., 500 Fifth Avenue, New York, New York 10110

First published in Great Britain in 1997 by Thames and Hudson Ltd, London

Library of Congress Catalog Card Number 97-60320

British Library Cataloguing-in-Publication Data
A catalogue record for this book is available from the British Library.

ISBN: 0-500-27985-3

Printed and bound in Italy

FRONT COVER:
Poncho *(poncho),* 1830, cat. no 155.

BACK COVER:
Woman's mantle *(llijlla),* ca. 1970, cat. no. 2.

TITLE PAGE:
Hair tie *(wata, watana),* mid-20th century, cat. no. 208.

CONTENTS

FOREWORD

Ethnographic textiles are among the fastest growing and most vital collections at the Fine Arts Museums of San Francisco. As often happens in museums, this previously modest collecting area was transformed by an important gift, the Caroline and H. McCoy Jones Collection of more than seven hundred Near Eastern and Central Asian carpets and other textiles, which arrived in San Francisco nearly twenty years ago. In 1992 Jeffrey Appleby brought a similar energy to the Museums with his substantial gift of fine Andean textiles. Textiles are arguably the most important art form among the indigenous peoples of the Andes, and the beautiful and powerful pieces in the Appleby collection represent textile traditions that stretch back to the earliest Andean cultures and continue through the colonial era. The acquisition of the Appleby collection has allowed us to create the contemporary context for this ancient art.

An undertaking such as this catalogue and its accompanying exhibition is the work of many people. Cathryn Cootner, formerly Curator of Textiles, and James Blackmon were instrumental in bringing the Appleby Collection to the Museums. Melissa Leventon, Curator of Textiles, and Diane Mott, Associate Curator of Textiles, have ably continued the work Cootner began, assisted by textile department volunteers Laura Erdos Fernandez, Alice Glasser, and Chana Motobu. The conservation and preservation work on the collection, under the supervision of Textile Conservator, Sarah Gates, has been spearheaded by textile conservation volunteers Barbara Arthur and Barbara Nitzberg, with the assistance of Lynn Armstrong, Jeanne Bean, Janet Glessner, Kathy Murphy, Zoe Pettijohn, Jean Scardina, Elise Schlick, and Tamsen Schwartzman. Barbara Arthur deserves special thanks for the many hours she devoted to assisting Margot Blum Schevill with cataloguing the collection. Schevill was also assisted by Wendy Berkelman and Tim Wells, and a number of scholars acknowledged by her elsewhere in the catalogue, and to whom the Museums are also grateful.

As always, William White, Director of Exhibition and Technical Production, has designed a handsome exhibition, which was expertly installed by Principal Technician Robert Haycock; Senior Technicians Everet Thomas, Margaret Thomas, and Rick Wilds; and Technicians Richard Biernacki and Delores Fontaine. Ron Rick, Chief Graphic Designer, Constance King, Senior Graphic Designer, and Dina Bernardin, Graphic Designer, have also contributed greatly to the exhibition's appearance. Kathe Hodgson, Coordinator of Exhibitions, helped keep the project running smoothly.

We are grateful to Mr. Appleby for his generous gift and for his contribution to the production of this catalogue; we also acknowledge funding from the Andrew W. Mellon Foundation Endowment for Publications and a grant from the National Endowment for the Arts, a Federal agency, for the cataloguing and photography of the collection.

HARRY S. PARKER III
Director of Museums
Fine Arts Museums of San Francisco

COLOMBIA

Mariana
Acosta
● Otavalo
★ Quito

ECUADOR

● Riobamba

Cañar

PERU

BRAZIL

Amazon River

HUÁNUCO

PASCO

Junín
● JUNÍN

★ Lima

CUZCO

Urubamba ● Calca
● ● ● Paurcatambo
▲ Cuzco
Cotabambas ●
APURÍMAC

LA PAZ

BOLIVIA

PUNO

● Charazani

Puno ● Ayata

Lake Titicaca

COCHABAMBA

Juli ● ▲ ★ La Paz

Cochabamba

PACIFIC OCEAN

Tiahuanaco ●
Achiri ● Calamarca
Sicasica ●

● Leque
● Challa
● Bolívar

● Oruro

● Macha

● Potolo
● Sucre

MOQUEGUA

Atacama Desert

Altiplano

ORURO

Potosí ●

● Tarabuco

CHILE

POTOSÍ

CHUQUISACA

- - **COUNTRY**
...... DEPARTMENT
● Town
★ Capital
▲ Weaving center and archaeological site
Andes Mountains

TO HONOR THE ANCESTORS: LIFE AND CLOTH IN THE ANDES

BY
LYNN A. MEISCH

Andean societies are among the most textile-oriented cultures in the world. The de Young Museum is fortunate to own especially fine examples of Andean textile artistry in the Jeffrey Appleby textile collection. These textiles, most dating from the nineteenth and twentieth centuries, but some from the colonial era, come from the modern countries of Argentina, Bolivia, Chile, Ecuador, and Peru, which formed part of the Inca empire in the fourteenth and fifteenth centuries (see map).

The word *Andes* refers to the second highest mountain range in the world, as well as to the surrounding region. The Andean *cordilleras* run like a spine down the South American continent, separating the Pacific coast, with its mangrove swamps in Ecuador and dry deserts in Peru and northern Chile, from the tropical rain forests of the Amazon basin (fig. 1). It is a region of dramatic contrasts and stunning beauty, home in ancient and modern times to a plethora of ethnic groups, cultures, and great civilizations that traded their raw materials and finished products, including textiles, across ecological zones.

It is difficult for outsiders to comprehend the importance of textiles to early and modern Andean people. In pre-Hispanic cultures, cloth and costume conveyed ethnic identity, wealth, social rank, marital status, age, and gender. Long before the Inca expansion, costume was used to mark ethnic affiliation, but the Incas mandated that the groups they conquered preserve their costume, especially their headdress and hairstyle, as a way to identify and control them (Cobo 1979 [1653], 190). The use of a distinctive hat or hairstyle to indicate a person's community continues to this day in many places (fig. 2).

In the Inca empire, weavings of the highest quality were sacrificed as offerings, woven for the dead, exchanged at important milestones in life, bestowed by the Incas as an honor, and supplied to the Inca state as tribute (Murra 1962). Chosen women (Q. *akllakuna*)[1] devoted their lives to spinning and weaving for the sun and the Inca state. When the Incas conducted a census of their empire and knotted the results on their counting strings (Q. *kipus*), they listed humans first, camelids (guanacos, vicuñas, llamas, and alpacas) second, textiles third, and ceramics fourth, before precious metals, gemstones, food supplies, and other important goods (Murra 1982). In many indigenous communities today the use of traditional clothing symbolizes a person's status as a civilized human being, and this is expressed in the Quechua languages. In Peru, a white or mestizo, the opposite of an indigenous person, is called *q'ara,* which is translated as "naked, uncultured, or uncivilized" (Mannheim 1991, 19). In Zumbagua, in Cotopaxi, Ecuador, old men call "young men *lluchu* ('naked' or 'skinned') if they dare walk publicly in the parish without poncho and hat" (Weismantel 1988, 7).

The Spanish influenced traditional dress in various ways after their invasion of the Andes in A.D. 1532, and subsequent conquest. They introduced new fibers (sheep's wool and silk) and new tools (carders, the spinning wheel, and treadle loom). Initially the Spanish prohibited *indígenas* from wearing European-style clothing in order to mark them as subordinate. After the great Andean rebellions

FIGURE 2
Little girl wearing a *montera* (S. brimmed hat), Isla Amantaní, Lake Titicaca, Peru. (Photo: Lynn Meisch)

FIGURE 3
Relatives of Mariana Chuquín (*l. to r.*, Nieves Pupiales, Manuel Pupiales, and Filomena Chuquín) in traditional dress, La Rinconada, Imbabura, Ecuador. (Photo: Lynn Meisch)

between 1780 and 1782, such garments as the *unku* (Q. tunic) and *llautu* (Q. Inca headgear), which symbolized Inca nationalism, were outlawed, but distinctive dress, whatever its components, has long served as an ethnic marker to distinguish the metaphorically clothed and civilized *indígenas* from naked and uncultured mestizos, whites, and Amazon rain forest dwellers.

During the colonial campaigns to extirpate idolatry in Peru, the Spanish learned that destroying the Andeans' wood or stone religious figures was not enough; they had to burn the cloth these statues were wrapped in (Arriaga 1968 [1621]). Clothes are still extremely important as emblems of identity, representing not only a person's community or ethnic group, but also his or her very essence. After a death in Abancay, Peru (Ackerman 1996 [1991]) and in Otavalo, Ecuador, ritual kin or relatives of a dead person wash all his or her bedding and clothes to rid these textiles of the person's smell, thus releasing the soul of the deceased. In Ayacucho, Peru, during the guerilla war between the Maoist group *Sendero Luminoso* (S. Shining Path) and the Peruvian government, families whose relatives were "disappeared" by either side held funerals with the missing person's clothing laid out in lieu of an actual body. A heartbreaking photograph of this practice was included on the cover of *1984 Peru Briefing,* published by Amnesty International.

Mariana Chuquín, an *indígena* (S. indigenous person) from Mariano Acosta in northern Ecuador, now living in San Francisco, told me that "traditional dress for us signifies our mother earth. We respect our ancestors who wore this dress when we wear it today. The dress of Mariano Acosta is sacred. It is completely handmade, requires much time to make, has an incomparable value, and cannot be bought or sold" (my translation from Spanish) (fig. 3). Breenan Conterón, an *indígena* from Ilumán, near Otavalo in northern Ecuador, also emphasized the connection between traditional dress and her ancestors: "I wear this dress every day, and when I leave my community and visit other cities in my country, Ecuador, I always wear this dress because in this way I honor and respect my ancestors, who fought to maintain their culture, tradition, and customs" (Meisch and Rowe, in press; my translation from Spanish).

Figure 4
Half an overskirt for mourning *(luto aksu),*
1950–1960; Quechua peoples. Tarabuco,
Chuquisaca, Bolivia. Catalogue no. 10.
(Appleby Collection 1992.107.136)

FIGURE 5
Melchora Vargas, of Chilla Apachita (near Candelaria), Tarabuco, Chuquisaca, Bolivia, weaving half of an *aksu* (Q. wrap skirt) on the frame loom. The white center stripe is the textile's heart, and the *chapuna,* a small, trapezoidal wooden tool, is near her foot. (Photo: Lynn Meisch)

Andean textiles have also been a medium for conceptualizing the world and for communicating complex ideas (Frame 1986; E. M. Franquemont 1986b). Complementary-warp weaves, in which two warp yarns are always paired and are essential to the structure of the fabric, embody the fundamental Andean concepts of reciprocity and complementarity. Frame has shown how early and modern Andeans visually pun with cloth by including representations of fabric structures within their textiles. For example, a pre-Hispanic tapestry contains images of twisted strands resembling plied yarn, and early turbans contain images of four-strand braids (Frame 1986, figures 19, 32).

The iconography of Andean textiles has long fascinated researchers. The motifs on many textiles are rich and complex and vary greatly among communities. In some places the motifs are simply customary or pleasing. They represent objects of everyday life (the sun, seeds, trees, birds, trains, rivers, even designs taken from children's school books, such as the elephants sometimes found on belts woven in Cañar, Ecuador), but do not carry heavy symbolic weight. In other communities, such as Choquecancha, Cuzco, Peru, the condor, feline, and serpent or toad motifs share the characteristics of ancient sky, earth, and water deities (Seibold 1992, 169–70). Many textiles in the department of Cuzco contain representations of feathered *ch'unchus* (Q. jungle dwellers), considered the opposite of civilized highlanders who wear clothes, a distinction that goes back to Inca times (Wilson 1996 [1991]).

In yet other communities, such as Tarabuco, Chuquisaca, Bolivia, the textiles represent a miniature world, with humans, land forms (the large plain-

weave areas are called the *pampa,* or plain [Q.], rivers, flora, fauna, and celestial motifs (Meisch 1986b, 1987a) (fig. 4). In Kaata, La Paz, Bolivia, the motifs of livestock, crops, and children on the headbands worn by women symbolize fertility (Bastien 1985 [1978], 13). Snail motifs have magical associations because snails carry their homes with them up and down the mountain and live on both land and water. Even the colors have meaning. On a Kaata poncho, wide red bands and bordering yellow, green, orange, and black stripes "represented the colors of the earth and sky blending together" (Ibid., 110). In other regions, colors have different meanings, and in some places they are simply "the custom."

In parts of the southern Andes today, weavers anthropomorphize cloth or textiles on the loom by giving them the names of human body parts. The center stripe is called the heart (Cereceda 1986; Meisch 1986b), and the side warps are called the mouth because they open and close to eat the wefts while the piece is being woven. The poor textile also suffers repeated blows on its heart from a tool called a *chapuna* (Q.) which is used to help change the sheds (fig. 5). The term comes from the Aymara verb *chapuña,* which means to hit someone with great force, usually in the chest (Meisch 1986b). Many Andean cultures distinguish grammatically between human and nonhuman, so giving textiles human characteristics elevates the cloth to the status of a living being. In fact, among the textiles given human body parts are little striped bags (A. *wayakas*) used to hold seeds, which literally contain the potential for new life.

Throughout the Andes, Aymara and Quechua speakers anthropomorphize such land forms as mountains, which are sacred and seen as having a head,

FIGURE 6
Woman spinning sheep's wool, Nitiluisa, Chimborazo, Ecuador. (Photo: Lynn Meisch)

FIGURE 7
Cañari weaver warping a belt, similar to the belt shown as catalogue no. 148. (Photo: Lynn Meisch)

bowels and heart, legs and toenails (Bastien 1985 [1978]; Carpenter 1982). The Aymara have "two bases or frames for naming shapes. The most general is pieces of cloth used in making clothing. The other basis for naming shapes is land forms" (Miracle and Yapita Maya 1981, 48). We say a shawl is shaped like a rectangle; the Aymara say a rectangle is shaped like a shawl. Humans, land, and cloth are sacred or holy and intimately related.

Spinning and weaving continue to be important in many communities, even as people in other areas prefer machine-made goods. When I finally learned to spin in Saraguro, Loja, Ecuador, my teachers said to me with obvious relief, "Now you are a woman; you can spin. Now you can get married." Although spinning is primarily females' work throughout the Andes (fig. 6), males sometimes spin, and in some regions, such as Cañar, Ecuador, males ply yarn. Warping and weaving using pre-Hispanic technology is primarily a female task in the southern Andes and a male one in north-central Peru, highland Ecuador, and parts of Colombia (fig. 7). There are also local variations in this pattern. In many communities weaving, like fine spinning, is still considered an essential skill for full participation in adult life. Alejandro Flores Huatta and his niece, Paula Quispe Cruz of Isla Taquile, Peru, who are both weavers, said,

> There are many weavers in Taquile. But not all women weave with the same skill. The finest weavers and weaving families are well known throughout the community. Each individual in Taquile wears the clothing identified with his or her own family. . . . All women must learn to weave before they are married; it is a requirement. (Flores Huatta and Quispe Cruz 1994, 168–70)

These weavers expressed the connection between textiles and their ancestors, as well as the sacred nature of cloth. They said of a wedding poncho, "This type of poncho must be used and it may be rented, but not loaned. . . . This poncho is sacred." (Ibid., 173)

The five contributors to this volume are spinners, weavers, designers, anthropologists, art historians, specialists in pre-Hispanic and ethnographic textiles, or some combination of the above. Amy Oakland Rodman traces the history of the highland weaving tradition, indicating the continuities and ruptures over millennia, especially in the vital southern Andes, the center of several great polities including Tiwanaku, later Aymara-speaking chiefdoms including the Colla and Lupaca, and the Incas.

Ed Franquemont, emphasizing that the true treasures of the Andes are the weavers themselves, raises important questions about the significance of museum collections and the effects of tourism and collecting on traditional textiles. His essay contributes to a growing body of work dealing with these questions (Stocking 1985; Messenger 1989; Price 1989; Vergo 1989; Karp and Lavine 1991; Karp, Kreamer, and Lavine 1992).

Andeans themselves are adding their voices to the discussion of cultural change and the preservation of their heritage. Aymara *indígenas,* consulting for the Museum of the American Indian in the United States, said:

One does not see the older type of weavings anymore, the ones with the combination of colors and large stripes. The modern young native generation is not interested anymore; they do not give any importance to those olden objects. . . . Yet our ancestors are still present and alive. Returning back home, we can weave exactly the same textiles as we see in the museum. These things are not that hard to do. (Quispe Fernández and Huanca Laura 1994, 149–50)

Margot Schevill, who analyzed and catalogued the collection, provides background on the collector and the collection, discussing how Appleby began the collection, and analyzing materials, techniques, and iconography.

In Ecuadorian Quichua, the word *ali* means both "good" and "slow." *Ali pacha,* good cloth, is both well made and slowly made, a concept that is the antithesis of our emphasis on speed and efficiency. Barbara Arthur examines the intricate, beautiful, and time-consuming finishing details with a weaver's appreciation of the work they entail. The textiles in the Appleby collection, representing countless hours of careful work, are indeed *ali pacha.*

---

1. The linguistic history of the Andes is complex, and most Andeans historically spoke several languages (Mannheim 1992), as do many people today. Two main indigenous languages are still spoken in the area represented by the Appleby collection. Aymara is used in the Andes of northern Chile and on the Bolivian and Peruvian altiplano including the Lake Titicaca region. The languages of the Quechua family, called Quichua in Ecuador, are spoken in northern Argentina, much of highland Bolivia, Peru, and Ecuador, and parts of Colombia and Brazil. Members of the tiny Chipaya ethnic group in Bolivia speak a language called Chipaya, and the Mapuche of southern Chile also speak an eponymous language. Many speakers of native languages speak Spanish as well.

The Andean languages were not written before the arrival of the Spanish, who used their own orthography to represent the sounds of native tongues, including phonemes, which have no Spanish equivalent. Spelling remains a controversial issue to this day. For example, the earliest Aymara dictionary lists "tunic" as *ccahua* (Bertonio 1984 [1612]); a modern dictionary spells it *khawa* (De Lucca 1983). We step squarely into this controversy by equivocating, using a phonemic alphabet in most instances and, in others, resorting to the more conventional or familiar spelling; Incas rather than Inkas. Readers should be aware that the spellings in many publications represent local usage or politically preferred orthographies, that some words have disappeared, new ones have taken their place, and the languages have borrowed from one another. In the interests of consistency, we have usually given only one spelling of a word and identify its origins by initials in parentheses: A.: Aymara; C.: Chipaya; M.: Mapuche; Q.: Quechua or Quichua; and S.: Spanish.

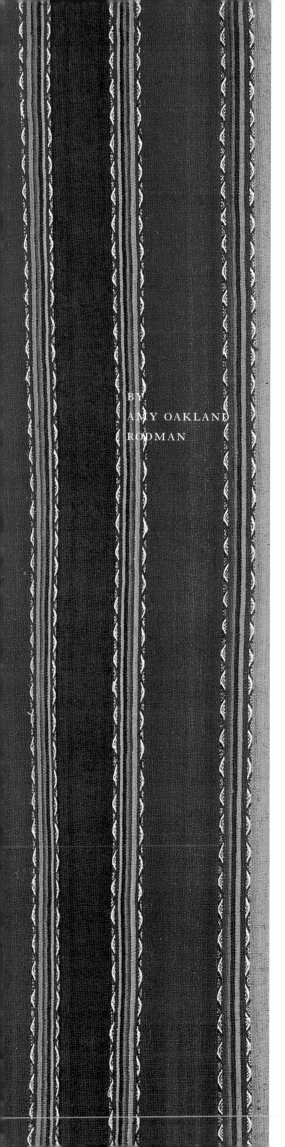

BY
AMY OAKLAND
RODMAN

WEAVING IN A HIGH LAND:
A CONTINUOUS TRADITION

The tradition of Andean highland weaving is elegant, ancient, and continuous. In South America, most archaeological textiles come from coastal cultures that developed in the arid regions along the Pacific Ocean. Early highland textiles have also been discovered, excavated along the desert coast, where they undoubtedly arrived by trade, and in protected caves in mountain valleys. It is now possible to discuss a separate highland textile tradition of the southern Andes, parallel to the traditions of the coast.

Fiber Sources

There has always been a ready supply of excellent fiber in South America. Inhabitants of the highlands favored the lustrous hair of the native American camelids, the guanaco and vicuña and the domesticated alpaca and llama (fig. 8). It is in this high, mountainous land that the llama was domesticated into an excellent pack animal whose hair was used for ropes, bags, and blankets, the alpaca was bred for a permanent fiber supply, and the vicuña's fine hair was coveted as the most highly prized fiber.

It is difficult to conceive of a period when Andean highlanders did not spin and weave camelid hair. Although it appears that weaving with a heddled loom appeared on the Peruvian coast during the second millennium b.c., fiber manufacture, cord, and net-making skills may have arrived with the first Americans sometime between twenty and twelve thousand years ago (Doyon-Bernard 1990; King 1978). South America's abundant resources provided more than one fiber source and separate textile traditions undoubtedly developed in different regions.

Fibers from plants such as *Furcrea* (a succulent, like the agave) were used by lowland tribes living in the wet regions of the eastern Andean slopes. Tribes living in this region today, and others in highland Ecuador and northeast Argentina, construct interlinked net bags and other cloth from native plants. Few archaeological textiles have survived in this moist climate, but collections in the archaeological museums of the universities of Sucre and Cochabamba, in Bolivia, do contain plant fiber net bags from highland archaeological sites, identifying early fiber traditions related to the eastern lowlands (Oakland 1986a).

Native Peruvian cotton was the principal fiber used by coastal dwellers. The coast of Peru and northern Chile is one of the driest deserts in the world, and these conditions have allowed for the preservation of large quantities of very early cotton textiles considered the foundation for South America's textile tradition (Bird and Mahler 1952; Bird, Hyslop, and Skinner 1985). Cotton grows today on the coast and in high valleys and is included in highland archaeological collections, but cotton was never the principal fiber choice in the highlands. Bright colors are difficult to achieve with dyes on cotton, but native Peruvian cotton exists in a variety of natural shades including white, cream, brown, red brown, and green grey (Vreeland 1986). Highlanders apparently discovered, even early on, that it is possible to dye camelid hair brilliant colors. Coastal

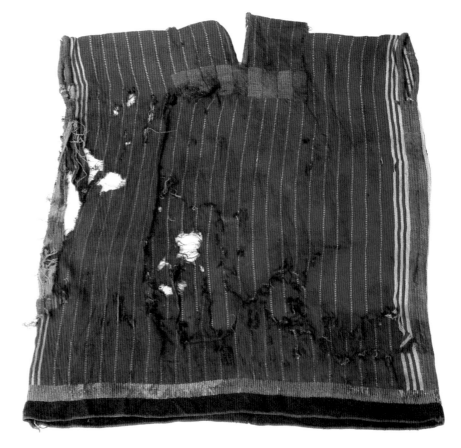

Andeans preferred predominantly cotton textiles decorated with slit-tapestry and weave structures patterned with the weft, the horizontal threads on a loom. The highland form of tapestry did not leave vertical slits, but was known for its tight interlocking weft threads, although most highland textiles were patterned with the warp, the loom's fixed set of vertical threads.

Spinning

Distinct spinning techniques appear to have separated highland and coastal traditions as well. Coastal cotton spinners used a fine spindle and whorl, which was rotated horizontally across the lap. Spinning off the tip of this spindle produces yarns with fibers aligned in a slant like that of the letter S. These S-spun yarns are almost always used as unplied yarn, but sometimes as doubled yarn by cotton weavers in northern Peru and Ecuador today (Meisch 1980b), a practice also noticed in ancient north-coast textiles (Rowe 1984).

Highland camelid fibers and sheep's wool today are spun differently, off the top of a drop-spindle, which produces yarns twisted in the opposite direction, slanting like the letter Z (fig. 9). These Z-spun yarns are always plied, producing a Z-spun, S-plied yarn (described as Z2S, meaning two Z-spun yarns plied in an S twist), a traditional yarn type found in virtually all yarns spun from camelid fiber both past and present.

Ancient Highland Textiles

Unfortunately, the earliest highland textiles are lost. Stone spear points and architectural features are all that remain from formative period highland archaeological sites in the south-central Andes (Bolivia, southern Peru, and northern Chile). Yarns spun from camelid hair and dating at least to the third millennium B.C. have been excavated in the Atacama Desert and further north along the Chilean desert coast (Dransart 1991; Rodman and True n.d.; True and Crew 1980). A variety of textile traditions existed along the Chilean north coast by the second millennium B.C. During this early Preceramic period in the southern Andes, several diverse cultures developed on the coast, along coastal rivers, and in the adjacent highlands.

Distinctive garment forms may have represented each culture even in this early period (Ulloa 1974, 1982). Cotton, plant fibers, and camelid hair were all used to create cords, twined mats, string skirts, mantles, loincloths, caps, and bags. A multitude of finely spun and plied camelid-fiber yarns were formed into enormous turbans, a notable male headdress during this period. Among the first artifacts recognizable as women's clothing were string skirts discovered along the southern coastal desert (Rodman and True n.d.; True and Nuñez 1971). Exotic feathers from tropical birds adorned headdresses, and mantles were made of local pelican pelts. Water bags were created from the skins of sea mammals, and chinchilla and viscacha hair was spun and sewn into furry blankets (Bird 1946; Dauelsberg 1974, 1985; Muñoz 1989; Nuñez 1989; Rivera 1991; Rodman and True n.d.; Southon, Rodman, and True 1995).

By the first millennium B.C., inhabitants of the south-central Andes, like those from the northern Andean regions, had developed a fully formed weaving tradition. Here, camelid fiber, not used on the northern coast, was used for tunics, turbans, twined and woven mantles, loincloths, and string skirts. Many early textiles were dyed a brilliant red color produced from the roots of a *Relbunium* species similar to the madder family (Dauelsberg 1963; Rodman and True n.d., Wallert and Boytner forthcoming).

In the following Alto Ramírez culture, men dressed in one of the most distinctive garment styles developed at that time, the last centuries B.C. through the first centuries A.D. Their costume included a tall, looped headdress patterned with rows of stepped designs in brilliant green, gold, red, and blue, worn with red and white striped shirts embroidered along the seams in wide red and blue stitching (fig. 10). The shirts or tunics were sometimes also decorated with tapestry borders with images of mountains, rayed faces, toads, and camelids. The Alto Ramírez style was discovered inland along the Azapa River valley near Arica, Chile, but the style appears highland in origin (Rivera 1991; Ulloa 1974).

Tiwanaku Textiles

The most important highland culture in the southern Andes was known as Tiwanaku, from the archaeological site of Tiwanaku with its famous standing stone monuments, located high in the windswept altiplano of the Lake Titicaca basin in Bolivia. Although textiles are rarely preserved on the altiplano, Tiwanaku textiles dating from the fifth to the tenth centuries have been recovered throughout Bolivia and northern Chile. Tiwanaku was the preeminent highland capital of a vast, long-standing religious polity. Tiwanaku's cultural influence was equally expansive and enduring. The site is known for its highly decorated stone carvings, but textiles and tablets of wood, patterned with Tiwanaku religious images, have been discovered in the Atacama Desert and in highland valleys where the preservation of usually perishable artifacts is much more complete than at Tiwanaku. These small-scale, portable objects are direct copies of the more permanent carved stone monuments found throughout the Tiwanaku highland site.

Tiwanaku weavings are among the finest of all Andean textiles. The thread counts are so fine on tapestry tunics and mantles uncovered in the Atacama Desert of northern Chile that they were called painted textiles when they were first excavated (Oakland 1986a, 1986b; Rodman and Cassman 1995). With yarn spun from only a few long hairs, much finished Tiwanaku cloth has the feel of a light, silk handkerchief. Tiwanaku textiles were also diverse, reflecting the variety of cultural traditions brought together during Tiwanaku's long period of influence. Techniques of tie-dyeing and patchwork, weft-interlocked tapestry, and warp-patterned weaves of brilliantly dyed camelid fiber were all part of the Tiwanaku tradition. Red, blue, green, and gold were emblematic Tiwanaku colors, and often mixed with deep maroons, pinks, and violets. It is possible that the southern Andes was always the center for indigo dyeing, and blue yarns were a hallmark of the area.

Embroidered Tiwanaku warp-faced textiles (fig. 11) often feature striping patterns quite similar to nineteenth- and twentieth-century mantles woven in the Lake Titicaca basin (fig. 12). It seems that, between 1000 and 1400, highland weavers developed an interest in overall patterning, combining warp-striping and warp-faced patterned weaves (Ulloa 1982; Rodman 1992a, 1992b). But smaller objects such as elaborately patterned narrow bands and bags woven with stripes of complementary-warp weaves, supplementary-warp weaves, and transposed warps, were also a feature of Tiwanaku textiles discovered throughout the highlands of the southern Bolivian Andes and in northern Chile (Oakland 1986a).

Bolivian collections from Mojocoya contain early examples of supplementary-warp weave on a paired ground, with the supplementary yarns changing faces between the warp pairs. It may be that this particular structure, so common to modern Andean weaving, was also commonly used in this region of the southern Andes during pre-Hispanic periods (Oakland 1986a; Rowe 1977). Complementary-warp weaves and double-cloth structures, popular with Andean weavers today, apparently developed in very early periods along the Peruvian coast, but the earliest preserved highland complementary-warp textiles are associated with Tiwanaku weaving (Oakland 1986a; Rodman 1992b).

The cultural power of Tiwanaku waned and the site was abandoned by the twelfth century, but the weaving tradition was not lost. Today, Aymara inhabitants of the Bolivian altiplano, termed the Colla by their Inca conquerors in the fifteenth century, continue the ancient highland weaving techniques. The Appleby textile collection is principally composed of modern textiles related to these southern highland Inca and Aymara traditions.

Aymara and Inca Textiles

Ancient Aymara textiles followed Tiwanaku prototypes. Elegant tunics and mantles were woven from brilliantly dyed and finely spun camelid fiber in warp-faced, warp-striped, and warp-patterned weaves (Adelson and Takami 1978; Adelson and Tracht 1983). Few pre-Hispanic Aymara archaeological textiles have been published, but historical documents and early dictionaries have aided research on ancient Aymara weaving traditions. Early Spanish chroniclers discussed headgear and clothing styles unique to the Colla in regions surrounding Lake Titicaca. Aymara garments were known for such specific colors as red, blue, and maroon, and the placement of wide and narrow warp stripes using simple, warp-faced plain weave.

By the fifteenth century, the powerful Incas were able to subjugate the

FIGURE 11
Tiwanaku warp-striped tunic with embroidered neck plaque from the Azapa Valley, near Arica, Chile. (Photo: Amy Rodman)

FIGURE 12
Woman's mantle *(wayllas),* 19th century;
Quechua/Aymara peoples. Acora pampa,
Puno, Peru. Catalogue no. 229. (Appleby
Collection 1992.107.96)

southern highland Aymara, and to incorporate Aymara territory into their vast empire, which stretched along much of western South America. At the time of the Spanish conquest in the sixteenth century, the most valued object in the empire was weft-faced tapestry known as *qumpi* (Q.) (Murra 1962; A. Rowe 1978; J. Rowe 1979). Other fine double-faced cloth woven by Collas was also called *qumpi,* or *lipi* (A.) (Desrosiers 1986). Although the Inca elite wore these elaborately patterned, weft-faced textiles, warp-patterned garments were undoubtedly more common to most highland Andeans. This warp-faced tradition continues in many communities surrounding the former Inca capital of Cuzco in the southern Peruvian highlands, within the regions of the former Aymara kingdoms of Bolivia, and in indigenous communities in Ecuador.

Andean Looms and Weaving Techniques

Before the arrival of the Spanish, various looms were used, all producing a textile with four finished sides or selvages. Coastal populations and groups living in the northern regions of Colombia and Ecuador generally preferred the backstrap loom because the warp tension is easily regulated with a simple shifting of the weaver's body forward or backward. The backstrap loom is also used in many parts of Bolivia, in the highlands around Cuzco for sheep's wool or camelid fiber warp-patterned weaves, and throughout Ecuador for weaving with a variety of fibers (fig. 13).

The most characteristic type of loom commonly used today in the southern highlands is the staked, horizontal, ground loom, a loom on which the tension is fixed because the loom bars are lashed to four stakes driven into the ground (fig. 14) (Cason and Cahlander 1976; Prochaska 1988). In some areas, such as Chuquisaca and Cochabamba in Bolivia, the loom bars are lashed to a frame that is leaned against the wall. Loom types are difficult to assess archaeologically, and few complete pre-Hispanic looms exist to aid in determining which types were used regionally in the past. Common to Andean weaving, whether on the backstrap, frame, or staked loom, is cloth finished along all four selvages. When the weaving is complete, the weaver removes the loom parts from the cloth instead of cutting the cloth from the loom.

Men are the principal weavers using pre-Hispanic technology in indigenous communities today in many parts of Colombia, Ecuador and northern Peru, as well as in some communities in Bolivia, northern Chile, and southern Peru. In this latter region, however, women generally weave most of their families' garments using the backstrap, staked, or vertical loom. Men knit caps, embroider on sewing machines, weave on treadle looms (fig. 15), and make ropes and intricate braids. There is no way of knowing if this division of labor was the practice in ancient periods, but it is quite possible (Meisch 1996 [1991]).

Today, long, lustrous alpaca hair is the most highly valued fiber, although sheep's wool, cotton, and synthetic yarns are also used. Contemporary weaving traditions of Tarabuco, near Sucre in Bolivia, are an exception with their cotton and wool mixtures (Meisch 1986b). Fine, white, cotton yarns are purchased for use in Tarabuco weaving, and archaeological collections from this region demonstrate that the ancient population also wove native cotton into shirts, bags, and belts, with dyed camelid hair used in the patterned areas (Oakland 1986a).

Dyes

Camelid-fiber textiles from archaeological collections of the southern highlands testify to a long and ancient tradition of dyeing based on knowledge of the

FIGURE 13
Cañari man weaving a waistband for a woman's gathered skirt. Note his tunic. (Photo: Lynn Meisch)

FIGURE 14
Horizontal staked loom in highland Bolivia. (Photo: Mike Rodman)

FIGURE 15
Man weaving on the treadle loom, Isla Taquile, Lake Titicaca, Peru. (Photo: Lynn Meisch)

Figure 16
Alonso Pilla Caiza of Salasaca, Tungurahua, Ecuador, with cochineal insects growing on opuntia cactus. His scarf is dyed with cochineal. (Photo: Lynn Meisch)

Figure 17
Woman's mantle *(llijlla),* 17th–18th century; Quechua peoples. Cuzco, Peru. Catalogue no. 197. (Appleby Collection 1992.107.88)

extraction of a wide range of natural dyes. Reds were produced from *Relbunium* and cochineal (fig. 16), blue and green from indigo, and violets were created from dye mixtures (Saltzman 1986; Wallert and Boytner forthcoming). These practices, which developed over several millennia, undoubtedly continued in many areas of the southern highlands well into the twentieth century, and are still practiced in parts of Ecuador. Antique textiles preserved in many communities today, especially in the region surrounding Lake Titicaca, are certainly part of this ancient highland tradition.

Colonial and Contemporary Andean Weaving

The Spanish conquest in the sixteenth century greatly altered every aspect of native life including native garment forms and textile techniques. One of the earliest textiles to combine European and Andean traditions is a lovely warp-patterned cloth that incorporates camelid fiber yarns with gold and other metallic threads within traditional warp-faced structures (fig. 17). This combination expresses the native Andeans' appreciation of finely woven cloth, as well as the Europeans' interest in precious metals. These warp-patterned Aymara textiles, woven with metallic threads, were considered high-status fabrics during the colonial period.

Today, highland textile traditions have certainly changed from the ancient past, and European textile techniques have been adapted to local purposes. The ubiquitous knitted cap, considered a native man's garment, is actually an introduced style, often made entirely of European materials: foreign needles, yarns, and dyes (fig. 18). In many contemporary communities, garment styles reflect Spanish peasant costume rather than indigenous loomed products. The man's sleeveless vest and the woman's full, gathered skirt were adopted during the eighteenth century, and have become part of styles that identify native groups today. Andeans found the European treadle loom useful in the production of yardage for trousers, dresses, shirts, and coats. In fact, the concept of tailoring a garment, that is, cutting shaped pieces from woven cloth, was a European introduction. The sewing machine offers an excellent, entirely new, opportunity for textile construction and decoration, and machine embroidery is done on clothes in some areas (Femenias 1987, 1995; Meisch 1987b).

FIGURE 18
Man's knitted cap; near Macha, Bolivia. (Photo: Mike Rodman)

FIGURE 19
Men from the altiplano, Bolivia. (Photo: Mike Rodman)

Andean garment styles today are dynamic, incorporating both cloth woven on the treadle loom and locally made traditional, four-selvage textiles. These are often worn with such commercially manufactured clothes as socks, shirts, blouses, petticoats, and sweaters (fig. 19). Throughout the Andes many communities continue ancient textile practices along with modern adaptations. Looms, fibers, and many garment forms still follow the ancient native tradition closely.

Contemporary Andean Costume and Highland Weaving
The contemporary Andean textile tradition includes modern Andean textiles based on such ancient types as the mantle, a long square or rectangular garment known by several terms depending on its gender association. When worn by women, the mantle is known as an *isallu* or *awayu* (A.), *llijlla, fachalina* (Q.), or *baita* (S. *bayeta*), and it is often held shut by a stickpin (*tupu* Q.). When worn by men, the mantle is called the *llakuta* (Q.), *wallas,* or *fullu* (A.). The woman's square or rectangular half- or full-body wrap skirt known as the *aksu, anaku* (Q.), or *urku* (A., Q.), is also directly related to ancient garments as is the man's tunic, called an *unku, kushma* (Q.), *khawa* (A.), or *ira* (C.). The many belts worn by males and females are called *chumpi* (Q.) or *wak'a* (A.); narrow bands and hair ties are known as *tulma* (Q.) or *t'isnu* (A.); bags as *wayaka* (A., Q.), *capacho* (S.), or *ch'uspa* (Q., meaning coca-leaf pouch); and small cloths used to hold food

or coca leaves as *tari* (A.), *inkuña* or *unkuña* (Q.). Even the poncho (etymology unknown, it may be Mapuche), a textile of colonial origin, is similar to the preconquest tunic but with the sides left unsewn.

Men in a few scattered communities continue to wear the tunic, which was originally considered essential to highland men's costume, and worn with a loin-cloth (Q. *wara*), mantle, and headdress. Men in Q'ero, Peru, Chipaya men from villages near Oruro, Bolivia, and Yura men from communities near Potosí, Bolivia, wear a tunic today as do men in Cañar and Saraguro, Ecuador (Meisch 1980a, 1981). Pre-Hispanic highland tunics were large, with the width draped over the shoulders and falling to the elbows or wrists, and the body of the tunic reaching below the knees. A poncho is the contemporary Andean tunic replacement in most areas, a versatile garment often worn over western-style trousers and shirt (see fig. 19).

Chipaya women, as well as women from communities north of Lake Titicaca near Charazani and Amarete, and some women in Chimborazo province in Ecuador (Meisch and Rowe, in press), wear a large dress with shoulder pins similar to the preconquest women's dress (fig. 20). Many women in indigenous communities wear some form of this wrap skirt, usually a much abbreviated but often highly patterned version. The wrap skirt is not worn alone however, but covers a large treadle-loomed and machine-stitched dress, the *almilla* (S.), or it might also cover a blouse and slip combination.

Contemporary Andean weaving is principally preserved in remote regions of the southern Peruvian and Bolivian highlands, throughout highland Ecuador, in parts of highland Chile, and in northern Argentina. Very little remains of the ancient native weaving tradition of the coast, but highland weaving continues as an integral component of indigenous life. The textile itself encodes both local, geographical information and deep, cosmological meaning (Bastien 1985 [1978]; Cereceda 1986; C. R. Franquemont 1986; Meisch 1986b, 1987a; Seibold 1992, 1995; Wilson 1996 [1991]).

Textiles are still the principal means of designating ethnic identity. Community-specific garment styles are evident throughout the Andes in notable patterns, colors, and garment forms. The very manner in which clothing is worn denotes cultural affiliation. Andean highland textiles today continue as a vital, adaptable, constantly changing, and clearly identifiable tradition.

Finely woven textiles are essential to highland Andean culture. In many native communities today no festival or ritual is complete without proper textiles (Medlin 1991; Meisch 1986b, 1996 [1991]; Seibold 1995; Zorn 1986, 1995). Special garments are woven for community celebrations, and the finest ancestral cloth is displayed during ritual days (fig. 21). Markets are also excellent opportunities for Andeans to exhibit the results of their weaving skills. Cloth remains the appropriate ceremonial gift, woven for baptisms, the first haircut ceremony, weddings, community leadership positions, *tinkus* (Q. ritual moiety battles), the saints in the church, and crosses carried in celebrations. More than a survival of ancient traditions, Andean textile style is characteristically a combination of the old and new. Universally, the cloth of the Andes is highly regarded for its finely spun fibers, brilliant colors, and intricate patterning. Woven in high lands, Andean textiles are recognized as among the most splendid and enduring of world traditions.

THE TRUE TREASURE OF
ANDEAN TEXTILES

BY
ED FRANQUEMONT

As curator of the American Museum of Natural History in New York, the late Junius Bird saw a great many textiles. Among them was always a certain number of fakes that were usually easily recognized because the skills of the faker were not even close to those of the original artist. But during the 1970s, he began to see a curious group of partially woven belt looms, ostensibly from the Late Intermediate period of Peru's central coast. The yarns were clearly ancient, the design vocabulary solidly within the style, and the hand of the weaver impeccably accurate. Yet, Dr. Bird felt uneasy about these pieces. The yarns seemed just too lively in the pattern sections to have been suspended in midwork for nearly a millennium, and the colors did not seem to be faded in the proper places. Eventually he found incontrovertible evidence in the shedding device of these half-woven looms. Instead of the clumsy heddle from Chancay culture, each loom had the distinctive self-adjusting heddle devised during the early years of the twentieth century by contemporary weavers of Cuzco, Peru (Junius B. Bird, personal communication).

Evidently a weaver from the Cuzco area had come to Lima and encountered the low value of her products compared to those looted from desert tombs. With the confidence and ambition typical of these people, she set about acquiring the yarn and wood necessary to recreate the design vocabulary, aesthetics, and touch of weavers who had been dead seven hundred years. She—probably there was a whole community of women—was betrayed only by an unwillingness to abandon a clearly superior technology, an oversight best explained by her lack of respect for the ability of outsiders to perceive such subtle differences in a backstrap loom. These contemporary Andean weavers were committing, without doubt, a self-conscious act of fraud in hopes of earning money from their art. But the fraud was truly magnificent—so ambitious and so successful that any weaver who has tried to re-create complex ancient Peruvian textiles must stand in awe of the power of these weavers' hands, their eyes, and especially their minds.

A second case of fraud is more recent, and perhaps more troubling. It concerns the so-called Aymara weavings (Adelson and Tracht 1983) that have circulated in the art markets of the developed world during the past two decades. Many of these textiles have been part of an international dispute that unites Bolivian *campesinos* (S. country people), United States customs officials, and some anthropologists against dealers and collectors of textiles, including some museums in the United States. The cloth commands a high price in art markets not only because the sense of design is remarkably congruent with that of western culture, but also because the sophisticated marketing techniques used by some dealers have cultivated a demand in the developed world. Much of the appeal has been built upon scarcity: Because this cloth dates to an earlier period and is now out of production, the limited number of pieces available adds the value of antiquity to the aesthetic beauty of the fabrics.

However, within a few years, this market strategy had been undone by the ingenuity and skills of contemporary Bolivian weavers who realized that the

Figure 22
Colonial-style coca bag *(ch'uspa),* late 16th–17th century; Quechua peoples. Cuzco, Peru. Catalogue no. 192. (Appleby Collection L96.120.3)

FIGURE 23
Woman's mantle *(llijlla),* mid-20th century;
Quechua peoples. Cuzco, Peru. Catalogue
no. 180. (Appleby Collection 1992.107.83)

simpler "Aymara" style of weaving brought much higher prices than did their
own weaving. Soon many weavers set about relearning to weave like this, and a
vigorous and faithful revival of the "Aymara" style was underway. "Fraud!" cried
the dealers. "We cannot tell the difference between the new and the old pieces!"
Certainly this would be a curious kind of fraud, with Bolivian weavers making
classic Bolivian cloth, in many cases doubtless the same cloth made by their
grandmothers, from handspun Bolivian yarn in Bolivia. But certainly here is
another magnificent case of textile brilliance, the revitalization of a dormant style.

These two cases demonstrate a fundamental truth often overlooked in
our appreciation of the remarkable Andean textiles: The real treasures of these
traditions are the weavers themselves. Each textile, ancient or modern, is the
handprint of a remarkable individual who represents through skills and perceptions a remarkable society. The command of the medium is so complete that,
with a little prodding from the marketplace, a weaver from contemporary
Cuzco can almost become one from the extinct Chancay culture, and contemporary Bolivian people can reanimate traditions of the past century. Working with
simple looms that present no technical barriers to any creative vision, Andean
weavers can do anything with fiber they can imagine; what they choose to make
reflects the critical role they play as custodians of a communal consciousness and
how they see the forces that affect their lives (fig. 22).

The Textile Medium in the Andes
Textiles have been the most important material commodity in the Andes for over
three thousand years. Bolstered by great support from governments and religious
institutions, Andean weavers stretched the limits of fiber art to encompass

domains we entrust to mathematics, literature, and precious metals, as well as the more ordinary functions of cloth. This expanded role of textile art seems unfathomable to those whose sense of textile treasure has been debased by the successes of the industrial revolution, yet it is wholly appropriate for this most complex multifaceted medium. Fiber is the quintessential labor-intensive medium, and as a result, the cultural imprint upon a textile is extremely strong. In the Andean societies of the past few centuries, individual artisans have controlled all of the skills and design decisions from raising the raw material by agriculture or husbandry through the production of a finished garment. Their products are almost entirely a result of what they think is good, proper, and beautiful (fig. 23).

Yet their notions of good, proper, and beautiful have also been shaped by the nature of textile processes. As weavers fashion cultural statements of fiber, the act of working conditions their minds to think in significant ways. As the French anthropologist Pierre Bordieu argues (1977), the actual practice of a complex cultural activity such as textile work teaches people how to perceive and understand the meaning of it, and this understanding in turn changes and enhances the manner in which people practice their culture. For fiber artists, this process of cultural and technical feedback takes place in many domains simultaneously, including, at least, the technical, kinetic, perceptual, intellectual, and aesthetic. Led by their hands and eyes to new perceptual skills, Andean weavers are able to produce their traditional fabrics because they think differently from most other people (fig. 24). Frame (1986) argues that pre-Columbian Andeans came to use the very structure of cloth itself as a motif in their art, and C. R. Franquemont (1986) has shown that fiber art forms the basis of a perceptual system applied to the natural world. In the Andean world, textiles have shaped culture as much as culture has influenced fiber art.

How Andean weavers think about their art has not been adequately researched in part because it has generally been assumed that textiles represent an impoverished analog of painting and literature. Yet it is clear that Andean fiber artists escape the sense of their work as a flat, visually dominated art like these other media. They are keenly aware of the motions of the yarns to form the primary structure of their work, and of the fact that it has thickness or three dimensions. They know what is happening on the interior of the cloth hidden from view of the casual observer, and can understand both surfaces of a fabric by looking at either. Weavers do not see their fabrics as static, but rather design and understand their cloth as kinetic, blowing in the breeze, filled with potatoes, or moving on a human body. They are especially sensitive to the tactile quality of the fabric, and usually explore an unfamiliar textile first with their hands rather than their eyes. We found that contemporary Inca weavers near Cuzco, in Peru, had difficulty recognizing their own work in high-quality color photographs, but could identify the fabrics from which balls of yarn had been raveled! Clearly this is a different way of experiencing cloth from that which is generally supposed by literate cultures.

As important and fascinating as it is, the mental equipment of Andean weavers has proved difficult to approach in the field. Textile skills are learned by repetitious practice of complex motor skills rather than through verbal explanation, producing a domain that is independent of language, more like music than like reading. Just as musicians can translate sounds into the motions of playing their instruments, weavers are able to translate visual information directly into kinetic activity without passing it through the filter of words in their minds. Even the very best of weavers are rarely able to express themselves

FIGURE 24
This photograph shows Cipriana Quispe, of Chinchero, Peru, at work on a complex complementary-warp weave belt. To follow the design without counting threads, she uses visual clues from the pattern held on many temporary shed swords. (Photo: Ed Franquemont)

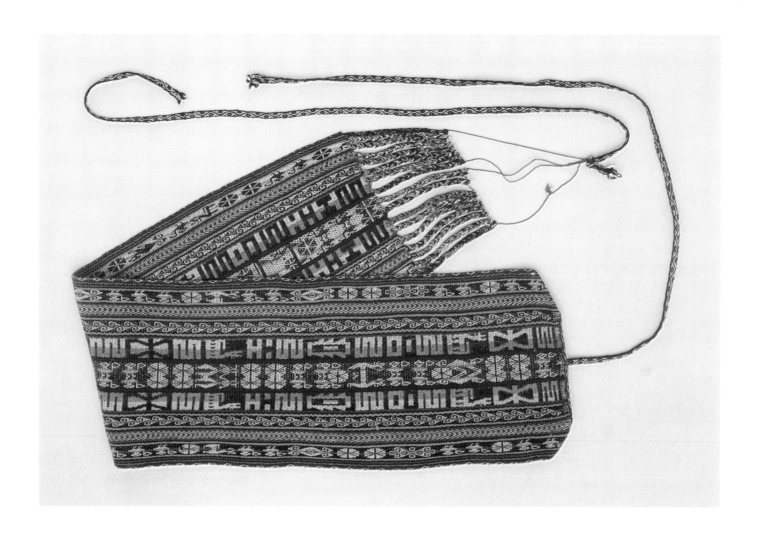

FIGURE 25
Belt *(wak'a),* ca. 1950; Quechua peoples.
Ayata, La Paz, Bolivia. Catalogue no. 76.
(Appleby Collection 1992.107.196)

FIGURE 26
Sabina Choque of Chinchero, Peru, at work
on a *wata.* Small groups of young shepherd
girls teach one another the basics of weaving
in making these useful, narrow fabrics.
(Photo: Ed Franquemont)

well in words about their work, which has inhibited the anthropological study of weavers and textiles for many decades. It has also made it difficult to reduce that which is truly meaningful about textiles to analysis and exposition in academic papers, or to presentation in graphic form. Andean weavers design their cloth for a society of people like themselves, where basic textile skills are universal, and clever process can be immediately understood along with beautiful design. To appreciate the Andean genius with cloth, it is imperative to experience the textiles at first hand, from differing distances and angles, through the hands as well as the eyes, and ideally with an understanding of the way they are made.

As it is free of language, textile activity has a tremendous potential as a way of exploring and representing other systems of knowledge that are not easily conveyed through words. Because it is easy for us to see how textiles express aesthetics and are used to reinforce social ordering through costume, the role of cloth as a finely tuned system of knowledge has been often overlooked, but is highly developed in Andean civilizations. Here fiber art is more like mathematics than it is like verbal skills, because the process of making textiles and the textiles themselves can explore and embody abstract ideas about the physical and social world that are impossible to explore in a linear medium such as language. Not only can information be nested at different levels, ranging from characteristics of the yarn to the process of manufacture to the decorative motifs to the garment design, but also all of these levels of meaning can be experienced simultaneously, and interact with one another (fig. 25).

Such a complex representational medium was difficult for western civilization to imagine until the advent of the information revolution in the past forty years, yet it was an integral part of the world view of even the most primitive Andean weaver. Indeed, ancient Andean people used the textile medium as the underlying matrix of one of the largest and most successful civilizations of the preindustrial world; the wisdom and understandings of this great civilization was coded not in language and written numbers but rather in fiber.

Even today, five hundred years after the European invasion, Andean weavers are custodians of the complex ideas that define their culture and of a sophisticated system of aesthetics and meaning. Through their cloth, it is possible to observe in tangible form the mind of a people solving complex problems of space and structure that require dealing with very large numbers and many possibilities. These textiles, especially costumes, also represent an "ethnic code" (C. R. Franquemont, 1986), human plumage so to speak, that is intentionally constructed or chosen by the user. This visible culture, defining and delineating one group from another, is the rarest of anthropological facts: a way to experience categories of people seen from the user's point of view, rather than as an analytical construct developed by a researcher. Through the clothes they make and wear, people reveal in a very profound way what they want to think about themselves and others, and they teach us to see the world as they do. Few other categories of anthropological evidence offer such great possibilities for expressing indigenous voices.

Weavers in the Andean World
The traditional Andean weaver of the Cuzco area learns the craft through a diffuse process by which an older generation of weavers passes skills to new weavers in ways that do not strictly follow family lines, and continue throughout a lifetime (Franquemont and Franquemont 1988). The critical phase occurs

just before adolescence, when girls spend most of their time in small peer groups tending flocks of sheep on the steep Andean hillsides. With the energy that children of other societies might use to teach one another games, Andean girls teach one another to weave small-scale fabrics (fig. 26). From this beginning, women move through a succession of age grades in which they learn new fabrics and new skills from older women, and eventually enter into a remarkable relationship with an older woman called *allwi masi* (Q. warping partners). This relationship amounts to an apprenticeship in Andean womanhood, and fosters a deep bond between women that continues for the rest of their lives. As a weaver reaches her middle years, she finds herself now the senior partner of *allwi masi* relationships, and in a position to pass on to younger weavers the nuances of a point of view that begins with textile activity, but soon encompasses all life experience. It is here in these women's groups that the essence of Andean identity is formed, the crucial perceptual skills are learned, and the intellectual system that underlies indigenous knowledge is mastered.

Yet for all the glory of the final products, the actual practice of weaving in the Cuzco region occurs in the humblest of circumstances. Despite the group energy of the early learning years and the romance of weaving on grassy hillsides, women usually weave in the dusty *kancha* (Q. courtyard) shared with barnyard animals in a house compound. Two or three generations of women may live around this compound, but usually only one is at the prime textile-producing stage of life. She works mostly during the dry season when demands of agriculture are low, and generally alone except for neighbors who tend to drop in at this time of the year in regular rounds of visits. It is common to see two or three women spinning and talking while their host weaves, but rarely does a woman weave away from her own home. Unless there is a daughter of an age to assume many household tasks, women work in *winay rutusqa* (Q. broken time), interrupted for many other household responsibilities. Nevertheless, they can be extraordinarily productive, and claim to produce as many as ten major pieces of cloth a year. Time studies (E. M. Franquemont 1986b) show that this work would fill more than twenty forty-hour weeks of loom time. Many women take great pride in their work and their identity as weavers, but the truth is that most traditional Andean weavers work mostly out of necessity, with no more joy in their work than women of developed societies find in cooking and housework (Goodell 1968).

In the Cuzco area, while weaving, sandwiched around other domestic and agricultural tasks, consumes nearly half of a woman's work year, the spinning of yarn for these fabrics requires even more time. Spindle work is a constant companion of all other parts of an Andean life, yet no weavers can hope to keep up with even their own personal requirements for yarn. Spinning and plying account for more than 60 percent of the time needed to produce even the most complicated Andean textile (E. M. Franquemont 1986a). This means a weaver must work from a store of yarn produced by younger and older women in her family, and with yarns spun by other women who form a wide network of social and family relations that each woman constructs throughout her life. This shared textile activity stitches together the women's community in the villages of the Cuzco area, with the weaver as the focal point of production.

As in most traditional, inwardly focused folk communities, goods are designed for use within the society itself, so weavers usually know firsthand those individuals who will wear or use their products. In fact, in Cuzco area communities, most end users of a weaver's products come from the same

network that produces the yarn with which she works. Occasionally, the very best weavers will work on a barter contract, receiving a sheep in return for weaving an exceptional cloth from yarn provided by the client. During the colonial period and continuing through the *hacienda* system, men and women were often required to weave as a tax paid to non-Indian masters who dominated their lives. Oppressive relationships like these may have been the origin of a disproportionate share of the cloth that finds its way into museums because it was collected and never used, but that is still a small percentage of the total output of an Andean community and a small percentage of the cloth we know from the Andes. Most fabrics made in the Cuzco area are designed by women for people they understand and care about, and are woven in part to express a great communal bond among them. It is this bond that fuels the great power of the cloth, and is the heart of the southern Andean textile tradition.

For Andean weavers, textile activity has never been a separate skill but rather an adjunct to a way of life and a source of group identity. Weavers have been the point of production for a large society for which cloth has a special role, and their dialogue with this society has been intimate. But the very societies that have nurtured weavers and their skills for thousands of years are now rapidly evolving. The industrial, transportation, and information revolutions have arrived in the Andes almost simultaneously, bringing cheap goods, foreign people and ideas, and new images conveyed through new media. Not only are the economic status and prestige value of being a weaver under assault by the intrusion of the money economy and mass media, but also the folk context that has supported the weavers is crumbling irrevocably. Andean identity lay for centuries at the village level; it now lies at ethnic and national levels where village folk costume has a different meaning that has attracted a wholly new audience.

Most weavers are now aware of the use of their products by people who are not of their society and who judge cloth by very different criteria from those assumed by the producers. The dialogue between weavers and their people has therefore quieted, and centuries-old standards of taste, quality, and value are proving unreliable. This shift in focus from inward to outward has produced a

FIGURE 27
Tourists buying—or not buying—textiles at the weekly market in Tarabuco, Bolivia. (Photo: Lynn Meisch)

FIGURE 28
Antonia Callañaupa selling textiles in the market in Chinchero, Cuzco district, Peru. (Photo: Lynn Meisch)

great strain within the productive modes of Andean people. Weaving traditions that have been monolithic and homogeneous are bifurcating: The majority of weavers need to make money and are working toward the market conditions; a few weavers are becoming fine artists by virtue of a concern with making textiles that respond to their own sense of value and quality.

For many Andean weavers today, market conditions control production decisions. Commonly, outside consumers of their products set quality standards. Few consumers understand the textiles technically or aesthetically, so the quality of work is slipping. Price is a paramount issue for most consumers, which not only erodes quality but also favors certain types of textiles that can be produced in the ideal price range. Cuzco area weavers, for instance, focus almost exclusively on belts that sell at prices most tourists are willing to pay for a memento of their trip. Price also influences the materials chosen for work. Because spinning yarn by hand consumes anywhere from 60 to 90 percent of production time for a textile, most people reject handspun yarn in favor of available machine-spun fibers. But even those people who have not felt the low-quality demand for textile goods from tourists are not immune to the market forces at work in the world today (figs. 27, 28). Franquemont and Franquemont (1978) demonstrated that indigenous weavers in Huancavelica, Peru, have enormous untapped productive capacity that could be mobilized by offers to pay for their products at a rate competitive with the lowest pay scales of their societies. These weavers do not produce much simply because there is no longer anyone to buy their products, and Cuzco weavers make the simplest fabrics they know because their consumers cannot tell the difference.

The weaving traditions of the contemporary Andes are also affected by other forces. In many places, it is now especially difficult to educate new weavers, as the demands of modern life and of the states within which these people live make it increasingly difficult to introduce even the most willing of children to fiber arts in any meaningful way. As formal school has replaced the herding experience in the Cuzco area, girls now learn to weave from older family members rather than from their peers, and practice in small snatches of available evening hours rather than during long, lazy days on the hillsides. The girls learn an abbreviated version of their textile traditions, and the bonding that later supports women's groups is severely compromised. Because textile activities are poorly rewarded in the money economy when compared to wage labor, few people invest the immense energy necessary to dominate their textile traditions. Textile activity suffers in prestige because it is viewed as being connected to old ways that have little place in a developing economy, and promises little power over the forces that young people see around them. Consequently the weavers of the contemporary indigenous world are frequently poor and marginalized members of their societies even when they are nominally venerated.

Collectors, Museums, and Indigenous Weavers

Jeffrey Appleby and other serious collectors form a countercurrent within the tide of low-quality demand washing across the Andes, and in many cases represent the best of the new audience for Andean cloth. They take time to learn the cultural landscape represented by the textiles they find, invest in relationships that bring high-quality fabrics to their attention, often spend enough energy to appreciate what we might call Andean visual "jazz," the nuances that make a particular piece special within a broader tradition. Collectors have now replaced the *hacendado* (S. hacienda owner), the colonial master, and even the Inca government in their thirst for the very best products of the Andean loom. In a very real sense, fiber art collectors have become, by their acquisitions, the keepers of the archive of Andean thought captured in cloth. The strength of this collection is an insistence that these traditions still course through the fingers of twentieth-century weavers, and this show provides a spectacular window into this remarkable tradition of these most enigmatic people. Expositions of actual fabrics can teach ways of seeing that cannot be approached through written text or photograph.

Despite the opportunities brought by museum collections, sometimes those who love the textiles the most present a great obstacle to the survival of the traditions that created them. Collectors and museums feel a special urgency to preserve traditions slipping over the horizon of history, and tend to favor an ordinary antique textile over a superior contemporary piece. This is a lesson well understood by Andean weavers who fake ancient Chancay belts, revitalize the nineteenth-century "Aymara" styles, or throw their cloth into the burro pen for a few weeks before sale. An ethnographic present constructed just over the horizon of contemporary times by the interests of collectors robs the tradition of the vitality necessary to promote experiments in fiber, colors, and design. Andean textile traditions have never been static, but today many weavers can do their very finest work only within rigid limits of style as interpreted by those outside their traditions; they can be innovative and creative only by working downward to the low-quality demand of the tourist market.

Museums have always been about objects, but Andean textiles today present great challenges to our understanding of what collections mean and do. It is certainly easier to appreciate these works of art in isolation, separated from the people who produced them, to ignore the weavers' poverty and romanticize their character. But in the Andes, the tradition bearers are still with us. Some of the very finest weavers in the world make beds in Cuzco hotels, sell soda pop in Bolivian train stations, or sit by dusty roads in Ecuador, wondering, perhaps, where, in the end, all this traffic will take them. Their fingers are alive with wisdom, knowledge, and perceptions that built one of the world's great civilizations, and they are now working not in service of their local community, but for a larger world. Here, museums broker the relationship between the developed world and indigenous weavers by choosing what is of value and what to display.

The challenge is not just to reach through the textile on the wall to teach museum goers about the people who made it, but also to reflect back to weavers how much we, their new constituency, value those who continue to make remarkable Andean textiles. This is a tough new challenge for scholar, collector, and museum, yet there is little choice but to meet it because there is no neutral ground. Every purchase made, each show hung, and every article written is eventually a message sent and received about what is good and valuable. We must be sure these messages say what we intend by including commissioned new cloth and even the weavers themselves in our work. Surely people matter at least as much as things, and if we value these textiles enough to worry about their survival, we should work diligently to find in our emerging global reality a significant place for the traditions that create them. After all, cloth is the imprint of Andean culture upon fiber; here we find the true treasure of Andean textile traditions, the weavers themselves.

THE JEFFREY APPLEBY COLLECTION OF ANDEAN TEXTILES

BY
MARGOT BLUM
SCHEVILL

Survival in the awesome landscape of the Andes requires courage and strength, and has engendered a unique aesthetic vision. As evidenced by the brilliant textiles of the Appleby collection, this vision has resulted in cloth that is a triumph of design, color, and imagery. The 240 pieces in the collection originated in the Andean highlands of Argentina, Bolivia, Chile, Ecuador, and Peru. The material is ethnographic and historic, but not pre-Hispanic, although many of the techniques practiced before the Spanish Conquest have persisted to the present. The pieces in the collection were made between the late-sixteenth and mid-twentieth centuries by artists of the loom who were predominantly Aymara, Quechua, Quichua, and Mapuche speakers.

Because Andean cloth and clothing differs among communities, a variety of information is conveyed through this medium to the informed viewer: age, community or region, ethnicity, status, class, religion, and more. Many of the textile artists who could have decoded this information are gone, but the fabric remains. Analyses of the cloth structure, contemporary analogies when appropriate, the published literature, and the consultants' expertise have revealed some of this lost information.

The Collector

According to Jeffrey Appleby, collectors are born, not made. While in high school, he started buying Art Deco ties from the Salvation Army and flea markets, thus amassing his first large collection. Appleby attended the University of New Mexico and studied architecture, but soon discovered that this profession was not for him. His grandmother and his parents, who are adventure travel trekkers, encouraged him to travel. Following their lead, he lived and traveled in Mexico, buying costumes in Oaxaca, and in Guatemala, where he bought more textiles. Returning to the United States, he sold what he had bought, and over the next few years began to develop an import business.

In 1975, at a flea market in California, Appleby made his first purchase of Andean textiles, two headbands (S. *winchas*), similar to that illustrated in fig. 29. That same year he decided to study in South America, to settle in La Paz in Bolivia, and to travel from there. Appleby also collected in Peru and made additional trips to Ecuador, Argentina, and Chile, buying from the indigenous peoples, intermediaries, other collectors, and shop owners and developing an appreciation for the range and beauty of Andean textiles. In 1978, he began assembling the collection that is now in the possession of the Fine Arts Museums of San Francisco.

By 1984, Appleby had settled in New Mexico, and he opened a store in Corrales. At a later date, he moved to his home town, Del Dios, California, and continued his business. He was able to upgrade his Andean collection by buying from collectors and dealers, and at Sotheby's in New York City. Cathryn Cootner, the former curator of textiles at the Fine Arts Museums of San Francisco, was instrumental in soliciting his collection for the museum. She

encouraged Appleby to include one really fine example of each textile by type and provenance, rather than multiple examples.

Still an avid collector, Appleby maintains twenty-five personal collections including Mexican serapes, Dayak beadwork and basketry from Borneo, Lakai embroideries from Uzbekistan, and photographs of tribal people for the stereopticon. Although he did not buy Andean textiles in their countries of origin after 1984, Appleby returned to Peru in April, 1996, to ascertain the origin of pieces about which he was unsure. In order to elicit further information, I met with Jeff several times. With the aid of a small color print and his notes, he displayed an extraordinary visual memory as he remembered where, when, and from whom he bought certain pieces. This information is woven into the catalogue raisonné descriptions. The collection reflects Jeffrey Appleby's tastes, preferences, aesthetic and scientific sensibilities, and goals, and as a whole provides an overview of three and one-half centuries of Andean textiles.

The Collection

The collection contains a wide range of garments and utilitarian and ceremonial cloths, including saddlebags, slings, and other material. Women's dress comprises fifty shoulder mantles, which are usually two pieces joined edge to edge,

FIGURE 29
Headband *(wincha),* ca. 1950; Quechua/Aymara peoples. Charazani, La Paz, Bolivia. Catalogue no. 92. (Appleby Collection 1993.107.225)

Headbands similar to this one were the first Andean textiles to catch Jeffrey Appleby's eye.

FIGURE 30
Full skirt *(urku),* ca. 1940; Quechua/Aymara
peoples. Charazani, La Paz, Bolivia.
Catalogue no. 64. (Appleby Collection
1992.107.129)

often with bindings on the outer selvages; two shawls, woven in one piece in a
long rectangular shape with decorative fringes; nine skirts, some half of a larger
cloth that was divided among daughters or for sale. Some of these garments are
worn wrapped around the body, sometimes on top of another skirt, others are
full, gathered skirts (fig. 30); six purses knitted in unusual shapes; three finely
woven headbands trimmed with beads and typical of the communities around
Charazani, La Paz, Bolivia; and nine hair ties, including a complex, long,
patterned band with other bands created from intersecting transverse warps.

Men's dress includes thirty-two ponchos, made of two pieces joined edge to
edge, with a neck opening and with edge bindings and fringes; four small
ponchos; twenty-six coca bags; complex textiles of patterned cloth with a strap,
edge bindings, fringes (fig. 31), and sometimes pockets and tassels; five scarves,
usually tan with stripes; two tunics, woven in one piece with a neck opening,
and sewn at the side seams with arm openings; three mantles with distinctive
stripes, made as one piece or of two pieces joined edge to edge; four hat bands;
and one pair of knitted leggings.

Textiles used by either males, females, or both include six slings, thirty-eight
belts, twenty-four knitted hats, and nine coca or ceremonial cloths. Other items
include three saddlebags, a colonial-style purse, and a piece of copper fringe.

Materials and Production
The weaving fibers come from the camelid family, which includes the llama,
alpaca, guanaco, and vicuña, native to the Andes, and from sheep introduced by
the Spanish. Throughout the highlands, it is common to see men, women, and

FIGURE 31
Poncho *(poncho),* ca. 1960; Quechua/Aymara peoples. Charazani, La Paz, Bolivia. Catalogue no. 62. (Appleby Collection 1992.107.115)

FIGURE 32
Hat *(chullu),* ca. 1950; Quechua peoples. Macha, Potosí, Bolivia. Catalogue no. 119. (Appleby Collection 1992.107.191)

children spinning. The yarn is spun in one direction and then two or more yarns are plied in the other direction. The most common direction for two-ply yarn in the central and southern Andes is Z2S. In the Cuzco area and in some parts of Bolivia, the spinning and plying direction is the opposite, S2Z, or backward spun. There is a Quechua term for this, *lluq'i,* and magical practices are often associated with this yarn (Meisch 1986a,b; Oakland 1982). *Lluq'i* often appears on the outer selvages of a garment alternating with Z2S-spun yarn, which creates a herringbone or V effect and also keeps the selvages from curling.

Thirty-five textiles from Peru and thirty from Bolivia have S2Z-spun yarn for the warp. Weavers less commonly use S2Z-spun yarn for the weft. Two belts from Challa Wacho, Apurímac (cat. no. 151, 152 [fig. 33]), and one mantle from Junín (cat. no. 211), woven in weft-faced tapestry technique, and twelve smaller pieces such as slings and belts from Bolivia, have this feature. For the warp, Andean spinners often produce overspun yarn, which kinks back on itself when not under tension and is very strong and fine. Many textiles with overspun yarn have a high warps-per-inch count, and the cloth has a fine hand or feel to it. Over time the cloth becomes softer and more malleable.

In the past, dyers produced a wide range of colors from such natural sources as cochineal, indigo (fig. 34), and mordanted combinations. By the late nineteenth century, synthetic dyes were available worldwide. Consequently, contemporary artisans may combine natural and synthetic dyes to produce the desired color.

The pre-Hispanic textile tradition of the Andean area is well known. These ancient textiles reveal a technical sophistication equal to or surpassing that of

FIGURE 33
Belt *(chumpi),* ca. 1950. Quechua peoples. Cotabambas, Apurímac, Peru. Catalogue no. 152. (Appleby Collection 1992.107.52)

FIGURE 34
Angel Fajardo weaving an indigo-dyed *ikat* shawl *(paño),* similar to that shown as catalogue no. 145. (Photo: Lynn Meisch)

contemporary Andean weavers. The staked loom and the backstrap loom and other body-tension looms are ancient forms. Men and women today continue to create four-selvage textiles with warp-faced patterns by means of a pick-up technique (fig. 35) called *pallay* or *agllana* (Q. to select). In some regions, the solid-colored plain-weave sections or *pampas* (Q.) are said to resemble the high plains; *pallay* is a metaphor for the mountains or for the plowed potato fields (C. R. Franquemont 1986).

Besides warp-faced plain weave, weavers employ various methods of pick-up patterning to create designs. Andean weavers generally created the patterning in the warp; the Maya weavers of Guatemala and Chiapas, in contrast, excel in supplementary-weft brocading. The most common Andean pick-up technique represented in the Appleby collection is complementary-warp weave, and there are 124 textiles in which this technique is used. Complementary-warp weave is a compound fabric structure with two sets of warps (interlacing with the weft) that are complementary to each other. The two sets of elements play equivalent and reciprocal parts on each face of the fabric, and the resulting textile is double faced.

There are twenty-seven textiles with supplementary-warp weave, in which extra warps are used for creating a pattern on a ground weave. These supplementary warps are not essential to the structure of the cloth. Another structure is double cloth, a compound fabric in which two separate weave structures, usually plain weave, are interconnected only where they exchange faces. There are thirty-six textiles in which this technique has been used. Eleven weavings have both complementary- and supplementary-warp weave structures, and eight have complementary-warp weave and double cloth.

Tubular edge bindings appear in fifty-six of the textiles as joining and decorative elements in coca bags, slings, and saddlebags, and on the outer selvages and neck openings of larger pieces. Plain-weave edge bindings with fringe decorate fifty-four of the ponchos and mantles, and tassels and pompoms appear on many of the coca bags and hats.

Color plays an integral role in Andean weaving. Spinners may combine two different colored yarns while plying. This technique, known as *ch'imi* (A.), creates a shimmering effect in the cloth. Eighteen Bolivian and five Peruvian textiles have this feature. Another color effect called *abrash* (Arabic for "mottled") is found in fourteen textiles with solid-colored plain-weave areas. This occurs because of variations in the dye bath or from dyeing the wool before it is spun. *Ikat,* a Malayan word, refers to resist or tie-dyeing done by binding warps or wefts at designated intervals before the yarns are woven, then immersing them in dye (fig. 36). When the bindings are removed and the textile is woven, patterns result from areas of yarn not penetrated by dye. Only two ponchos in the collection have *ikat* warps.

The iconography also is an important element in Andean textiles. In some examples it may represent a kind of abstract text; in other textiles actual words and letters are woven into the fabric. Broad categories include human, animal, bird, celestial, and geometric motifs. One bird image present in nineteen different textiles is that of the condor, the largest bird in the Andes, which soars high above the mountains and carries messages to the mountain gods or to the sun. Viscachas, burrowing rodents native to the Andes and a relative of the chinchilla, appear frequently; with their long ears and bushy tails, they look like a cross between a rabbit and a squirrel. Images of *ch'unchus,* who represent jungle *indígenas,* are common in cloths from Q'ero, Cuzco, Peru.

Intricate geometric patterns that Ed Franquemont identified with Quechua

FIGURE 35
Woman's mantle *(awayu),* late 19th century;
Quechua/Aymara peoples. Challa,
Cochabamba, Bolivia. Catalogue no. 22.
(Appleby Collection 1992.107.121)

FIGURE 36
Arcelia Pérez wrapping the design for a
woman's shawl *(S. paño)* with agave fiber.
(Photo: Lynn Meisch)

names dominate the complementary- and supplementary-warp patterning of many Peruvian and Bolivian textiles. Images often are abstract and highly stylized, conforming to the accepted regional or community styles. For example, the imagined beasts or birds woven into a half *aksu* (Q. wrap skirt) from Potólo, Chuquisaca, Bolivia, are part of this community's shared visual vocabulary (fig. 37). Other strange animals appear in belts from Leque, Cochabamba, Bolivia (fig. 38). Such colonial-influenced motifs as flowers, mermaids, men and women in fancy dress, and double-headed eagles, symbols of the Hapsburgs, appear on some of the older pieces (fig. 39). Not all textiles have *pallay* or *agllana.* The multicolored, vertically striped cloths from Bolivia are beautifully balanced and resemble abstract paintings. As Franquemont noted, in the 1980s these cloths caught on with dealers, who marketed them with great success to collectors abroad.

One of the highlights of the collection is the group of thirty-two striped ponchos, some of which are exceptionally large and may have been woven as tribute to the *hacienda* owner. One of the oldest ponchos, ca. 1830 (cat. no. 155, fig. 39), came from Mamara, in the province of Grau, Apurímac, Peru. It was handed down from one generation to the next by the women in one family and was never worn by the men. The poncho has warp stripes with two-color complementary-warp patterning and is made of seven pieces sewn together. Such colonial motifs as double-headed eagles and mermaids are woven into one of the stripes. In addition, the poncho contains a complete poem expressing the despair of someone, perhaps the owner, Colonel Humberto Cruz, who was an

FIGURE 38
Belt *(wak'a),* ca. 1950; Quechua/Aymara peoples. Leque, Cochabamba, Bolivia. Catalogue no. 30. (Appleby Collection 1992.107.207)

FIGURE 39
Poncho *(poncho),* 1830; Quechua peoples. Mamara, Apurímac, Peru. Catalogue no. 155. (Appleby Collection L96.120.1)

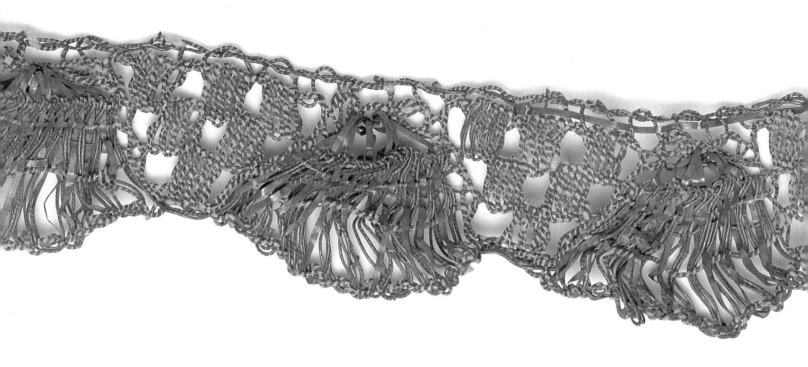

FIGURE 40
Saddlebags *(alforjas),* 18th–19th century; Aymara peoples. Oruro, Bolivia. Catalogue no. 114. (Appleby Collection 1992.107.180)

FIGURE 41 (above)
Copper fringe, 19th century; Spanish. Cuzco, Peru. Catalogue no. 193. (Appleby Collection 1992.107.7)

FIGURE 42
Lappeted hat, 18th century; Quechua/Spanish. Cuzco, Peru. Catalogue no. 196. (Appleby Collection 1992.107.44)

officer in the War of Independence and later in the army of the Bolivian-Peruvian Confederation (1835): "My pleasure is finished, my glory is destroyed, as he who lost what he desired, Ay! I do not know what to do" (my translation). Perhaps this was a popular song of the day.

A pair of saddlebags or *alforjas* (S.) (cat. no. 114, fig. 40) from the department of Oruro, Bolivia, are of special interest. They are made of warp-faced plain weave and multicolored knotted pile. The knotting technique appears to be of European origin, although there is a pre-Hispanic antecedent, the Huari knotted-pile hats. Other pile structures are found in Huancavelica, Peru. The iconography includes large lions, surrounded by birds and hearts, which are familiar heraldic images. A small piece of copper fringe from the town of Cuzco, Peru (cat. no. 193, fig. 41), appears to be lacework of copper scallop strips worked in with yellow-green cotton or camelid yarn. Appleby suggested that the fringe was used on dresses. The lappeted hats from Cuzco (cat. no. 195 and 196) are outstanding. The imagery, embroidered on natural linen, suggests a European-influenced court scene, as well as Indians from the rain forest (the *ch'unchus* mentioned above) with tall feather headdresses. Gracing the back of one hat (cat. no. 42) is the Hapsburg eagle, symbolic of the Spanish conquerors who altered, but did not completely destroy, Andean lifeways after their arrival.

NOTE

I would like to acknowledge the assistance of the following people, who aided me in various ways during the cataloguing of the Appleby textile collection: Jeffrey Appleby, who, during several sessions with me in 1995 and 1996, supplied additional information on each piece, along with collection history; Barbara Arthur, who lent her weaver's golden eye and knowledge to the analyses of each textile; Tim Wells and Wendy Berkelman, who contributed their time and expertise; Dr. Luis Becu, Ruth Corcuera, Diana S. Rolandi de Perrot, and Carola Segura, textile scholars from Buenos Aires, Argentina; the consultants, Ed Franquemont, Lynn A. Meisch, Amy Oakland Rodman, and Cynthia LeCount; and Melissa Leventon, curator of textiles of the Fine Arts Museums of San Francisco.

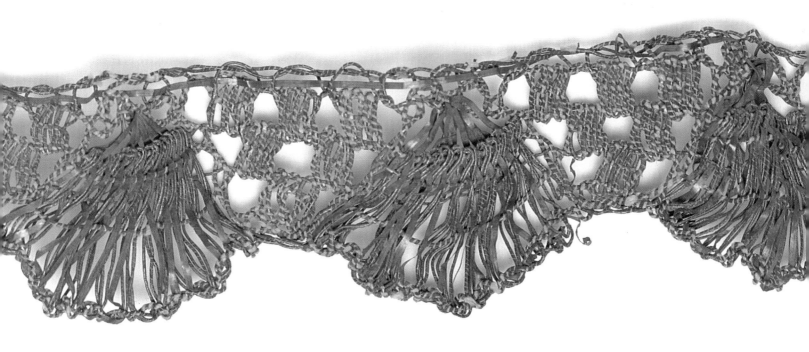

WOVEN JEWELS: THE FINISHING DETAILS

BY
BARBARA ARTHUR

Often it is the finishing details that define a weaving as exceptional in its beauty and creativity. These embellishments serve as inspirations to me as a weaver. As we were studying the Appleby collection, I was always drawn to the fine details, and admired the weavers' skill in creating such unique and beautiful finishes. Most of the weave structures found in these details are hand-manipulated with a backstrap loom setup.

The single bands for hats and ties often are created with a complementary-warp weave. This weave structure has the following characteristics: (1) the pattern is integral to the basic weave structure; (2) the two sets of warps are contrasting in color; (3) the length of the floats alternates; (4) the alignment of the warps is alternate or diagonal; (5) the cloth is almost always double faced.

Many of the hat bands and ties are double cloth (cat. no. 126, fig. 43). They often have oblique interlaced units (braids) at both ends, and the tassels are created by drawing the yarn through the ends and binding it. Some are very finely woven of commercial cotton sewing thread. The images may include condors, other birds, rodents, and four-legged animals (fig. 44).

Hair Ties

Some of the ties (such as fig. 45, cat. no. 164) that women in parts of the Andes wear as part of their traditional clothing (fig. 46) are beautiful, intricate, two-color, complementary-warp weave bands. Many are ingenious in design and technology, with intersecting transverse warps added at intervals along the warp as the weaving progresses. They are woven from the center out to the ends. The yarn is very tightly spun, plied, and finely woven. The added bands have different patterns, but are similar in iconography and color. Some of the trans-verse warps are not complementary-warp weave but are alternating float weave or crossed-warp weave structures. The loose warps create fringes (cat. no. 163, fig. 47). The main band often has a structure of discontinuous warps, which dovetail or interlock around a common weft at the center of the tie (fig. 48). This technique is used in Peru for a change in color patterning. In some areas, two girls usually work together in the making of a warp. The transverse warps are threaded through every other warp of the main band and are woven from the center out to the ends.

Headbands

Most of the headbands are warp-faced double cloth (cat. no. 93, fig. 49). Some are embellished with small glass beads that are added to the side selvages and included in the weft yarn. At one end, multicolored warp ends are grouped, bound together in pairs with a figure-eight stitch, turned on edge, and stitched through all the pairs at half-inch intervals. Some bands have narrow ties added, which are woven with a flat crossed-warp weave. This is achieved when a warp crosses over or under an adjacent warp element and is kept in place by the inter-lacing of a weft. It is then recrossed to the original warp order. A common design is the diamond.

FIGURE 43
Hatband *(t'isnu),* ca. 1970; Quechua/Aymara peoples. Llallagua, Potosí, Bolivia. Catalogue no. 126. (Appleby Collection 1992.107.217)

FIGURE 44
Detail of figure 43.

FIGURE 45
Double hair tie *(wata, watana),* mid-20th century; Quechua peoples. Lares, Cuzco, Peru. Catalogue no. 164. (Appleby Collection 1992.107.14)

FIGURE 46
Indígenas in the market at Tarabuco, Bolivia. Note the beautiful hair ties and fine *aksus* (Q. overskirts) on the girls and the beautiful poncho on the man. (Photo: Lynn Meisch)

FIGURE 47 (left)
Hair tie *(wata, watana),* early to mid-20th century; Quechua peoples. Lares, Cuzco, Peru. Catalogue no. 163. (Appleby Collection 1992.107.12)

FIGURE 48 (far left)
Detail of figure 47.

FIGURE 49 (below)
Headband *(wincha),* ca. 1950; Quechua/Aymara peoples. Charazani, La Paz, Bolivia. Catalogue no. 93. (Appleby Collection 1992.107.226)

Figure 50
Coca bag *(ch'uspa)* late 19th century (detail of strap); Aymara peoples. Luribay, La Paz, Bolivia. Catalogue no. 72. (Appleby Collection 1992.107.167)

Figure 51
Bag *(capacho),* ca. 1950; Quechua peoples. Ayata, La Paz, Bolivia. Catalogue no. 74. (Appleby Collection 1992.107.163)

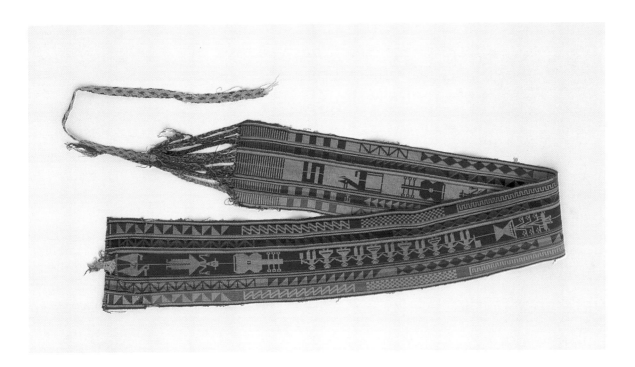

Straps for Bags and Belts

Most bag straps are patterned in complementary-warp pick-up or *pallay* (cat. no. 72, fig. 50). Occasionally, supplementary-warp patterning is used in their construction (cat. no. 74, fig. 51). When not in use for the design, the supplementary warps float on the back, and the design is not the same on both sides. This weave creates long floats that are tied down at intervals with weft yarns.

Belts usually have narrow ties added to both ends. Many are oblique interlaced units and some are crossed-warp weaves. One tie (cat. no. 98, fig. 52) has a weave structure that is unique in this collection. The band is woven with two sets of warps and multiple wefts, which act as oblique interlacements at the center and edges of the band. The visual imagery represents plied yarns or the fabric of twining, an ancient Andean method of visual punning (Frame 1986).

FIGURE 52
Belt *(chumpi),* ca. 1940; Quechua peoples. Northern Yungas, La Paz, Bolivia. Catalogue no. 98. (Appleby Collection 1992.107.197)

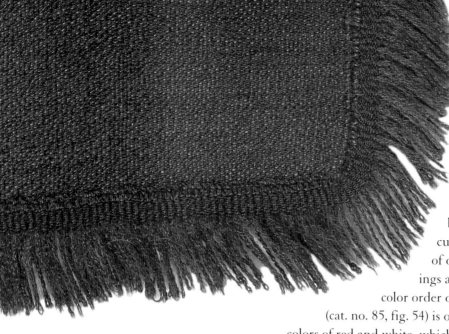

Edge Bindings

The edge bindings are functional as well as decorative. On large weavings, they protect the cloth's edges from wear. Many ponchos have a separately woven, flat, plain-weave band sewn around the edges with the ancient stitch, similar to a figure eight (cat. no. 90, fig. 53). Some examples have fringe created from extralong edge-binding wefts, which are either cut or looped and curl back around themselves at the ends as a result of overspun yarn (cat. no. 85). Plain-weave edge bindings also may include design elements patterned by the color order of the warps. The edge binding on one poncho (cat. no. 85, fig. 54) is one-fourth-inch wide, plain weave, in alternating colors of red and white, which create a checkerboard pattern. The fringe is one and one-fourth inches long and is made of multicolored wefts that are looped. Frequently the four corners of a poncho are turned under before the edge binding is added.

Other edge bindings are created with complementary-warp weave. One scarf (cat. no. 48, fig. 55), is woven in one long piece with three narrow bands on each end, which are sewn together and to the scarf itself. The three narrow patterned bands are woven with a complementary-warp weave. The fringes (fig. 56) are four inches long, black, looped, and created by the wefts of the bottom band.

The tubular edge binding is a warp-faced structure (cat. no. 76, fig. 25). In Peru and Bolivia, it may be woven onto a larger finished cloth, appearing as a border applied to bags, shawls, carrying cloths, and ponchos (Cahlander, Cason, and Houston 1978). The warps are held in place on the edges of the larger cloth by a spiraling weft, which passes through edge binding warps and the cloth edge in a circular direction. This process of passing the weft through the warps in the same direction draws the side selvages together to create a tube, which encases the edge of the larger cloth. The weft is held on a needle so it can pass through the cloth edge and the warps with each new shed. The tubes are woven in plain weave and in various patterns and colors including diagonal stripes, checks, and zigzag lines with diamonds (cat. no. 137, fig. 57). Some tubular edge bindings are plain weave with color substitution. When the warps are not being used in the color pattern area, they float inside the tube.

A Favorite Edge Binding

The diamond motif found in the crossed-warp tubular weave is one of the most fascinating and beautiful embellishments in Andean textiles and appears on the edges of ponchos, shawls, bags (cat. no. 39, fig. 58), and sometimes on belts. The tubular structures are woven without heddles. A forked stick is used to organize the warps and hold the cross in place. The pattern is created by crossed and diverted warps. The two colors in the center of the diamonds also are

FIGURE 53
The fringe on a small ch'imi poncho
(ponchito ch'imi), 19th century; Aymara peoples. La Paz, Bolivia. Catalogue no. 90. (Appleby Collection 1992.107.119)

FIGURE 54
Multicolored fringe on a black poncho
(poncho), late 19th century; Aymara peoples. Achiri, La Paz, Bolivia. Catalogue no. 85. (Appleby Collection 1992.107.117)

TRADITIONAL TEXTILES OF THE ANDES

FIGURE 55
Scarf *(chalina)*, late 19th century; Aymara peoples. Calamarca, Las Paz, Bolivia. Catalogue no. 48. (Appleby Collection 1992.107.155)

FIGURE 56
Detail of figure 55.

FIGURE 57
Man's mantle *(llakuta),* 19th century;
Aymara peoples. Potosí, Bolivia. Catalogue
no. 137. (Appleby Collection 1992.107.149)

diverted from side to side on the inside of the binding. At least three colors of
warp are used for the diamond pattern. Usually more colors are added for the
unpatterned areas.

The diamond motif tubular edge binding may be used on bags to join the
side seams (fig. 59) and bind the top edges. Pockets are created by extralong
warps woven separately, pulled forward, and incorporated into the rest of the
bag, and tubular edge bindings may be used on the pocket edges. Many of the
small bags are embellished with a combination of tubular edge bindings, tassels,
pompoms, beads, scallops, and silver coins.

The amount of time invested in these finishing details is incalculable, and
these bands, edge bindings, tassels, headbands, and hair ties are like woven
jewels adorning the people wearing Andean cloth. Such textiles truly honor the
ancestors of the spinners and weavers who made them.

FIGURE 58
Coca bag *(ch'uspa)*, ca. 1900; Aymara
peoples. Calamarca, La Paz, Bolivia.
Catalogue no. 39. (Appleby Collection
1992.107.166)

FIGURE 59
Detail of figure 58.

Catalogue Raisonné of the Jeffrey Appleby Collection of Andean Textiles

by Margot Blum Schevill

This catalogue raisonné of textiles from the Jeffrey Appleby collection follows a specific format, comprising the following elements:

Country of origin—by alphabetical order: Argentina, Bolivia, Chile, Ecuador, Peru; province or department

Item number (i.e., catalogue number); English name (foreign name); approximate date of manufacture—provided by the collector, with additional comments by the consultants

Colors, fibers—color terminology was derived by Barbara Arthur from *Creative Color* by Faber Birren (1961).

We described what we saw, although what we called beige was probably white when the textile was new. We noted our first impression and then discovered that under magnification a more accurate reading was possible. For example, what at first we called black was often dark purple.

Camelid (alpaca, llama, vicuña) fibers and sheep's wool are the most common, but in recent times synthetic yarn has become popular among urban Andeans, and cotton appears occasionally.

Fabrication—the weaving, knitting, or interlacing process. The terminology is derived from *The Primary Structure of Fabrics* by Irene Emery (1966) and *Warp-Patterned Weaves of the Andes* by Ann P. Rowe (1977).

Dimensions—length, or warp, first, then the width, or weft. Unwoven warps, such as belt fringes, are included in the length measurement.

Description—shape, visual impression, including iconography, and some technical features; provided by the cataloguers. Comments come from the collector, consultants, personal communications, and secondary sources. For direct quotation, the source is identified by name. Otherwise the information is woven into the body of the comments. The word *unique* is used to indicate that the collector or the consultants have never seen a similar example. Descriptive words, such as *abrash* (Arabic for "mottled" and here meaning the shimmering effect created by variations in the dye bath) and *ch'imi* (an Aymara word for yarn that has been plied of different colors or shades of yarn), are particular visual features of some of these textiles. Occasionally the termination area of a four-selvage cloth is referred to; this is also known as the terminal zone or area. It is woven last because, when a textile is almost finished, there is a space between two completed areas that is meticulously filled in, often with a needle. This area is visible on textiles because the patterning is usually abandoned and the texture of the cloth changes. Most of the two-piece textiles are joined by the ancient stitch, a figure-eight form.

Origin of the textile—by country, department, province (in Ecuador provinces are the equivalent of departments), region, and town. This information was provided by the collector unless otherwise indicated in the comments.

Linguistic affiliation—of the group that created the textile. Some of the older pieces were woven in areas in which at the time only Aymara was spoken but where now Quechua is also used. In those areas, belts, for example, will be known both as *wak'a,* the Aymara word, and *chumpi,* the Quechua word.

Yarn spin—the direction of the warp and weft yarn. Z2S indicates that Z-spun yarn is plied into an S spin; S2Z, an S-spun yarn plied into a Z spin (less common and sometimes referred to as *lluq'i,* a Quechua word meaning left and associated with magical practices); Z2S4Z is Z-spun yarn plied into an S-spun yarn, which is plied into four Z-spun yarns.

Warp and weft count, or *sett*—given in inches; epi means ends per inch, ppi means picks or wefts per inch, and the gauge for knitted textiles is spi: stitch per inch. The count was made in plain-weave and stockinette-knit areas. For double cloth, the count was of the top layer only.

Provenance—where and when the collector acquired the textile.

References—the primary and secondary sources of the information included in the comments; complete references appear in References and Works Consulted, page 146.

Notes: Cross-references to catalogue items that are illustrated are set in italics.

The linguistic origin of foreign words used in this catalogue is indicated by the abbreviations A. for Aymara, Q. for Quechua (Quichua in Ecuador), and S. for Spanish.

ARGENTINA
CHUBUT

1. **Belt** *(traruchiripa),* mid-20th century
Multicolored sheep's wool or camelid hair,
synthetic, and cotton
Woven in warp-faced plain and one-color
supplementary-warp weaves
Length: 70½ in., 172.8 cm; *width:* 3 in.,
7.6 cm

A long belt patterned in geometric motifs
of predominantly handspun and commercial yarn, with a warp fringe on both ends.
It differs in color and texture from Mapuche
belts from Chile) (see cat. no. 142, *143*). It
may have been woven on a vertical loom as
illustrated in Nardi and Saugy (1982). Rowe
(1977) discusses Mapuche (Araucanian)
belts. For further information on highland
Argentine textiles, see Rolandi de Perrot
and Jiménez de Pupareli (1983–1985).

Origin: Argentina, Chubut, Esquel
Linguistic Affiliation: Mapuche
Yarn Spin: Ground- and supplementary-warp
spin, Z2S, S2Z; weft, S2Z
Warp and Weft Count: 44 epi, 18 ppi
Provenance: Esquel, Chubut, Argentina, n.d.
References: Nardi and Saugy 1982, 58; Rolandi
de Perrot and Jiménez de Pupareli 1983–1985;
Rowe 1977, 40, fig. 39

1992.107.19

BOLIVIA
CHUQUISACA

2. **Mantle, woman's** *(llijlla),* ca. 1970
See fig. 37, p. 44.
Black, magenta, and multicolored sheep's
wool or camelid hair
Woven in warp-faced plain and two-color
complementary-warp weaves in alternate
and diagonal alignment
Length: 40 in., 101.6 cm; *width:* 45 in.,
114.3 cm

A large mantle of two pieces with solid-
colored and patterned stripes joined edge to
edge. There is a crochet edge binding on all
outer selvages. It is a more recent example
from Jainina with typical iconography
for this area. Images include birds and
geometric motifs within birds, checkerboard, imaginary animals and birds, an
imagined bestiary. Images are randomly
placed with zigzag lines. See also cat. no.
5, *6,* 7.

Origin: Bolivia, Chuquisaca, Oropeza, Potólo,
Jainina
Linguistic Affiliation: Quechua
Yarn Spin: Ground- and complementary-warp
spin, Z2S; weft, Z2S
Warp and Weft Count: 60 epi, 18 ppi
Provenance: San Francisco, California, 12/78

1992.107.130

Cat. no. 1

TRADITIONAL TEXTILES OF THE ANDES

3. **Skirt** *(aksu)*, 1940–1950
Brown, blue, shades of red, multicolored, and *ch'imi* sheep's wool or camelid hair
Woven in warp-faced plain and two-color complementary-warp weaves in alternate and diagonal alignment
Length: 33 in., 83.8 cm; width: 44 in., 111.8 cm

A medium-size skirt of solid-colored and animal-, bird-, and geometric-patterned stripes joined edge to edge. The two pieces are patterned differently, one side with imaginary bird and animal images, the other with narrow complementary-warp patterned stripes, one of which includes birds and viscachas. The diamond motifs are from Ravelo.

Origin: Bolivia, Chuquisaca, Oropeza, Potólo, Ravelo
Linguistic Affiliation: Quechua
Yarn Spin: Ground- and complementary-warp spin, Z2S; weft, Z2S
Warp and Weft Count: 92 epi, 18 ppi
Provenance: San Francisco, California, 12/78; originally bought in Sucre, Bolivia, in 1976
Reference: Ed Franquemont, personal communication, January 1996

1992.107.133

4. **Belt** *(chumpi)*, ca. 1960
Magenta, black, and multicolored sheep's wool or camelid hair
Woven in warp-faced double cloth
Length: 36 in., 91.5 cm; width: 1½ in., 3.8 cm

A medium-size belt of double cloth, patterned overall with animal and bird images such as condors and llamas, also imaginary animals. There are oblique interlaced units on one end and ties at both ends. Typical colors and images for this area.

Origin: Bolivia, Chuquisaca, Oropeza, Potólo
Linguistic Affiliation: Quechua
Yarn Spin: Warp and weft spin, Z2S
Warp and Weft Count: 48 epi, 18 ppi
Provenance: La Paz, Bolivia, 2/78

1992.107.224

5. **Festival poncho** *(poncho capote)*, ca. 1950
Maroon, magenta, red, multicolored, and *ch'imi* sheep's wool or camelid hair
Woven in warp-faced plain and two-color complementary-warp weaves in diagonal alignment
Length: 43½ in., 110.5 cm; width: 43 in., 109.2 cm

A medium-size poncho of solid-colored and animal-, bird-, and geometric-patterned stripes with remnants of a fringe; two pieces are sewn edge to edge, and there is a neck opening. Colors used to be pink, blue, green, and red; now they are pink and black.

Cat. no. 6

Maroon warp yarn is of black and red fibers that were combed together before spinning. A bright color palette. Images appear to be birds, cows, monkeys, humped llamas, and other imaginary animals. See also cat. no. 6.

Origin: Bolivia, Chuquisaca, Oropeza, Potólo
Linguistic Affiliation: Quechua
Yarn Spin: Ground- and complementary-warp spin, Z2S; weft, Z2S
Warp and Weft Count: 72 epi, 18 ppi
Provenance: San Francisco, California, 5/82

1992.107.113

6. **Festival poncho** *(poncho capote)*, ca. 1970
Red, dark maroon, and multicolored sheep's wool or camelid hair and multicolored acrylic
Woven in warp-faced plain and two-color complementary-warp weaves in diagonal alignment
Length: 45¾ in., 116.2 cm; width: 45 in., 114.3 cm

A very large fringed poncho of solid-colored and animal-, human-, and geometric-patterned stripes in two pieces, joined edge to edge, with a neck opening. There is an edge binding on all outer selvages with a multicolored acrylic fringe that may have been added later. Images include figures on

horses—a play on positive and negative space—in bottom right hand corner, wolves, birds, radiating diamonds, and imaginary figures. See also cat. no. 5.

Origin: Bolivia, Chuquisaca, Oropeza, Potólo
Linguistic Affiliation: Quechua
Yarn Spin: Ground- and complementary-warp spin, Z2S; weft, Z2S
Warp and Weft Count: 64 epi, 12 ppi
Provenance: San Francisco, California, 4/82

1992.107.114

7. **Half skirt** *(aksu)*, 1940–1950
Pink, dark blue, red, and multicolored sheep's wool or camelid hair
Woven in warp-faced plain and two-colored complementary-warp weaves in diagonal alignment
Length: 32½ in., 82.6 cm; width: 24½ in., 62.2 cm

Half of a woman's skirt, one piece, with animal-, bird-, and geometric-patterned and solid-colored stripes with a three-color tubular edge binding on three sides. Images include a human figure with upraised hands on a four-legged animal, catlike creatures, and geometric motifs. Rodman commented that sometimes *aksus* are separated so that they can be divided among relatives. Meisch

Cat. no. 8

Cat. no. 9

noted that such pieces are also sometimes separated for sale.

Origin: Bolivia, Chuquisaca, Oropeza, Potólo
Linguistic Affiliation: Quechua
Yarn Spin: Ground-warp spin, Z2S; complementary-warp spin, Z2S, S2Z; weft, Z2S
Warp and Weft Count: 64 epi, 19 ppi
Provenance: Sucre, Bolivia, 2/78
Reference: Lynn A. Meisch, Amy Oakland Rodman, personal communications, 1995

1992.107.135

8. Coca bag *(ch'uspa)*, ca. 1970

Red, beige, and multicolored sheep's wool, white cotton
Woven in warp-faced plain and two and three-color complementary-warp weaves
Length: 7⅜ in., 18.7 cm; width: 8 in., 20.3 cm

A small bag, one piece, in solid-colored and animal-, bird-, and geometric-patterned stripes joined at side seams with a tubular edge binding. Figurative patterns in beige and maroon are on one side; the other side is plain weave. There is one pocket, a strap, and a decorative finish on the bottom with pompoms, which are also on the pocket. The images are of llamas and horses in horizontal patterns and of birds and stars or seed pods turned sideways in vertical stripes. One row of patterning is along the top of the back together with blocks of color in four patterned bands. Coca bags like this resemble pre-Inca prototypes from Nazca and Ica, Peru. Men put lime or quinua, an ash catalyst for coca, in the tiny pocket called *uñita* (from Q. *uni,* baby animal). This

bag is so tightly woven that it is stiff, and the motifs pop out because the red sheep's wool is twice as thick as the white cotton. Several communities in this area weave this bag.

Origin: Bolivia, Chuquisaca, Yamparáez, Tarabuco, Candelaria
Linguistic Affiliation: Quechua
Yarn Spin: Ground-warp spin, S3Z; complementary spin, Z2S, S2Z; weft, S2Z
Warp and Weft Count: 112 epi, 38 ppi
Provenance: La Paz, Bolivia, 3/78
References: Meisch 1986b, fig. 21; 1987a, 53; Wasserman and Hill 1981, 17, pl. 25

1992.107.183

9. Small poncho *(luto unku),*

early 20th century
Gray-green, black, and dark blue sheep's wool or camelid hair
Woven in warp-faced and two-color complementary-warp weaves
Length: 17½ in., 44.5 cm; width: 24½ in., 62.2 cm

A small poncho of two pieces in solid-colored and geometric-patterned stripes, sewn together edge to edge, with a neck opening. A plain weave edge binding is sewn to all outer selvages with remnants of fringe created by the wefts of the edge binding. The high warp count results in many very fine geometric patterns. Franquemont and Meisch commented that this style of poncho is worn over the shirt and under the larger poncho.

Origin: Bolivia, Chuquisaca, Yamparáez, Tarabuco
Linguistic Affiliation: Quechua
Yarn Spin: Ground- and complementary-warp spin, Z2S; weft, Z2S
Warp and Weft Count: 136 epi, 22 ppi
Provenance: La Paz, Bolivia, 4/77
References: Meisch 1986b, fig. 5; Ed Franquemont, Lynn Meisch, personal communications, January 1996

01992.107.102

10. Half overskirt for mourning *(luto aksu),* 1950–1960

See fig. 4, p. 11.
Black, maroon, beige, multicolored, and *ch'imi* sheep's wool
Woven in warp-faced and two-color complementary-warp weaves
Length: 43⅜ in., 110.2 cm; width: 27⅞ in., 71 cm

A half skirt, one piece, with solid-colored and figurative-patterned stripes and three-color tubular edge binding on three outer selvages. Images include horses with flags, abstract birds, and flowers. Interesting use of positive and negative space in which faces are visible. Extensive use of *ch'imi* yarn in various color combinations, also in the tubular edge binding and narrow bands of complementary-warp weave, which contrast with the dominant black, beige, and maroon coloring. Meisch commented that this is a half *luto aksu;* the zigzag design is called *mayu k'inku* (Q. meandering river) and the horses with flags are carnival horses.

Origin: Bolivia, Chuquisaca, Yamparáez, Tarabuco, Candelaria

Cat. no. 11

Cat. no. 12

Linguistic Affiliation: Quechua
Yarn Spin: Ground-warp spin, Z2S, S2Z, complementary-warp spin, Z2S; weft Z2S
Warp and Weft Count: 40 epi, 14 ppi
Provenance: Albuquerque, New Mexico, 12/77
References: Meisch 1986b; 1987a; Lynn Meisch, personal communication, January 1996

1992.107.136

COCHABAMBA

11. **Coca bag** *(ch'uspa),* late 19th century
Rose and multicolored camelid hair
Woven in warp-faced plain, two- and three-color complementary, and double-cloth weaves
Length: 8⅝ in., 22 cm; width: 10¼ in., 26.4 cm

A medium-size bag, one piece, with solid-colored and geometric-patterned stripes joined at sides with plain-weave tubular edge binding, which also is on the bottom. Multicolored tassels are on the sides and bottom. There are remnants of a strap on the inside. Today the people of Bolívar speak Quechua, but when this cloth was woven, the language there was Aymara. Rodman commented that the dyes were natural with the exception of pink and that this is typical Aymara weaving. Because "the [old-style] cloth" is not being woven now, these bags are brought out for fiestas and "danced."

Origin: Bolivia, Cochabamba, Arque, Bolívar
Linguistic Affiliation: Quechua/Aymara
Yarn Spin: Ground-, complementary-, and double-cloth warp spin, Z2S; weft, Z2S
Warp and Weft Count: 64 epi, 18 ppi

Provenance: San Francisco, California, 6/79
Reference: Amy Oakland Rodman, personal communication, 1995

1992.107.170

12. **Coca bag** *(ch'uspa),* late 19th century
Shades of red with purple, beige, and multicolored sheep's wool or camelid hair
Woven in warp-faced plain and two-color complementary-warp weaves
Length: 9⅞ in., 25.1 cm; width, 12½ in., 31.8 cm

A large bag, one piece, with one side of geometric-patterned stripes and the other side of warp-faced plain weave. A three-color tubular edge binding joins the two sides and continues along the top edges. A three-color plain-weave strap is sewn to inside corners and multicolored tassels are added to bottom of bag. This may be a saddlebag that was converted to a coca bag. Saddlebags are woven in one piece with one half patterned and the other side, which is next to the animal, not patterned. A natural dye palette.

Origin: Bolivia, Cochabamba, Arque, Bolívar
Linguistic Affiliation: Quechua/Aymara
Yarn Spin: Ground- and complementary-warp spin, Z2S; weft, Z2S
Warp and Weft Count: 48 epi, 18 ppi
Provenance: La Paz, Bolivia, n.d.

1992.107.184

13. **Hat** *(lluchu),* 20th century
Multicolored sheep's wool or camelid hair
Knitted in stockinette, garter, loop, and eyelet stitches; color patterning, circular

knitting on straight needles
Length: 14¾ in., 37.5 cm; width: 9 in., 22.9 cm

A long hat, one piece, with multicolored geometric patterning in a series of wave designs. Turned-back cuff on bottom creates an unusual shape similar to those from Muñecas, La Paz, as represented in LeCount (1990). Also multicolored loops on bottom edge of cuff and a tassel on top. An unusual specimen.

Origin: Bolivia, Cochabamba, Arque, Bolívar
Linguistic Affiliation: Quechua/Aymara
Yarn Spin: Spin, Z2S
Gage: 14 spi
Provenance: Del Dios, California, 6/81
Reference: LeCount 1990, 54

1992.107.190

14. **Little poncho** *(ponchito),* late 19th century
Red and multicolored sheep's wool or camelid hair
Woven in warp-faced plain, two- and three-color complementary-warp, alternating float weaves, and warp-faced double cloth
Length: 43½ in., 110.5 cm; width: 34⅞ in., 88.6 cm

A medium-size poncho, two pieces, of solid-colored and geometric- and floral-patterned stripes joined edge to edge, with a neck opening. Technically and visually complex with a range of colors and of pattern weaves. A natural dye palette. Illustrated in Wasserman and Hall (1981) as a rare ceremonial poncho, the design representing a floral vine of the Andean highlands.

Cat. no. 15

Origin: Bolivia, Cochabamba, Arque, Bolívar
Linguistic Affiliation: Quechua/Aymara
Yarn Spin: Ground-, complementary-, and
double-cloth warp spin, Z2S; weft, Z2S
Warp and Weft Count: 72 epi, 18 pp
Provenance: San Francisco, California, 2/83;
belonged to the Alawi family from the Jorenko
estancia
Reference: Wasserman and Hill 1981, pl. 13
1992.107.105

15. Overskirt *(aksu, urku)*, late 19th century
Rose and multicolored sheep's wool or
camelid hair
Woven in warp-faced plain and two-color
complementary-warp weaves
Length: 47 in., 119.4 cm; width: 55⅝ in.,
141.3 cm

A large overskirt, two pieces, with solid-
colored and patterned stripes in geometric,
bird, and human images, joined edge to
edge. Patterning is different on both pieces,
and there is a dark green, plain-weave
tubular edge binding on all outer selvages.
Images include Ss, crosses, a woman with
her arms up, and large and small birds.
Solid rose areas on outer selvages are
warped with Z2S, Z2S, and S2Z in
sequence, which creates a diamond pattern,
not a herringbone effect. Center rose area
has a richness and depth of color because
of the *ch'imi* combinations of brown with
rose, purple, and red. It resembles an *urku*
published in Adelson and Tracht (1983, 108,
pl. 40). A finely woven textile, a natural dye
palette.

Origin: Bolivia, Cochabamba, Arque, Bolívar
Linguistic Affiliation: Quechua/Aymara
Yarn Spin: Ground-warp spin, Z2S, S2Z; comple-
mentary-warp spin, Z2S; weft, Z2S
Warp and Weft Count: 80 epi, 18 ppi
Provenance: Chapare, 3/84; from a family that
had moved from Bolívar, Cochabamba
Reference: Adelson and Tracht 1983, 108–109
1992.107.146

16. Bag *(ch'uspa)*, late 19th century
Rose and multicolored sheep's wool or
camelid hair
Woven in warp-faced plain and two-color
complementary-warp weaves
Length: 13⅝ in., 34.5 cm; width: 13¼ in.,
33.7 cm

A large bag, one piece, of solid-colored and
patterned stripes with geometric, bird, and
rayed star motifs and a four-color tubular
edge binding on sides and top. There is a
strap, and multicolored tassels are attached
to sides and bottom of bag. A natural dye
palette. See also cat. no. 17.

Origin: Bolivia, Cochabamba, Tapacarí, Challa
Linguistic Affiliation: Quechua/Aymara
Yarn Spin: Ground- and complementary-warp
spin, Z2S; weft, Z2S
Warp and Weft Count: 68 ppi, 20 ppi
Provenance: San Francisco, California, 5/82
1992.107.174

17. Bag *(ch'uspa)*, late 19th century
Rose, olive, and multicolored sheep's wool
or camelid hair

Woven in warp-faced plain and two color
complementary-warp weaves
Length: 11⅛ in., 28.3cm; width: 12⅝ in.,
32.1 cm

A medium-size bag, one piece, of solid-
colored and patterned stripes with
geometric and bird images, and a four-color
tubular edge binding on sides, top, and on
bottom; a strap and multicolored tassels at
top, bottom, and sides. A natural dye
palette. See also cat. no. 16.

Origin: Bolivia, Cochabamba, Tapacarí, Challa
Linguistic Affiliation: Quechua/Aymara
Yarn Spin: Ground- and complementary-warp
spin, Z2S; weft, Z2S
Warp and Weft Count: 64 epi, 20 ppi
Provenance: La Paz, Bolivia, 4/80
1992.107.175

18. Bag *(ch'uspa)*, ca. 1960
Multicolored camelid hair
Woven in warp-faced double cloth
Length: 7⅛ in., 18.1 cm; width: 6¾ in.,
17.1 cm

A small bag, two pieces, in patterned
double cloth with human, floral, animal,
and geometric images, a new, multicolored
strap, four-color tubular edge binding on
sides and top, and multicolored wool trim
and tassels on the bottom. Large condors
dominate the iconography. In design, there
is little relationship to earlier bags; this style
became popular in the mid-twentieth
century. Unusual to have a bag with two
pieces sewn together at bottom. Rodman
commented that commercial, synthetic,
multicolored yarn is valued by *indígenas,*
and that the fiber of the bag is camelid and
the dyes synthetic. The image of a man and
woman with small llamas has pre-Hispanic
antecedents.

Origin: Bolivia, Cochabamba, Tapacarí, Challa
Linguistic Affiliation: Quechua/Aymara
Yarn Spin: Warp spin, Z2S; weft, Z2S
Warp and Weft Count: 60 epi, 18 ppi
Provenance: La Paz, Bolivia, 6/80
Reference: Amy Oakland Rodman, personal
communication, 1995
1992.107.176

19. Knit Bag *(monedero)*, early 20th century
Multicolored sheep's wool and alpaca
Knitted in stockinette stitch with color
geometric patterning; circular knitting
on straight needles
Length: 7¼ in., 18.4 cm; width: 5½ in.,
14 cm

A medium-size bag—sometimes known as
monederos (S. coin bags)— with triangular-
shaped appendages knitted onto the bottom,
ties and tassels, and a strap on top. The

Cat. no. 18

Cat. no. 19

Cat. no. 20

stepped motifs are typical of Challa. The bottom is shaped like a llama, and the appendages resemble the head, tail, tummy or udders, and four legs of the animal.

Origin: Bolivia, Cochabamba, Tapacarí, Challa
Linguistic Affiliation: Quechua/Aymara
Yarn Spin: Spin, Z2S
Gage: 14 spi, 6 spc
Provenance: La Paz, Bolivia, 6/80
Reference: LeCount 1990, 70, no. 8 in pl. 9

1992.107.177

20. **Belt** *(chumpi),* ca. 1940
Beige, brown, pink, and red sheep's wool or camelid hair
Woven in warp-faced double cloth
Length: 42 in., 106.7 cm; width: 2½ in., 6.4 cm

A medium-size belt, one piece, patterned overall in mostly geometric, floral, and bird images with fifteen oblique, interlaced units on one end. This example came from the northern Challa area. Images include condors, large and small birds (some with flowers in their mouths), snakes, a large geometric motif with sixteen faces attached, and small floral motifs. Sections alternate in brown with beige, and beige with brown with a pink-red narrow stripe in center. Brown weft may be alpaca. See cat. no. 21.

Origin: Bolivia, Cochabamba, Tapacarí, Challa
Linguistic Affiliation: Quechua/Aymara
Yarn Spin: Double-cloth warp spin, Z2S; weft, Z2S
Warp and Weft Count: 72 epi, 18 ppi
Provenance: La Paz, Bolivia, 3/78

1992.107.210

21. **Belt** *(chumpi),* ca. 1940
Beige, dark purple, pink, multicolored, and *ch'imi* sheep's wool or camelid hair
Woven in warp-faced double cloth
Length: 42⅞ in., 108.9 cm; width: 4⅞ in., 12.4 cm

A medium-size, wide belt, one piece, patterned overall with geometric and bird motifs and nineteen oblique, interlaced units with ties on one end and ties on other end. Images include condors, small birds, and large hooked geometric motifs. More stylized images in regular repeats in contrast to cat. no. 20.

Origin: Bolivia, Cochabamba, Tapacarí, Challa
Linguistic Affiliation: Quechua/Aymara
Yarn Spin: Double-cloth warp spin, Z2S; weft, Z2S
Warp and Weft Count: 68 epi, 10 ppi
Provenance: La Paz, Bolivia, 3/78

1992.107.211

22. **Woman's mantle** *(awayu),* late 19th century
See fig. 35, p. 43.
Black and multicolored sheep's wool or camelid hair
Woven in warp-faced plain and two- and three-color complementary-warp weaves and warp-faced double cloth
Length: 46½ in., 118.1 cm; width; 44½ in., 113 cm

A large mantle, two pieces, sewn together edge to edge, with large, solid black stripes, or *pampas,* and patterned stripes, or *pallay,* in geometric and bird motifs with a plain-weave tubular edge binding on all outer selvages. Rodman commented that S2Z and Z2S yarns warped in adjacent groups create a herringbone effect on outer borders so that the piece will lie flat. Yorke (1980) mentioned that the double-cloth bands in weavings from this area are called *kurti.* A very nice example.

Origin: Bolivia, Cochabamba, Tapacarí, Challa
Linguistic Affiliation: Quechua/Aymara
Yarn Spin: Ground-warp spin, Z2S, S2Z; complementary-warp spin, Z2S; weft, Z2S
Warp and Weft Count: 64 epi, 16 ppi
Provenance: New York, New York, 12/85
References: Yorke 1980, 22–23; Amy Oakland Rodman, personal communication, 1995

1992.107.121

23. **Woman's overskirt** *(aksu),* late 19th century
Ch'imi and multicolored sheep's wool or camelid hair
Woven in warp-faced plain and two-color complementary-warp weaves
Length: 56⅛ in., 142.6 cm; width: 51⅜ in., 130.5 cm

A large, woman's overskirt, two pieces, sewn together edge to edge, patterned in geometric, bird, and animal images, and solid-colored stripes with a five-color tubular edge binding on all outer selvages. Patterned stripes are different on both cloths. The S2Z- and Z2S-warp yarns create a herringbone effect in the outermost stripes. A very fine old textile in excellent condition. Published in Adelson and Tracht (1983), who commented that the matrimonial style of *urku,* which predominates in the Bolívar region, was actually widespread throughout all of northern Potosí and southern Cochabamba. Also see fig. 31, which shows how the garment was worn.

Origin: Bolivia, Cochabamba, Tapacarí, Challa
Linguistic Affiliation: Quechua/Aymara
Yarn Spin: Ground-warp spin, S2Z, Z2S; complementary-warp spin, Z2S; weft, Z2S
Warp and Weft Count: 68 epi, 18 ppi
Provenance: San Francisco, California 10/82
Reference: Adelson and Tracht 1983, 108–109

1992.107.144

24. **Half woman's overskirt** *(aksu),* late 19th century
Black, rose, and multicolored sheep's wool or camelid hair
Woven in warp-faced plain and two-color complementary-warp weaves
Length: 62½ in., 158.8 cm; width: 30⅜ in., 77.2 cm

One piece, half of a woman's skirt, with solid black, or *pampas,* areas and pink geometric- and bird-patterned, or *pallay,* stripes, and a plain-weave tubular edge binding on three outer selvages. Half of one of the great Challa *aksus* noted for their clarity of design; *aksus* were sometimes divided up among family members. A natural dye palette. Lovely hand, fine old cloth. Exceptionally nice termination area for a Bolivian weaving; placed almost in the center, an unusual feature.

Origin: Bolivia, Cochabamba, Tapacarí, Challa
Linguistic Affiliation: Quechua/Aymara
Yarn Spin: Ground-warp and complementary-warp spin, Z2S; weft, Z2S
Warp and Weft Count: 64 epi, 18 ppi
Provenance: La Paz, Bolivia, 4/80

1992.107.145

25. **Poncho** *(poncho),* late 19th century
Blue, red, beige, multicolored, and *ch'imi* sheep's wool or camelid hair
Woven in warp-faced plain and two-color complementary-warp weaves
Length: 72 in., 183 cm, width: 64 in., 162.6 cm

A large poncho, two pieces, sewn together edge to edge, with a neck opening, and solid-colored and geometric- and bird-patterned stripes. Other ponchos from this area have black stripes. In good condition because they were rarely used; one of three such ponchos known. It is beautifully woven; pink wefts show through to give sparkle and texture. Narrow blue stripes at side edges are of S2Z-spun yarn. Very discrete termination area with a symmetrical organization of stripes. It resembles cat. no. 136, a smaller poncho from northern Potosí, in layout and complementary-warp design. A natural dye palette. A fine old textile.

Origin: Bolivia, Cochabamba, Tapacarí, Challa
Linguistic Affiliation: Quechua/Aymara
Yarn Spin: Ground-warp spin, Z2S, S2Z; complementary-warp spin, Z2S; weft, Z2S
Warp and Weft Count: 48 epi, 16 ppi
Provenance: Santa Fe, New Mexico, 8/85

1992.107.109

Cat. no. 32

26. **Coca bag** *(ch'uspa)*, late 19th century
Dark orange-red, beige, and multicolored
sheep's wool or camelid hair
Woven in warp-faced plain and two- and
three-color complementary-warp weaves
Length: 9¼ in., 23.5 cm; width: 1⅛ in.,
2.9 cm

A medium-size bag, one piece, sewn
together at bottom, with solid-colored and
geometric- and bird-patterned stripes. The
sides are joined by a three-color tubular
edge binding that continues on the top
edges. There are three rows of multicolored
fringe tassels. A natural dye palette. Designs
are similar to those on the woman's mantle,
cat. no. 33.

Origin: Bolivia, Cochabamba, Tapacarí, Leque
Linguistic Affiliation: Aymara
Yarn Spin: Ground- and complementary-warp
spin, Z2S; weft, Z2S
Warp and Weft Count: 40 epi, 16 ppi
Provenance: La Paz, Bolivia, 3/79

1992.107.169

27. **Hatband** *(t'isnu)*, ca. 1950
Multicolored sheep's wool or camelid hair
Woven in warp-faced double cloth
Length: 23 in., 58.4 cm; width: ⅜ in., 1 cm

A long, narrow band in patterned double-
cloth with multicolored pompoms at both
ends. Very imaginative images including
bats, viscachas, monkeys, llamas, spiders,
octupi, and the letter S. Finely woven, so
each image is clearly delineated. Pompoms
may be a combination of commercial and
handspun yarn.

Origin: Bolivia, Cochabamba, Tapacarí, Leque
Linguistic Affiliation: Quechua/Aymara
Yarn Spin: Double-cloth warp spin, Z2S; weft, Z2S
Warp and Weft Count: 96 epi, 22 ppi
Provenance: La Paz, Bolivia, 1/76

1992.107.204

28. **Belt or hatband** *(t'isnu)*, ca. 1950
White, red, and multicolored sheep's wool
and camelid hair
Woven in warp-faced double cloth
Length: 30½ in., 77.5 cm; width: 1⅛ in.,
3 cm

A medium-size belt or hatband, one piece,
in patterned stripes, with oblique, interlaced units at each end. Images include a
wonderful parade of large animals such as
llamas, viscachas, a monkey with eyes and
mouth, other rodents; long tails a prominent
feature. A more classic style, not as complex
as cat. no. 29.

Origin: Bolivia, Cochabamba, Tapacarí, Leque
Linguistic Affiliation: Quechua/Aymara
Yarn Spin: Double-cloth warp spin, Z2S, weft, Z2S
Warp and Weft Count: 56 epi, 20 ppi
Provenance: La Paz, Bolivia, 1/76

1992.107.205

29. **Belt or hatband** *(t'isnu)*, ca. 1940
Beige, pink, and multicolored sheep's wool
or camelid hair
Woven in warp-faced double cloth
Length: 39½ in., 100.3 cm; width: ⅞ in.,
2.2 cm

A long belt or hatband, one piece, in
patterned stripes with oblique, interlaced
units at each end. Leque figurative work

special; a classic example with abstract
images of large and small birds, rodents,
geometrics, and florals. More difficult to
read than those in cat. no. 28. Dense warp
count, very finely woven.

Origin: Bolivia, Cochabamba, Tapacarí, Leque
Linguistic Affiliation: Quechua/Aymara
Yarn Spin: Double-cloth warp spin, Z2S, weft, Z2S
Warp and Weft Count: 100 epi, 24 ppi
Provenance: La Paz, Bolivia, 2/76

1992.107.206

30. **Belt** *(wak'a)*, ca. 1950
See fig. 38, p. 45.
Dark brown, yellow, and multicolored
sheep's wool or camelid hair
Woven in warp-faced double cloth
Length: 33⅛ in., 84.1 cm; width: 4¾ in.,
12.1 cm

A medium-size belt, one piece, in
geometric-, animal-, and bird-patterned
stripes with eight oblique, interlaced units
on one end. There are several styles of belts
for this region; in this example, the images
are large and readable and include fish, a
nursing cow, a person sitting on a horse,
horses, squirrels, imagined beasts, and
hooks or waves. Yorke (1980) commented
that the women's belts from this area are
among the widest in Bolivia and that the
phantasmagoric figures make them easily
identified. See also cat. no. 31, *32*.

Origin: Bolivia, Cochabamba, Tapacarí, Leque
Linguistic Affiliation: Quechua/Aymara
Yarn Spin: Double-cloth spin, Z2S; weft, Z2S
Warp and Weft Count: 44 epi, 14 ppi
Provenance: La Paz, Bolivia, 2/78
Reference: Yorke 1980, 18

1992.107.207

31. **Belt** *(wak'a)*, ca. 1940
Multicolored sheep's wool or camelid hair
Woven in warp-faced double cloth
Length: 28⅛ in., 71.4 cm; width: 5 in.,
12.7 cm

A small belt, one piece, with geometric-,
animal-, and bird-patterned stripes. At
one end, interlaced groups of multicolored
warps are worked into twenty oblique,
interlaced units that create a unique finish.
Images are large and readable and include
camels, viscachas, rodents, and other horned
beasts arranged asymmetrically across the
textile. See also cat. no. 30, *32*.

Origin: Bolivia, Cochabamba, Tapacarí, Leque
Linguistic Affiliation: Quechua/Aymara
Yarn Spin: Double-cloth warp spin, Z2S; weft, Z2S
Warp and Weft Count: 40 epi, 12 ppi
Provenance: La Paz, Bolivia, 4/77

1992.107.208

Cat. no. 34

32. **Belt** *(wak'a),* ca. 1950

   Pink, dark purple, and multicolored sheep's
   wool or camelid hair

   Woven in warp-faced double cloth

   Length: 40⅝ in., 103.2 cm; width: 6⅛ in.,
   15.6 cm

   A large belt, one piece, in geometric-, bird-,
   and animal-patterned stripes, with eleven
   oblique, interlaced units at one end. This
   belt is similar in images and colors to cat.
   no. 29, although the style is crisper and
   tighter. Images are much smaller than those
   in cat. no. 30 or 31, and include condors,
   dogs, rodents, llamas, and a variety of small
   birds.

   Origin: Bolivia, Cochabamba, Tapacarí, Leque
   Linguistic Affiliation: Quechua/Aymara
   Yarn Spin: Double-cloth spin, Z2S; weft, Z2S
   Warp and Weft Count: 60 epi, 16 ppi
   Provenance: La Paz, Bolivia, 2/78

   1992.107.209

33. **Woman's mantle** *(awayu),* late 19th century

   Rose and multicolored sheep's wool or
   camelid hair

   Woven in warp-faced plain and two-color
   complementary-warp weaves

   Length: 38¾ in., 98.4 cm; width: 43½ in.,
   110.5 cm

   A medium-size mantle, two pieces, sewn
   together edge to edge, with large rose
   colored areas or *pampas* and geometric and
   bird-patterned *pallay.* A four-color tubular
   edge binding is on all outer selvages. The
   mantles with complementary-warp weave
   stripes are said to be an older style than
   those in double cloth. Color changes in
   tubular edge binding are beautifully done.
   Bird images similar to those in cat. no. *22,*
   a mantle from Challa. Striping on outer
   edges combines narrow, black, S2Z-spun
   yarn stripes with light rose, Z2S-spun yarn
   creating a herringbone effect. A natural dye
   palette. See also cat. no. *34.*

   Origin: Bolivia, Cochabamba, Tapacarí, Leque
   Linguistic Affiliation: Aymara
   Yarn Spin: Ground-warp spin, Z2S, S2Z;
   complementary-warp spin, Z2S; weft, Z2S
   Warp and Weft Count: 40 epi, 14 ppi
   Provenance: La Paz, Bolivia, 4/77

   1992.107.125

34. **Woman's mantle** *(awayu),* ca. 1950

   Black, red, and multicolored sheep's wool or
   camelid hair

   Woven in warp-faced plain and warp-faced
   double-cloth weaves

   Length: 37⅞ in., 96.2 cm; width: 48⅞ in.,
   124.1 cm

   A large mantle, two pieces, sewn together
   edge to edge, with large solid-colored and

Cat. no. 35

Cat. no. 36

Cat. no. 38

palette. Published in LeCount (1990), who also commented that this is one of two known specimens; the other one published in Taullard (1949). Abstract bar designs above figures may be some kind of value system.

Origin: Bolivia, western Cochabamba
Linguistic Affiliation: Aymara
Yarn Spin: Spin, Z2S
Gage: 16 spi, 6½ spc
Provenance: La Paz, Bolivia, 4/81
References: LeCount 1990, 70, pl. 9 and 105; Taullard 1949; Cynthia LeCount, personal communication, October 1995

1992.107.171

LA PAZ

36. **Woman's mantle** *(awayu),* late 19th century
Blue, red, multicolored, and *ch'imi* sheep's wool and camelid hair
Woven in warp-faced plain and two-color complementary weaves
Length: 34⅛ in., 86.7 cm; width: 43 in., 109.2 cm

A large mantle, two pieces of unequal size joined edge to edge, with solid-colored and geometric-, bird-, animal-, and floral-patterned stripes, and a four-color tubular edge binding on all outer selvages. The actual center of the piece is a complementary-warp weave stripe, and the joining is to one side of that. The style is unusual because of narrow patterned bands of potato hook motifs. The sway-backed bovine is a common motif in textiles from this region (see cat. no. *46*).

Origin: Bolivia, La Paz, Aroma, Calamarca, Collana
Linguistic Affiliation: Aymara
Yarn Spin: Ground- and complementary-warp spin, Z2S; weft, Z2S
Warp and Weft Count: 48 epi, 14 ppi
Provenance: Del Dios, California, 3/81

1992.107.124

37. **Little poncho** *(ponchito),* late 19th century
Dark blue, brown, rose, and multicolored sheep's wool
Woven in warp-faced plain and two-color complementary-warp weaves
Length: 28½ in., 72.4 cm; width: 39¼ in., 99.7 cm

A medium-size garment, two pieces, joined edge to edge in solid-colored and geometric-, bird-, and star-patterned stripes. A rare example; only six of this style are known. The iconography is diverse and dense, and it is not absolutely bilaterally symmetrical in patterning. This textile is published in Collier, Mendoza de Rick, and Berger (1981). Adelson and Tracht (1983) show a similar one.

double-cloth stripes. A classic *awayu* from this period with walking fish and other creatures rendered in the double cloth areas in beige and red. The images stand out in contrast to the red and black solid-colored areas. See also cat. no. 33.

Origin: Bolivia, Cochabamba, Tapacarí, Leque
Linguistic Affiliation: Quechua/Aymara
Yarn Spin: Ground- and double-cloth warp spin, Z2S; weft, Z2S
Warp and Weft Count: 56 epi, 12 ppi
Provenance: La Paz, Bolivia, 2.78

1992.107.131

35. **Knit Bag** *(ch'uspa),* ca. 1940
Beige, tan, brown, and black sheep's wool and camelid hair
Knit in stockinette and garter stitches, with a scalloped edging or *pica pica;* color patterning, circular knitting on straight needles
Length: 12 in., 30.5 cm; width: 6½ in., 16.5 cm

A medium-size bag, one piece, color patterning in human, animal, and geometric images with one tie and five tassels on sides and bottom. Large images of bulls, llamas, and men and women wearing headdresses and holding hands. Probably all natural colors; strong, bold imagery in muted color

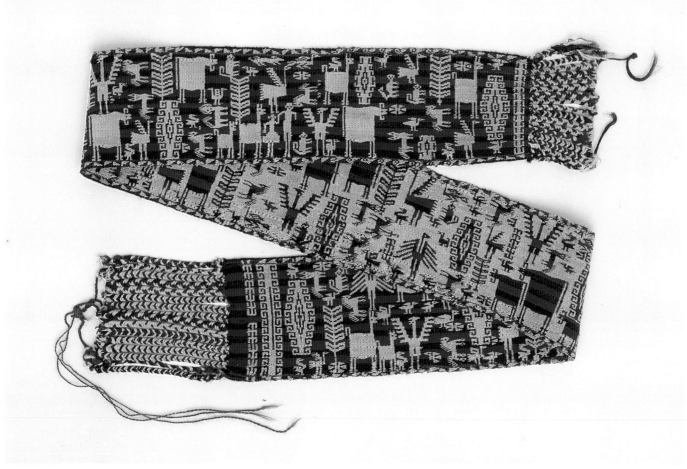

Cat. no. 41

Origin: Bolivia, La Paz, Aroma, Calamarca, Collana
Linguistic Affiliation: Aymara
Yarn Spin: Ground- and complementary-warp spin, Z2S; weft, Z2S
Warp and Weft Count: 52 epi, 14 ppi
Provenance: San Francisco, 5/81
References: Adelson and Tracht 1983, 68, pl. 9; Collier, Mendoza de Rick, and Berger 1981, 33, no. 46

1992.107.107

38. **Skirt** *(urku)*, ca. 1900
Black, multicolored, and *ch'imi* sheep's wool or camelid hair
Woven in warp-faced plain and two-color complementary-warp weaves
Length: 124 in., 315 cm; *width:* 24⅞ in., 63.2 cm

A full, gathered skirt, one long piece, in solid-colored and geometric-, bird-, and animal-patterned stripes and a plain-weave tubular edge binding on one side only. End selvages are joined by dovetailing warp loops along loom cord. Opening at waist. Exceptionally long piece. Similar skirts are published in Adelson and Tracht (1983) and in Adelson and Takami (1978).

Origin: Bolivia, La Paz, Aroma, Calamarca, Santiago de Llallagua
Linguistic Affiliation: Aymara
Yarn Spin: Ground- and complementary-warp spin, Z2S; weft, Z2S
Warp and Weft Count: 40 epi, 16 ppi
Provenance: La Paz, Bolivia, 5/78
References: Adelson and Takami 1978, 28; Adelson and Tracht 1983, 110–11

1992.107.126

39. **Coca bag** *(ch'uspa)*, ca. 1900
See figs. 58, 59, p. 57.
Multicolored sheep's wool or camelid hair
Woven in warp-faced plain and two-color complementary-warp weaves
Length: 7¼ in., 18.4 cm; *width:* 8¾ in., 22.2 cm

A small bag, one piece, of solid-colored and geometric-patterned stripes; joined at side seams with a three-color tubular edge binding that continues along the top edges. There are three pockets created by extra-long warps, forty-one multicolored tassels on bottom of bag and pockets, one other tassel, and remnants of a strap. A very festive *ch'uspa;* design and details are beautifully executed.

Origin: Bolivia, La Paz, Aroma, Calamarca
Linguistic Affiliation: Aymara

Yarn Spin: Ground- and complementary-warp spin, Z2S; weft, Z2S
Warp and Weft Count: 80 epi, 18 ppi
Provenance: Santa Fe, New Mexico, 8/85

1992.107.166

40. **Belt** *(wak'a),* late 19th century
Beige, multicolored, and *ch'imi* camelid hair
Woven in warp-faced double cloth
Length: 48⅝ in., 123.5 cm; *width:* 5⅜ in., 13.7 cm

One long, wide belt patterned with a variety of images, and with fringes on ends of oblique, interlaced units at both ends. There are two styles of belts from this region: one with images that are uniform and lined up (as in this example) and the other with free-form animals. Iconography includes sway-backed four-legged animals, llamas, condors, trees, birds, a human under a llama within a frame and variations of same, like a coat-of-arms. Rich iconography. This belt is published in Collier, Mendoza de Rick, and Berger (1981). Rowe (1977) discusses the belts from the south of Lake Titicaca, which have a variety of animal motifs and the device of using one set of warps in white and the other set striped, a double-cloth technique also found in Charazani, Bolivia. See also cat. no. *41.*

Cat. no. 43

Origin: Bolivia, La Paz, Aroma, Calamarca
Linguistic Affiliation: Aymara
Yarn Spin: Double-cloth warp spin, Z2S, weft, Z2S
Warp and Weft Count: 72 epi, 14 ppi
Provenance: La Paz, Bolivia, 3/79
References: Collier, Mendoza de Rick, and Berger 1981, no. 41; Rowe 1977, 95

1992.107.201

41. **Belt** *(wak'a),* late 19th century
Beige, multicolored, and *ch'imi* sheep's wool or camelid hair
Woven in warp-faced double cloth
Length: 67 in., 170.2 cm; width: 4¾ in., 12.1 cm

A long, wide belt patterned with a variety of images with oblique interlaced units and ties at both ends. The randomly spaced, highly diversified imagery includes condors, two-headed and other birds, bovines, llamas, men and women, monkeys, viscachas, dogs, horses, men riding horses, one large geometric repeat with hook shapes surrounding it, and bands of hook shapes. See also cat. no. 40.

Origin: Bolivia, La Paz, Aroma, Calamarca
Linguistic Affiliation: Aymara
Yarn Spin: Double-cloth warp spin, Z2S; weft, Z2S
Warp and Weft Count: 72 epi, 14 ppi
Provenance: Corrales, New Mexico, 4/86

1992.107.202

42. **Hatband** *(t'isnu),* late 19th century
Beige and multicolored sheep's wool or camelid hair and horsehair
Woven in warp-faced double cloth
Length: 24 in., 61 cm; width: ⅞ in., 2.2 cm

A small band, one piece, patterned with a variety of images, and with oblique interlaced units on one end and warp fringe on the other end. Images include sway-backed cows, condors, little horses and birds, and arches, which may be the Tiwanaku arch that used to be woven into pre-Hispanic textiles, but is now just a design element. Horsehair wefts in two separate sections.

Origin: Bolivia, La Paz, Aroma, Calamarca
Linguistic Affiliation: Aymara
Yarn Spin: Double-cloth warp spin, Z2S; weft, Z2S
Warp and Weft Count: 72 epi, 22 ppi
Provenance: La Paz, Bolivia, 1/76

1992.107.203

43. **Coca cloth** *(inkuña),* late 19th century
Gray, tan, brown, multicolored, and *ch'imi* sheep's wool or camelid hair
Woven in warp-faced plain and two-color complementary-warp weaves
Length: 26½ in., 67.3 cm; width: 25⅝ in., 65.1 cm

A small, almost square cloth with solid-colored and patterned stripes. Iconography includes the same sway-backed four-legged animals as in cat. no. 36 and *46,* but here there is a rider on most of them; also a double-headed condor and birds in the narrow complementary-warp stripes. Figure work areas make this a special piece; one image is said to be the gateway of the sun at Tiwanaku.

Origin: Bolivia. La Paz, Aroma, Calamarca
Linguistic Affiliation: Aymara
Yarn Spin: Ground- and complementary-warp spin: Z2S; weft, Z2S
Warp and Weft Count: 52 epi, 12 ppi
Provenance: Austin, Texas, 1/87

1992.107.151

44. **Hat** *(lluchu),* 1950–1975
Multicolored and *ch'imi* sheep's wool or camelid hair
Knit in stockinette, garter, *pica pica* or scallop stitches; color patterning, circular knitting on straight needles
Length: 13½ in., 34.3 cm; width: 9½ in., 24.1 cm

A medium-size hat, one piece, with animal-, bird-, and geometric-patterned and solid-colored stripes and an elongated topknot. Images include sway- and straight-backed horses and bovines, condors, double-headed birds, and waves. LeCount (1990) commented that the iconography on caps made between approximately 1950 and 1975 has an orderly placement, shows a great variety, and is often very detailed. Motifs neatly arranged right side up in rows separated by narrow pattern bands; a *punta* row found near the top is rare, seen only on *chullus* here and in the Sicasica area. Some of these images appear in graph 6 on page 92 of LeCount's book. A natural dye palette. Presence of *ch'imi* yarn gives rich visual effect.

Origin: Bolivia, La Paz, Aroma, Calamarca
Linguistic Affiliation: Aymara
Yarn Spin: Spin, Z2S
Warp and Weft Count: 14 spi
Provenance: San Francisco, California, 3/81
Reference: LeCount 1990, 55

1992.107.188

45. **Hat** *(lluchu),* ca. 1970–1980
Red and multicolored sheep's wool and camelid hair
Knit in stockinette, garter, and popcorn stitches; color patterning, circular knitting with straight needles
Length: 10½ in., 26.7 cm; width: 9 in., 22.9 cm

A medium-size hat, one piece, with solid-colored and bird-, animal-, and

Cat. no. 44

Cat. no. 45

geometric-patterned stripes. Ear flaps were added, and there is an unusual topknot with one strand of yarn. Tiny white birds and circle motifs not confined within stripes or bands but cross them randomly. Lovely color use in ear flaps. LeCount commented that this is the only known specimen from Calamarca with ear flaps; may be a modern anomaly.

Origin: Bolivia, La Paz, Aroma, Calamarca
Linguistic Affiliation: Aymara
Yarn Spin: Spin, Z2S
Gage: 18 spi
Provenance: La Paz, Bolivia, 5/83
Reference: Cynthia LeCount, personal communication, October 1995

1992.107.189

46. **Woman's mantle** *(awayu),* late 19th century
Brown, beige, multicolored, and *ch'imi* sheep's wool or camelid hair
Woven in warp-faced plain and two-color complementary-warp weaves, and warp-faced double cloth
Length: 38 in., 96.5 cm; width: 42½ in., 108 cm

A large mantle, two unequal-sized pieces sewn together edge to edge, of solid-colored and animal-, bird-, geometric-, and floral-patterned stripes. A rare feature is the three rows of figures in each double-cloth band; another feature is that the center seam is off center and the figurative band is in the center of textile. Iconography includes four-legged, sway-backed animal images, viscachas, birds including the condor, and hooklike geometrics. A beautiful piece. Yorke (1980) commented that the distinctiveness of Calamarca garments lies in their bold designs and a color arrangement that, in the *awayus,* favors an unusual amount of white.

Origin: Bolivia, La Paz, Aroma, Calamarca
Linguistic Affiliation: Aymara
Yarn Spin: Ground-, complementary-warp, and double-cloth spin, Z2S; weft, Z2S
Warp and Weft Count: 56 epi, 14 ppi
Provenance: San Francisco, California, 7/85
Reference: Yorke 1980, 16

1992.107.122

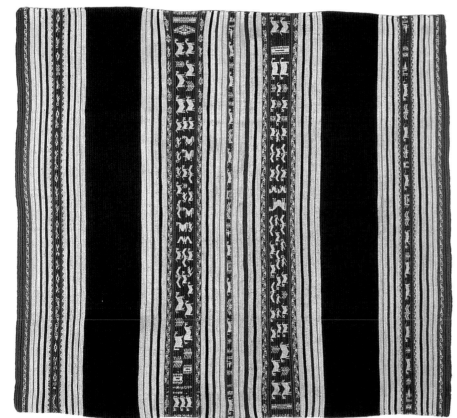

Cat. no. 46

47. **Woman's mantle** *(iskayu),* late 19th century
Red, dark blue, and multicolored sheep's wool or camelid hair
Woven in warp-faced plain and two-color complementary-warp weaves
Length: 29 in., 73.7 cm; width: 48½ in., 123.2 cm

A medium-size mantle, two pieces, sewn together edge to edge with solid-colored and floral-, bird-, and geometric-patterned stripes. The two pieces are not woven with

Cat. no. 47

the same designs in the patterned stripes. There is an *abrash* effect in solid-colored stripes. A fine example with figurative work, usually just stripes. Adelson and Tracht (1983) commented that the *iskayu* was the oldest and most important ceremonial mantle worn by Aymara women during the post-conquest period. Similar mantles with variations of broad and narrow stripes appear in almost all Aymara areas.

Origin: Bolivia, La Paz, Aroma, Calamarca
Linguistic Affiliation: Aymara
Yarn Spin: Ground- and complementary-warp spin, Z2S; weft, Z2S
Warp and Weft Count: 52 epi, 16 ppi
Provenance: Austin, Texas, 1/87
Reference: Adelson and Tracht 1983, 78
1992.107.148

48. **Scarf** *(chalina),* late 19th century
See figs. 55, 56, p. 55.
Tan, multicolored, and *ch'imi* sheep's wool and camelid hair
Woven in warp-faced and two-color complementary-warp weaves
Length: 69½ in., 176.5 cm; width: 14 in., 35.6 cm

One long piece of solid-colored and bird-, floral-, and geometric-patterned stripes with

three narrow patterned bands on each end that are sewn together and to the scarf itself. There is black fringe on both ends. The weaver probably wove three complementary warp-patterned bands, then cut them, sewed them together with tan warp yarn, and attached them to the scarf. Tan yarn may be alpaca or vicuña for it has a soft hand.

Origin: Bolivia, La Paz, Aroma, Calamarca
Linguistic Affiliation: Aymara
Yarn Spin: Ground- and complementary-warp spin, Z2S; weft, Z2S
Warp and Weft Count: 68 epi, 16 ppi
Provenance: La Paz, Bolivia, 3/82
1992.107.155

49. **Sling** *(honda),* early 20th century
Multicolored sheep's wool or camelid hair
Woven in weft-faced tapestry weave
Length: 42¾ in., 108.6 cm; width: 1¼ in., 3.2 cm

A medium-size sling, one piece, with a slit cradle in the center that has multicolored fringes on both sides of it and three-color, tubular long braids on both ends. A classic Calamarca sling. Cradle images are of horses or bovines. Fringed slings may have served ceremonial functions. Similar to a

sling published in Cahlander (1980). See also cat. no. *50.*

Origin: Bolivia, La Paz, Aroma, Calamarca
Linguistic Affiliation: Aymara
Yarn Spin: Tapestry-weave yarn spin, S2Z; weft, S2Z; fringe, Z2S
Warp and Weft Count: 22 ppi
Provenance: La Paz, Bolivia, 5/80
Reference: Cahlander 1980, 11, pl. 8
1992.107.228

50. **Sling** *(honda),* early 20th century
Multicolored sheep's wool or camelid hair
Woven in weft-faced tapestry
Length: 55½ in., 141 cm; width: 1 in., 2.5 cm

A long sling, one piece, with a slit cradle in the center that has multicolored fringes on both sides of it with three- and four-color, long, tubular sling braids on both ends. One braid has a loop. A ceremonial piece, beautiful colors. See also cat. no. 49.

Origin: Bolivia, La Paz, Aroma, Calamarca
Linguistic Affiliation: Aymara
Yarn Spin: Tapestry-weave yarn spin, S2Z; weft, S2Z
Weft Count: 26 ppi
Provenance: La Paz, Bolivia, 5/80
1992.107.229

Cat. no. 50

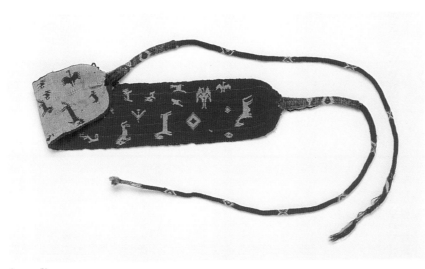

Cat. no. 51

Cat. no. 52

Cat. no. 53

51. **Sling** *(honda),* ca. 1930
Red, beige, and multicolored sheep's wool
or camelid hair and horsehair
Woven in warp-faced double cloth
Length: 52 in., 132 cm; width: 2½ in., 6.4 cm

A large sling, one piece, with animal, bird,
and geometric motifs, and three-color long
braids on both ends with fringes. One braid
has a loop. Iconography is similar to that of
cat. no. *44,* a *lluchu* from Calamarca, which
has motifs placed as randomly as they are in
this example. The cradle is woven, not slit
tapestry, as are cat. no. 49 and *50.* Cahlander
(1980) describes the braid construction.
Probably a ceremonial sling.

Origin: Bolivia, La Paz, Aroma, Calamarca
Linguistic Affiliation: Aymara
Yarn Spin: Double-cloth warp spin, Z2S, S2Z;
weft, horsehair
Warp and Weft Count: 64 epi, 20 ppi
Provenance: La Paz, Bolivia, 4/83
Reference: Cahlander 1980, 78

1992.107.232

52. **Sling or dancing tie** *(wichi wichi),*
early 20th century
Multicolored sheep's wool and camelid hair
Woven in weft-faced tapestry weave
Length: 18¼ in., 46.3 cm; width: 1½ in.,
3.8 cm

A medium-size sling or dancing tie, one
piece, with a four-part cradle in the center
and one long and one short four-color
tubular braid on each end. One has a
pompom and a loop; the other has horsehair
and wool tassels and pompoms. For ceremonial functions fruit is placed in a *wichi
wichi,* and the sling is "danced." Examples
of *wichi wichis* in Cahlander (1980).

Origin: Bolivia, La Paz, Aroma, Calamarca
Linguistic Affiliation: Aymara
Yarn Spin: Tapestry-yarn spin, S2Z, Z2S; weft,
S2Z, Z2S
Weft Count: 28 ppi
Provenance: La Paz, Bolivia, 4/83
Reference: Cahlander 1980, 10–13, pl. 5, 6

1992.107.231

53. **Coca bag** *(ch'uspa),* late 19th century
Black, beige, rose, and multicolored sheep's
wool and camelid hair
Woven in warp-faced plain and two-color
complementary-warp weaves
Length: 9½ in., 24.1 cm; width: 11½ in.,
29.2 cm

A medium-size bag, one piece, in solid-
colored and geometric-patterned stripes
joined at side seams with three-color
tubular edge binding, which also continues
along top edges. There is a strap, and nineteen multicolored tassels along the bottom

and lower edges of the bag. Sicasica weavers use black stripes to set off patterned ones and spin the yarn tightly in order to create small fine patterns. A natural dye palette. See also cat. no. 57, a woman's mantle, which also has large black stripes.

Origin: Bolivia, La Paz, Aroma, Sicasica
Linguistic Affiliation: Aymara
Yarn Spin: Ground- and complementary-warp spin, Z2S; weft, Z2S
Warp and Weft Count: 76 epi, 22 ppi
Provenance: La Paz, Bolivia, 4/80

1992.107.168

54. **Coca cloth** *(inkuña),* mid- to late 19th century
Multicolored camelid hair
Woven in warp-faced plain, two-color complementary, and alternating float weaves
Length: 25 in., 63.5 cm; width: 31 in., 78.7 cm

A medium-size cloth, one piece, of solid-colored and geometric-patterned stripes with a four-color tubular edge binding on four selvages and four tassels. The alternation of narrow alternate-float stripes with mostly solid-colored stripes makes a beautiful effect. The piece has a soft hand. The tones of the natural grays are striated. A colorful palette created by natural dyes.

Origin: Bolivia, La Paz, Aroma, Sicasica
Linguistic Affiliation: Aymara
Yarn Spin: Ground- and complementary-warp spin, Z2S; weft, Z2S
Warp and Weft Count: 64 epi, 16 ppi
Provenance: Corrales, New Mexico, 8/84

1992.107.150

55. **Poncho** *(poncho),* mid-19th century
Black and multicolored sheep's wool and camelid hair
Woven in warp-faced plain and two-color complementary-warp weaves
Length: 50½ in., 128.3 cm; width: 48 in., 122 cm

A large poncho, two pieces, in predominantly solid-colored black and geometric-patterned stripes joined together edge to edge with a neck opening. A black plain-weave edge binding with a blue fringe created by the wefts is sewn to all selvages. The side corners are turned up. A natural dye palette, similar in coloring and striping to other ponchos in the collection; see cat. no. 104, 162, 163.

Origin: Bolivia, La Paz, Aroma, Sicasica
Linguistic Affiliation: Aymara
Yarn Spin: Ground- and complementary-warp spin, Z2S; weft, Z2S; fringe, Z2S4Z
Warp and Weft Count: 88 epi, 16 ppi
Provenance: La Paz, Bolivia, 3/79

1992.107.106

Cat. no. 54

Cat. no. 55

Cat. no. 56

56. **Poncho** (*poncho*), late 19th century
Red, pink, dark blue, and multicolored camelid hair
Woven in warp-faced, two-color complementary, and alternating float weaves
Length: 75¾ in., 192.4 cm; width: 64½ in., 163.8 cm

A very large poncho, two pieces, in solid-colored and bird- and geometric-patterned stripes, joined edge to edge, with a neck opening. The edge binding of the neck and on the selvages is alternating float weave, which produces a checkerboard pattern. There are multicolored fringes added to all the edge bindings. The four corners are turned up, and there is an *abrash* effect in red, blue, and pink stripes. A natural dye palette. This textile was published in Wasserman and Hill (1981).

Origin: Bolivia, La Paz, Aroma, Sicasica
Linguistic Affiliation: Aymara
Yarn Spin: Ground- and complementary-warp spin, Z2S; weft, Z2S; fringe, Z2S4Z
Warp and Weft Count: 38 epi, 12 ppi
Provenance: Del Dios, California, 3/80
Reference: Wasserman and Hill 1981, pl. 9
1992.107.110

57. **Woman's mantle** (*awayu*), mid-19th century
Purple and multicolored camelid hair
Woven in warp-faced, two-color complementary, one-color supplementary, and alternating float weaves
Length: 47⅛ in., 119.7 cm; width: 33½ in., 85.1 cm

A medium-size mantle, two pieces, with narrow solid-colored and geometric- and bird-patterned stripes sewn together. A three-color, flat edge binding on all outer selvages. Typical of Lake Titicaca area textiles with older designs and dense warp count. *Abrash* effect in purple stripes. A natural dye palette. A very fine piece.

Origin: Bolivia, La Paz, Aroma, Sicasica
Linguistic Affiliation: Aymara
Yarn Spin: Ground-, complementary-, and supplementary-warp spin, Z2S; weft, Z2S
Warp and Weft Count: 112 epi, 20 ppi
Provenance: San Francisco, California, 7/85
1992.107.142

58. **Poncho** (*poncho*), early 20th century
Dark red, multicolored, and *ikat* sheep's wool
Woven in warp-faced plain weave
Length: 67⅜ in., 171 cm; width: 53½ in., 135.9 cm

A large poncho, two pieces, with solid-colored and *ikat* stripes sewn together edge to edge. There is a neck opening banded with pleated *ikat* cloth, and a plain-weave

striped cloth edge binding is sewn onto all outer selvages. Very fine wool, may be from merino sheep, and overspun. Most ponchos from this town are very long, possibly woven on a treadle loom, then cut and bound. No one knows how the *ikat* technique developed in Ulla Ulla. The use of *ikat* in eighteenth-, nineteenth-, and twentieth-century Bolivian textiles is rare. Gisbert, Arze, and Cajias (1992) discussed zones where *ikat* is woven, and commented that the three zones that use *ikat* are Ulla Ulla in Charazani and Calcha and Yura in Potosí. Wasserman and Hill (1981) describe ikat designs in a Charazani *llijlla* as "painted-warp[s]." An extremely elegant textile, a lovely hand, fine control of tie and dye with unusual color choices.

Origin: Bolivia, La Paz, Caupolín, Charazani, Ulla Ulla
Linguistic Affiliation: Quecha/Aymara
Yarn Spin: Ground-warp spin, Z2S; weft, Z2S
Warp and Weft Count: 92 epi, 20 ppi
Provenance: Cuzco, Peru, 5/80
References: Gisbert, Arze, and Cajias 1992, 272, fig. 91; Wasserman and Hill 1981, pl. 2
1992.107.116

59. **Bag** (*capacho*), ca. 1940
Dark green, orange-red, and multicolored camelid hair
Woven in warp-faced plain and two-color complementary-warp weaves
Length: 11 in., 28 cm; width: 15 in., 38 cm

A large bag, one piece, in solid-colored and geometric- and bird-patterned stripes with a double-cloth strap and four pockets created by longer warps that are open on the inside. The lime catalyst chewed with coca leaves is kept in these pockets. The sides are joined by commercial bias tape, which continues along the top selvages. The pockets are trimmed with multicolored beads. The tassels also are beaded, some with small coins on the end—Bolivian *cinco centavo* pieces; two are dated 1873 and 1883. Girault (1969) illustrates geometric motifs similar to those in this textile, which are associated with the *Callawayas* or *Qollahuayas*, medicine men who use these bags to hold herbs; some designs are reserved for their use. Relates to a pair of saddlebags from this region, see cat. no. *63*, in coloring and patterns. Beading is exceptionally fine.

Origin: Bolivia, La Paz, Caupolín, Charazani
Linguistic Affiliation: Quechua/Aymara
Yarn Spin: Ground- and complementary-warp spin, Z2S; weft, Z2S
Warp and Weft Count: 40 epi, 18 ppi
Provenance: San Francisco, California, 2/86
Reference: Girault 1969, 45
1992.107.161

60. **Belt** (*wak'a*), ca. 1950
Beige, maroon, and multicolored sheep's wool or camelid hair
Woven in warp-faced double cloth
Length: 47¾ in., 121.3 cm; width: 3 in., 7.6 cm

A medium-size belt, one piece, patterned with geometric, animal, and bird images. At one end warp ends are wrapped in groups, and there is one warp-faced plain-weave strap at each end. Images are horses, frogs, birds, and a radiating star placed in distinct blocks.

Origin: Bolivia, La Paz, Caupolín, Charazani
Linguistic Affiliation: Quechua/Aymara
Yarn Spin: Double-cloth warp spin, Z2S; weft, Z2S
Warp and Weft Count: 60 epi, 14 ppi
Provenance: La Paz, Bolivia, 2/76
1992.107.193

61. **Belt** (*chumpi*), early 20th century
Beige, maroon, purple, and multicolored sheep's wool or camelid hair
Woven in warp-faced double cloth
Length: 67¾ in., 172 cm; width: 1¾ in., 4.4 cm

A long, narrow belt, one piece, patterned in floral, animal, and bird images. At one end there is a long narrow tie of two oblique, interlaced units; at the other end, eleven oblique, interlaced units woven and sewn together. Images include large and small horses (some paired), llamas, monkeys, and a bird next to a flower.

Origin: Bolivia, La Paz, Caupolín, Charazani
Linguistic Affiliation: Quechua/Aymara
Yarn Spin: Double-cloth warp spin, Z2S; weft, Z2S
Warp and Weft Count: 84 epi, 14 ppi
Provenance: La Paz, Bolivia, 2/76
1992.107.194

62. **Poncho** (*poncho*), ca. 1960
See fig. 31, p. 41.
Dark red and multicolored sheep's wool or camelid hair
Woven in warp-faced plain and double cloth
Length: 53⅜ in., 135.6 cm; width: 52⅞ in., 134.3 cm

A large poncho, two pieces, with solid-colored and animal-, bird-, and geometric-patterned stripes joined edge to edge. There is a neck opening with two-color cross-knit loop stitch edge binding, and a plain-weave edge binding sewn to all outer selvages. The edge binding wefts create multicolored fringes. The four corners are turned up. Ponchos from this area are rare. There is a predominance of horses in the iconography, along with humans, and various types of birds and llamas. Girault (1969) illustrates

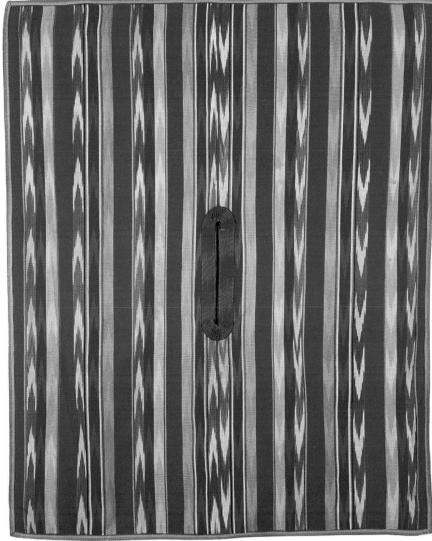

Cat. no. 58

Cat. no. 59

Cat. no. 63

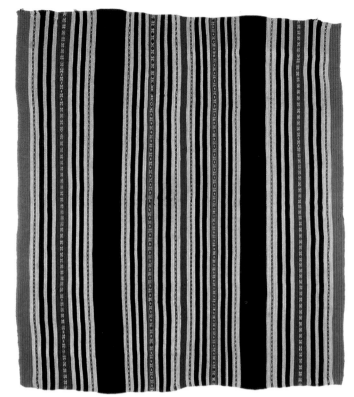

Cat. no. 67

geometric motifs, similar to those in this textile, that were associated with the *Callawayas* or *Qollahuayas,* medicine men. Wasserman and Hill (1981) commented on the hooked designs—"several angular and curved or 'hooked' variations of the scroll motif: *wajrapallay* [Quechua] said to depict the snail or cornucopia"—and said that these ponchos were worn for festive occasions. See also Bastien (1985 [1978], 110) for comments on the snail motif. Rodman added that the cross-knit loop stitch is a pre-Columbian technique for finishing textiles.

Origin: Bolivia, La Paz, Caupolín, Charazani
Linguistic Affiliation: Quechua/Aymara
Yarn Spin: Ground- and double-cloth warp spin, Z2S; weft, Z2S
Warp and Weft Count: 48 epi, 16 ppi
Provenance: La Paz, Bolivia, 1/79
References: Bastien 1985 (1978), 110; Girault 1969, 45; Wasserman and Hill 1981, 10; Amy Oakland Rodman, personal communication, 1995

1992.107.115

63. **Saddlebags** *(alforja),* ca. 1960
Green, red, and multicolored sheep's wool or camelid hair
Woven in warp-faced plain weave and warp-faced double cloth
Length: 35¼ in., 89.5 cm; width: 13¼ in., 33.7 cm

One long piece, folded back on both ends to create two pouches, with geometric-, human-, animal-, and bird-patterned and solid-colored stripes. A bias tape edge binding is sewn onto all selvages, and two multicolored pompoms are placed at diagonal corners. *Callawayas* or *Qollahuayas* wear them over their shoulders, carrying herbs in them. The central motif, a variation of the scroll, is very finely done in contrast to that on cat. no. *77,* a full skirt. Images of camelids, birds, a man and woman standing together holding hands, diamond with rays. Possibly a ceremonial textile because of fine weaving and little wear. See also cat. no. *59,* which is similar in coloring and patterns, for additional comments.

Origin: Bolivia, La Paz, Caupolín, Charazani
Linguistic Affiliation: Quechua/Aymara
Yarn Spin: Ground- and double-cloth warp spin, Z2S; weft, Z2S
Warp and Weft Count: 68 epi, 20 ppi
Provenance: La Paz, Bolivia, 2/78

1992.107.160

64. **Full skirt** *(urku),* ca. 1940
See fig. 30, p. 40.
Orange-red and multicolored sheep's wool or camelid hair
Woven in warp-faced plain, two-color complementary, alternating float, and warp-faced double-cloth weaves
Length: 26½ in., 67.3 cm; width: 37¼ in., 94.6 cm

One long piece, joined at end selvages with solid-colored and geometric-patterned stripes, has two rows of stitching to create pleats. Width measurement refers to the waist, not the bottom of the skirt, which is 162⅜ inches. Dwight Heath commented that this skirt style is worn only on special occasions; everyday skirts are less full and do not have patterned bands and stripes. See also cat. no. *59.*

Origin: Bolivia, La Paz, Caupolín, Charazani
Linguistic Affiliation: Quechua/Aymara
Yarn Spin: Ground-, complementary-, and double-cloth warp spin, Z2S; weft, Z2S
Warp and Weft Count: 40 epi, 16 ppi
Provenance: La Paz, Bolivia, 3/81
Reference: Heath, in Schevill 1986, 108

1992.107.129

65. **Coca or ceremonial cloth** *(inkuña),*
19th century
Multicolored and *ch'imi* camelid hair
Woven in warp-faced plain weave
Length: 36 in., 91.4 cm; width: 32½ in., 82.6 cm

A medium-size cloth of multicolored stripes with a four-color tubular edge binding on all outer selvages. Color stripe order almost symmetrical across piece. Cloths like these may be used for carrying coca or as *mesas* (S. tables) for offerings, as seen in a figure

Cat. no. 68

Cat. no. 69

in Adelson and Tracht (1983). Lovely range of colors. *Ch'imi* yarn enhances the visual impression. A natural dye palette.

Origin: Bolivia, La Paz, Ingavi, Tiahuanaco
Linguistic Affiliation: Aymara
Yarn Spin: Ground-warp spin, Z2S, S2Z; weft, Z2S
Warp and Weft Count: 64 epi, 20 ppi
Provenance: La Paz, Bolivia, 5/78
Reference: Adelson and Tracht 1983, 116, fig. 33
1992.107.154

66. **Woman's mantle** *(awayu),* late 19th century
Black and multicolored camelid hair
Woven in warp-faced plain and two-color complementary-warp weaves
Length: 41 in., 104.1 cm; width: 35 in., 89 cm

A medium-size mantle of two pieces, with solid-colored and geometric- and bird-patterned stripes, joined edge to edge. A Lake Titicaca-style piece with a natural dye palette. Subdued coloring, very tasteful and classic. See also cat. no. 67.

Origin: Bolivia, La Paz, Ingavi
Linguistic Affiliation: Aymara
Yarn Spin: Ground- and complementary-warp spin, Z2S; weft, Z2S
Warp and Weft Count: 80 epi, 18 ppi
Provenance: Corrales, New Mexico, 1/82
1992.107.140

67. **Woman's mantle** *(awayu),* mid- to late 19th century
Black, multicolored, and *ch'imi* camelid hair
Woven in warp-faced plain and two-color complementary-warp weaves.
Length: 40⅜ in., 102.5 cm; width: 35½ in., 90.2 cm

A medium-size mantle of two pieces with solid-colored and geometric-patterned stripes sewn together edge to edge. A Lake Titicaca-style textile known for the black and white stripes. The design layout is almost symmetrical on both sides, and images include star shapes. Outer edges are of varying shades of pink, giving a rich textural effect. A natural dye palette. See also cat. no. 66.

Origin: Bolivia, La Paz, Ingavi
Linguistic Affiliation: Aymara
Yarn Spin: Ground- and complementary-warp spin: Z2S; weft, Z2S
Warp and Weft Count: 80 epi, 28 ppi
Provenance: New York City, New York, 12/85
1992.107.141

68. **Hand warmers** *(guantes),* early 20th century
Green and multicolored sheep's wool
Knitted in stockinette, garter, moss, eyelet stitches with beads; color patterning, circular knitting on straight needles
Length: 5⅛ in., 13 cm; width: 4¼ in., 10.8 cm

Two small pieces with additional appendages for thumbs, and multicolored glass seed beads added in selected areas. Designs are geometric, floral, and letters. The word segnor *(señor)* is outlined with white beads. Published in LeCount (1990); fingerless gloves appear in figure 6.5. LeCount also commented that very few beaded pairs exist, and that fingerless gloves are still worn by market women. During the post-colonial times, knit purses, mittens, and baby caps of vicuña were popular among upper-class women of the Cuzco, La Paz, and Potosí areas.

Origin: Bolivia, La Paz, Lake Titicaca
Linguistic Affiliation: Aymara
Yarn Spin: Spin, Z2S
Gage: 15 spi
Provenance: La Paz, Bolivia, 4/82
References: LeCount 1990, 60, 69, pl 8; Cynthia LeCount, personal communication, October 1995
1992.107.185a,b

69. **Hat, beaded** *(lluchu),* early 20th century
Light pink and multicolored sheep's wool or camelid hair
Knitted in stockinette and garter stitches with beads; color patterning, circular knitting on straight needles
Length: 14½ in., 36.8 cm; width: 7½ in., 19.1 cm

A long hat, one piece, with white glass seed bead patterning and one tassel on top. Three

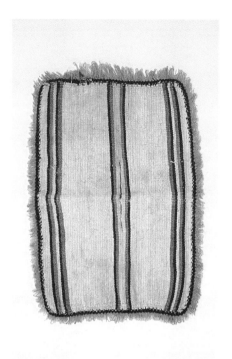

Cat. no. 71

Cat. no. 72

Cat. no. 73

rows of edging on the bottom and geometric patterning. LeCount (1990) discussed beaded hats, and this particular one; beaded hats without ear flaps are worn by women for fiestas and other special occasions; examples like this are rare. LeCount also commented that rainbow striping is typical of a particular area.

Origin: Bolivia, La Paz, Lake Titicaca
Linguistic Affiliation: Aymara
Yarn Spin: Spin, Z2S
Gage: 10½ spi
Provenance: La Paz, Bolivia, 5/78
References: LeCount 1990, 28, fig. 3.9, 54, 69, pl. 8; Cynthia LeCount, personal communication, October 1995

1992.107.186

70. **Hat, beaded** (*lluchu*), early 20th century
Pink with beige sheep's wool or camelid hair
Knitted in stockinette, garter, scallop stitches with beads; color patterning, circular knitting on straight needles
Length: 14⅝ in., 37.1 cm; width: 8 in., 20.3 cm

A medium to large hat, one piece, with allover patterning in multicolored glass seed beads. There is beaded scalloped edging on the bottom, and one multicolored tassel on the top. Rich iconography includes crowns, double-headed birds, lions, and stars, which may reflect colonial influence; also birds sitting on plant stalks, and men and women with yellow hats. Published in LeCount (1990); see also cat. no. 69. LeCount also commented on the interesting juxtaposition of a row of Inca stars above a row of crowns; the only other example is in the Museo Etnografía in La Paz.

Origin: Bolivia, La Paz, Lake Titicaca
Linguistic Affiliation: Aymara
Yarn Spin: Spin, Z2S
Gage: 10 spi
Provenance: La Paz, Bolivia, 5/80
References: LeCount 1990, 8, fig. 3.9, 69, pl. 8; Cynthia LeCount, personal communication, October 1995

1992.107.192

71. **Miniature saint's poncho** (*poncho santo*), 19th century
Beige with rose, yellow-green, and tan camelid hair
Woven in warp-faced plain weave
Length: 8 in., 20.3 cm; width: 5½ in., 14 cm

A miniature poncho, one piece, with stripes in the center and outer selvages, and a neck opening created by discontinuous wefts. There is an edge binding and fringe created by the wefts of the edge binding on all outer selvages. Candle wax and one pink weft

1½ inches in center of fifth row suggest that this textile served ceremonial purposes. Bruce (1986) discussed archaeological precedence for miniature textiles as offerings. A natural dye palette.

Origin: Bolivia, La Paz, Lake Titicaca
Linguistic Affiliation: Aymara
Yarn Spin: Ground-warp spin, Z2S; weft, Z2S
Warp and Weft Count: 80 epi, 24 ppi
Provenance: La Paz, Bolivia, 4/82
Reference: Bruce 1986

1992.107.235

72. **Coca bag** *(ch'uspa),* late 19th century
See fig. 50, p. 52.
Shades of red and multicolored sheep's wool or camelid hair
Woven in warp-faced plain, two-color complementary-, and one-color supplementary-warp weaves
Length: 9 in., 22.9 cm; width: 10½ in., 26.7 cm

A medium-size bag, one piece, of solid-colored and geometric-patterned stripes with nineteen tassels and a patterned strap. There is a multicolored tubular edge binding along the top and sides of the bag. The strap is original, a rare feature, and is finely woven with small designs. A natural dye palette.

Origin: Bolivia, La Paz, Loayza, Luribay
Linguistic Affiliation: Aymara
Yarn Spin: Ground-, complementary-, and supplementary-warp spin, Z2S; weft, Z2S
Warp and Weft Count: 96 epi, 26 ppi
Provenance: La Paz, Bolivia, 6/80

1992.107.167

73. **Bag** *(capacho),* late 19th century
Multicolored sheep's wool or camelid hair
Woven in warp-faced plain and one-color supplementary-warp weaves
Length: 7¼ in., 18.4 cm; width: 13¼ in., 33.7 cm

A medium-size bag, one piece, of solid-colored and geometric-patterned stripes. The sides are joined by a plain-weave tubular edge binding, also along top edges. There is a wide strap sewn to the inside corners and four tassels on the sides and bottom corners. The supplementary-warp yarn is S2Z spun. Long termination areas on the bottom of each side. A natural dye palette. A more recent version of this type of bag, cat. no. 74, is illustrated as figure 51. Yorke (1980) discusses weaving techniques from this area and commented on the Yanahuaya style to the east, which is characterized by supplementary-warp floats on a paired warp ground, the technique employed in this bag and cat. no. 74.

Cat. no. 75

Origin: Bolivia, La Paz, Muñecas, Ayata
Linguistic Affiliation: Quechua
Yarn Spin: Ground- and supplementary-warp spin, Z2S, S2Z; weft, Z2S
Warp and Weft Count: 88 epi, 18 ppi
Provenance: San Francisco, California, 10/82
Reference: Yorke 1980, 24

1992.107.162

74. **Bag** *(capacho),* ca. 1950
See fig. 51, p. 52.
Beige and multicolored sheep's wool or camelid hair
Woven in warp-faced plain, two-color supplementary, and alternating float weaves
Length: 9 in., 22.9 cm; width: 12½ in., 31.8 cm

A medium-size bag, one piece, of solid-colored and geometric-patterned stripes. The sides are joined with a tubular edge binding, also along top edges. There is a wide strap sewn to the inside corners; at one end the warps are worked into two oblique, interlaced units, and five large, cut-pile pompoms are attached to the sides and bottom. The tassels differ from others in the collection, and the supplementary warp is of S2Z-spun yarn. For an older version of this bag, see cat. no. 73.

Origin: Bolivia, La Paz, Muñecas, Ayata
Linguistic Affiliation: Quechua
Yarn Spin: Ground- and supplementary-warp spin, Z2S, S2Z; weft, Z2S
Warp and Weft Count: 64 epi, 14 ppi
Provenance: La Paz, Bolivia, 3/78
Reference: Yorke 1980, 24

1992.107.163

75. **Belt** *(chumpi),* ca. 1950
Brown and beige sheep's wool or camelid hair
Woven in two-color complementary-warp weave
Length: 46 in., 116.8 cm; width: 1¾ in., 4.4 cm

A medium-size belt, one piece, in overall human, animal, and geometric patterning with four and five oblique, interlaced units, plied ties, and one tassel at each end. Images are clearly delineated and imaginative, and include condors, double-headed eagles, other birds, women, men, children, fish, a double-headed frog, a man on a horse, and a winged man. In some sections, a brown weft is used, in others, beige. Black alpaca in tassels; most of the yarn probably sheep's wool. A densely packed warp with a very fine weft.

Origin: Bolivia, La Paz, Muñecas, Ayata
Linguistic Affiliation: Quechua
Yarn Spin: Complementary-warp spin, Z2S; weft, Z2S
Warp and Weft Count: 120 epi, 20 ppi
Provenance: La Paz, Bolivia, 4/80

1992.107.195

76. **Belt** *(wak'a),* ca. 1950
See figure 25, page 32.
Multicolored sheep's wool or camelid hair
Woven in warp-faced plain and two-color complementary-warp weaves
Length: 38½ in., 97.8 cm; width: 7⅞ in., 20 cm

A wide belt, one piece, in solid-colored and geometric-, human-, bird-, and animal-patterned stripes. There are seventeen oblique, interlaced units at one end and ties on both ends, and a five-color tubular edge binding on three outer selvages. Two corners are turned back and stitched. The belt has nine different rows of images, and the weaver played around with letters as design elements. Even though they did not read, the weavers knew that letters imparted meaning. Images include llamas, birds, women and men holding hands, and geometrics, which may be block lettering such as M, O, H, and W. This is a beautifully woven belt with a softer hand than found in other examples. It may have served a special function, as the addition of tubular edge binding along with long patterned ties

Cat. no. 77

Cat. no. 79

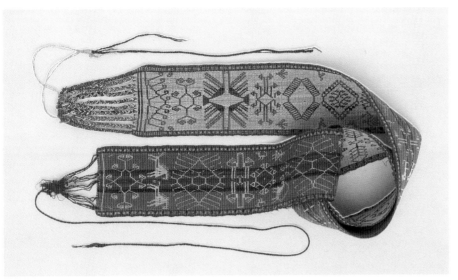

Cat. no. 82

is unusual. Because of overspun yarn, tie ends naturally re-ply themselves onto each other so no unraveling takes place.

Origin: Bolivia, La Paz, Muñecas, Ayata
Linguistic Affiliation: Quechua
Yarn Spin: Ground- and complementary-warp spin, Z2S; weft, Z2S
Warp and Weft Count: 56 epi, 16 ppi
Provenance: La Paz, Bolivia, 1/79

1992.107.196

77. Coca or ceremonial cloth (inkuña),
early 20th century
Red and multicolored sheep's wool
Woven in warp-faced plain and two-color complementary weaves
Length: 38½ in., 97.8 cm; width: 45⅜ in., 115.3 cm

A large cloth, two pieces, sewn together at center, with solid-colored and human-, geometric-, and animal-patterned stripes. There is a two-color tubular edge binding on all outer selvages. Clearly delineated images include men and women with hands joined, horses, viscachas, and radiating diamonds. The narrow bands of dark blue and white in diagonals set off the whole piece.

Origin: Bolivia, La Paz, Omasuyos, Achacachi
Linguistic Affiliation: Aymara
Yarn Spin: Ground- and complementary-warp spin, Z2S; weft, Z2S
Warp and Weft Count: 72 epi, 22 ppi
Provenance: La Paz, Bolivia, 3/82

1992.107.128

78. Bag (capacho), 19th century
Red, beige, and multicolored camelid hair
Woven in warp-faced plain, two-color complementary, and alternating float weaves
Length: 7½ in., 19.1 cm; width: 13¾ in., 34.9 cm

A large bag, one piece, with solid-colored and geometric-patterned stripes. It is joined at the sides by a tubular edge binding, which continues along top edges, and there is a strap and nine multicolored tassels at the sides and bottom. A Lake Titicaca-style piece, it resembles a bag from Achiri, Pacajes (see cat. no. 81) in coloring, striping pattern, and tassels. A natural dye palette.

Origin: Bolivia, La Paz, Omasuyos
Linguistic Affiliation: Aymara
Yarn Spin: Ground- and complementary-warp spin, Z2S; weft, Z2S
Warp and Weft Count: 80 epi, 18 ppi
Provenance: Corrales, New Mexico, 10/81

1992.107.164

79. Poncho (poncho), late 19th century
Cream and multicolored sheep's wool or camelid hair
Woven in warp-faced plain and two-color complementary-warp weaves
Length: 71 in., 180.3 cm; width: 62½ in., 158.8 cm

A large poncho, two pieces, with a few narrow, solid-colored and geometric-patterned stripes, joined edge to edge, with a neck opening. There is a plain-weave edge binding with multicolored fringe created by the edge binding wefts on all outer selvages. The textile has a soft hand, and the warp and weft count is low. Local designs and a natural dye palette.

Origin: Bolivia, La Paz, Omasuyos
Linguistic Affiliation: Aymara
Yarn Spin: Ground- and complementary-warp spin, Z2S; weft, Z2S
Warp and Weft Count: 48 epi, 16 ppi
Provenance: Corrales, New Mexico, 8/85

1992.107.118

80. Skirt (urku), early 20th century
Black, red, and multicolored camelid hair
Woven in warp-faced plain and two-color complementary-warp weave
Length: 25 in., 63.5 cm; width: 36⅜ in., 92.4 cm

A medium-size skirt, one piece, with ends sewn together to create a tube and gathered into a waistband. There are solid-colored and geometric- and bird-patterned stripes, and a plain-weave edge binding on the hem selvage. Pleated skirts were adopted from the Spanish and a half *urku* is often worn on top of a pleated skirt. A natural dye palette. Designs are similar to those of a poncho from the same province, illustrated in cat. no. 79.

Origin: Bolivia, La Paz, Omasuyos
Linguistic Affiliation: Aymara
Yarn Spin: Ground- and complementary-warp spin, Z2S; weft, Z2S
Warp and Weft Count: 52 epi, 16 ppi
Provenance: La Paz, Bolivia, 4/81

1992.107.127

81. Coca bag (ch'uspa), late 19th century
Multicolored camelid hair
Woven in warp-faced plain and two-color complementary-warp weaves
Length: 7 in., 17.8 cm; width: 9½ in., 24.1 cm

A medium-size bag, one piece, of solid-colored and geometric-patterned stripes with twenty-two multicolored tassels and a narrow strap. The sides are joined with a plain-weave tubular edge binding, which is also along the top edges. This bag is in the Lake Titicaca-style with symbols like those on textiles from Sicasica, and resembles bags from the Lake Titicaca area in Peru. It may be an early piece from Taquile, in Peru. A natural dye palette. See also cat. no. 224, a bag from Huancané, Puno, in Peru.

Origin: Bolivia, La Paz, Pacajes, Achiri
Linguistic Affiliation: Aymara
Yarn Spin: Ground- and complementary-warp spin, Z2S; weft, Z2S
Warp and Weft Count: 82 epi, 28 ppi
Provenance: La Paz, Bolivia, 4/77

1992.107.165

82. Belt (wak'a), early 20th century
Beige, red, multicolored, and *ch'imi* camelid hair
Woven in warp-faced plain, two-color complementary, and alternating float weaves
Length: 53⅛ in., 134.9 cm; width: 3⅛ in., 7.9 cm

Cat. no. 83

A medium-size belt, one piece, with overall patterning. On one end there are ten multi-colored, oblique, interlaced units with ties, and on the other end groups of yarn create a very long tie. The images are finely delineated and represent horses, men and women, and geometric and abstract floral motifs. A synthetic dye palette. Relates to another belt with the same origin, cat. no. 83.

Origin: Bolivia, La Paz, Pacajes, Achiri
Linguistic Affiliation: Aymara
Yarn Spin: Ground- and complementary-warp spin, Z2S; weft, Z2S
Warp and Weft Count: 104 epi, 18 ppi
Provenance: La Paz, Bolivia, 3/78

1992.107.199

83. **Belt** *(wak'a),* early 20th century
Red-orange, beige, multicolored, and *ch'imi* camelid hair
Woven in warp-faced plain, two-color complementary, and alternating float weaves
Length: 39⅜ in., 100 cm; width: 2½ in., 6.4 cm

A medium-size belt, one piece, with overall patterning and nineteen multicolored, oblique, interlaced units on one end. Images of llamas, birds, rodents, and large and small geometric motifs are clearly delin-eated, a result of color contrast and the fineness and density of the warp. Relates to another belt with the same origin, cat. no. *82.*

Origin: Bolivia, La Paz, Pacajes, Achiri
Linguistic Affiliation: Aymara
Yarn Spin: Ground- and complementary-warp spin, Z2S; weft, Z2S
Warp and Weft Count: 116 epi, 18 ppi
Provenance: La Paz, Bolivia, 5/80

1992.107.200

84. **Poncho** *(poncho),* mid- to late 19th century
Pink and multicolored camelid hair
Woven in warp-faced plain weave
Length: 82¾ in., 210.2 cm; width: 72½ in., 184.2 cm

A very large poncho, two pieces, sewn together edge to edge, with a neck opening, and three-color plain-weave edge binding sewn to cloth on all outer selvages. A multicolored fringe is created by wefts of the edge binding, and the four corners are turned back and stitched. Internal stripes of S2Z-spun yarn are placed next to stripes of Z2S-spun yarn, giving a herringbone effect. This style of poncho has been called a horseman's poncho, but this term is con-tested. Some researchers think that they may have been woven by poor villagers as tribute to the *hacienda* owner; others suggest that the *hilacata* or headman wore them. A fine old textile with a natural dye palette.

Origin: Bolivia, La Paz, Pacajes, Achiri
Linguistic Affiliation: Aymara
Yarn Spin: Ground-warp spin, Z2S, S2Z; weft, Z2S
Warp and Weft Count: 60 epi, 18 ppi
Provenance: La Paz, Bolivia, 2/78

1992.107.111

85. **Poncho** *(poncho),* late 19th century
See fig. 54, p. 54.
Black and multicolored camelid hair
Woven in warp-faced plain weave
Length: 65¾ in., 167 cm; width: 49 in., 124.5 cm

A large poncho, two pieces, sewn together edge to edge, with a neck opening. There is a plain-weave edge binding in alternat-ing colors, which creates a checkerboard pattern, sewn to all outer selvages. A multi-colored fringe is created by the wefts of the edge binding, and the four corners have been turned back and stitched. There are narrow bands of S2Z-spun yarn in the outer black stripes. Ponchos with black stripes alternating with multicolored stripes are typical of Pacajes. Very fine termination area. A natural dye palette.

Origin: Bolivia, La Paz, Pacajes, Achiri
Linguistic Affiliation: Aymara
Yarn Spin: Ground-warp spin, Z2S, S2Z; weft, Z2S
Warp and Weft Count: 100 epi, 20 ppi
Provenance: San Francisco, California, 12/78

1992.107.117

86. **Woman's mantle** *(awayu),* mid-19th century
Multicolored camelid hair
Woven in warp-faced plain, two-color complementary, and alternating float weaves
Length: 41 in., 104.1 cm; width: 28 in., 71.1 cm

A medium-size mantle, two pieces, joined edge to edge with geometric-patterned stripes and a four-color tubular edge binding on all outer selvages. Dense iconography in narrow patterned stripes and beautiful color changes. A dominant motif is a radiating star or *chaska*. Fine hand, lovely old textile. An exceptionally fine *awayu*, with a natural dye palette. Similar to an *awayu* from Sicasica, Aroma, cat. no. 57.

Origin: Bolivia, La Paz, Pacajes, Corocoro
Linguistic Affiliation: Aymara
Yarn Spin: Ground- and complementary-warp spin, Z2S; weft, Z2S
Warp and Weft Count: 92 epi, 24 ppi
Provenance: La Paz, Bolivia, 4/82

1992.107.143

87. **Belt** *(wak'a),* early 20th century
Red, beige, and multicolored camelid hair
Woven in warp-faced plain and two-color complementary weaves
Length: 48 in., 121.9 cm; width: 6 in, 15.2 cm

A medium-size, wide belt, one piece, with solid-colored and geometric- and bird-patterned stripes with fourteen multicolored, knotted, oblique, interlaced units on one end and remnants of a tie on the other end. A classic *wak'a* from this area with wide figure bands into which images of potato hooks and stars are woven. A synthetic dye palette.

Origin: Bolivia, La Paz, Pacajes, Santiago de Machaca
Linguistic Affiliation: Aymara
Yarn Spin: Ground- and complementary-warp spin, Z2S; weft, Z2S
Warp and Weft Count: 132 epi, 20 ppi
Provenance: Cuzco, Peru, 3/81

1992.107.198

88. **Coca or ceremonial cloth** *(inkuña),* early to mid-19th century
Tan and multicolored camelid hair
Woven in warp-faced plain weave
Length: 30 in., 76.2 cm; width: 31 in., 78.7 cm

A medium-size cloth, one piece, with solid-colored stripes, and narrow stripes with alternating warp color order, which creates a dotted effect. S2Z-spun yarn appears in outer solid-colored brown stripes. Same warp set-up and colors as one pictured in Adelson and Tracht (1983). Beautiful overall design and colors. A natural dyes palette. Similar in coloring and stripe arrangement to an *iskayu* from the same province; see cat. no. *89.*

Origin: Bolivia, La Paz, Pacajes
Linguistic Affiliation: Aymara

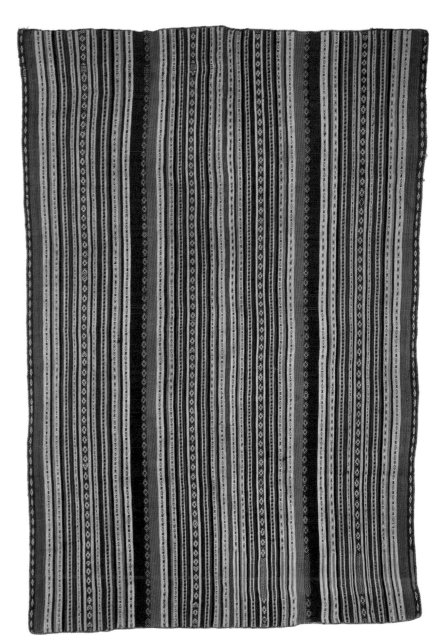

Cat. no. 86

Cat. no. 87

Cat. no. 89

Yarn Spin: Ground-warp spin, Z2S, S2Z; weft, Z2S
Warp and Weft Count: 60 epi, 18 ppi
Provenance: La Paz, Bolivia, 4/80
Reference: Adelson and Tracht 1983, 117
1992.107.153

89. **Woman's mantle** *(iskayu),* early to mid-19th century
Tan, multicolored, and *ch'imi* camelid hair
Woven in warp-faced plain and two-color complementary-warp weaves
Length: 36½ in., 92.7 cm; width: 45½ in., 115.6 cm

A medium-size mantle, two pieces, of solid-colored stripes, joined edge to edge. There is one narrow, geometric-patterned stripe at the center. An unusual feature is the joining at center with a complementary-warp weave band. Other published examples from this area and time-frame also have this feature. A similar *iskayu* is published in Siegel (1991). A natural dye palette. *Ch'imi* yarn of tan and rose in S2Z spin creates an *abrash* effect. A very fine, old textile. It resembles an *inkuña* from the same province, cat. no. 88, in color and use of S2Z-spun yarn.

Origin: Bolivia, La Paz, Pacajes
Linguistic Affiliation: Aymara
Yarn Spin: Ground- and complementary-warp spin, Z2S, S2Z; weft, Z2S
Warp and Weft Count: 80 epi, 20 ppi
Provenance: Corrales, New Mexico, n.d.
References: Adelson and Tracht 1983, 78; Siegel 1991, 46
1992.107.152

90. **Small ch'imi poncho** *(ponchito ch'imi),* 19th century
See fig. 53, p. 54.
Rose and black *ch'imi* camelid hair
Woven in warp-faced plain weave
Length: 49 in., 124.5 cm; width: 45 in., 114.3 cm

A small poncho, two pieces, sewn together edge to edge, with a neck opening, which is finished in green blue buttonhole stitch. There is a plain-weave edge binding on all outer selvages and a green blue fringe created by the wefts of the edge binding. The style—a salt-and-pepper effect created by overall *ch'imi* yarn—is unusual. The impact of the *abrash* is deep and resonant, like a paint-drenched canvas.

Origin: Bolivia, La Paz, Pacajes
Linguistic Affiliation: Aymara
Yarn Spin: Ground-warp spin, Z2S; weft, Z2S
Warp and Weft Count: 60 epi, 16 ppi
Provenance: Corrales, New Mexico, 4/86
1992.107.119

91. **Man's tunic** *(khawa),* early 19th century
Rose camelid hair
Woven in warp-faced plain weave
Length: 42½ in., 108 cm; width: 39 in., 99.1 cm

One piece, with a neck opening created by discontinuous wefts, and the sides not sewn together. There are two gold silk ribbons woven into tunic below the neck opening, and a plain-weave two-color tubular edge binding is present on all outer selvages. Three inches in from side selvages, Z2S-, Z2S-, and S2Z-spun yarns are placed side by side making a distinctive texture. Old garments like these were found on the trail from Potosí to Lima and have become family heirlooms. There is another tunic in the collection, see cat. *214,* from Moquegua, Peru. Adelson and Tracht (1983) commented that the earliest Aymara *ponchitos* were made in the tunic tradition. They consist of a one-piece, warp-faced rectangle with a discontinuous-weft neck slot and follow a tunic pattern; the main distinction between a *khawa* and a *ponchito* is that the sides on the *ponchito* are not sewn together.

Origin: Bolivia, La Paz, Pacajes
Linguistic Affiliation: Aymara
Yarn Spin: Ground-warp spin, Z2S, S2Z; weft, Z2S
Warp and Weft Count: 60 epi, 22 ppi
Provenance: La Paz, Bolivia, 2/79
Reference: Adelson and Tracht 1983, 60
1992.107.12

92. **Headband** *(wincha),* ca. 1950
See fig. 29, p. 39.
Beige, red, and multicolored sheep's wool and camelid hair
Woven in warp-faced double cloth
Length: 20 in., 50.8 cm; width: 3 in., 7.6 cm

A wide headband, one piece, of geometric-, human-, animal-, and bird-patterned double-cloth with white beads on the side selvages. There are twenty-four multi-colored, wrapped warp units at one end attached to two-color, crossed-warp weave ties and a beaded tassel, and a short tie on the other end. The beads are added in the weft passes. This style of headband has three lines of figure work with a variety of figures in the center. The side pieces have hooked motifs. Images include couples, two women, and birds with flowers. Headbands from this area include S2Z-spun yarn and are worn by Charazani women. A finely woven piece. See also cat. no. 59, a large bag from Caupolín, in the Charazani region, and two other headbands, cat. no. 93 (figure 49) and 94.

Cat. no. 90

Origin: Bolivia, La Paz, Saavedra, Charazani
Linguistic Affiliation: Quechua/Aymara
Yarn Spin: Double-cloth warp spin, Z2S, S2Z; weft, Z2S, Z6S
Warp and Weft Count: 100 epi, 24 ppi
Provenance: Corrales, New Mexico, 6/87
1992.107.225

93. **Headband** *(wincha),* ca. 1950
See fig. 49, p. 51.
Beige, red, and multicolored sheep's wool and camelid hair
Woven in warp-faced double cloth
Length: 19½ in., 49.5 cm; width: 1¾ in., 4.4 cm

A medium-size headband, one piece, of animal-, human-, and geometric-patterned double-cloth with blue and yellow beads on the side selvages. There are twenty-three multicolored, wrapped warp units at one end and long, two-color, crossed-warp weave ties at both ends with wrapped tassels. The beads are added in the weft passes. In contrast to that of cat. no. *92,* this style is predominantly figurative. Images include fantastic animals, a heraldic image with one wing, birds, double-headed horses, a woman with a wide petticoat, viscachas, and a radiating star. See also cat. no. 94.

Origin: Bolivia, La Paz, Saavedra, Charazani
Linguistic Affiliation: Quechua/Aymara
Yarn Spin: Double-cloth warp spin, Z2S, S2Z; weft, Z2S, S2Z
Warp and Weft Count: 98 epi, 28 ppi
Provenance: Corrales, New Mexico, 9/82
1992.107.226

94. **Headband** (wincha), ca. 1940
Beige, orange, and multicolored sheep's wool and camelid hair
Woven in warp-faced plain and two-color complementary-warp weaves
Length: 24 in., 61 cm; width: 1¾ in., 4.4 cm

Cat. no. 97

A medium-size headband, one piece, with overall geometric patterning and multi-colored beads on side selvages. There are eleven multicolored, oblique, interlaced units at one end and two long, four-color, tubular plain-weave ties at both ends. The beads are added in the weft passes. This represents another style, different from that of cat. no. 92 and 93 (fig. 49), with a single stripe of pattern work with scroll motif and complementary-warp weave instead of double cloth. Girault (1969) identifies a similar structure in a bag from Wata Wata.

Origin: Bolivia, La Paz, Saavedra, Charazani
Linguistic Affiliation: Quechua/Aymara
Yarn Spin: Ground- and complementary-warp spin, Z2S; weft, Z2S
Warp and Weft Count: 96 epi, 32 ppi
Provenance: Corrales, New Mexico, 9/82
Reference: Girault 1969, 152–53, fig. 82

1992.107.227

95. **Woman's mantle** *(awayu),* ca. 1950
Red, beige, and multicolored sheep's wool and camelid hair
Woven in warp-faced plain, two-color complementary, and warp-faced double-cloth weaves
Length: 36 in., 91.4 cm; width: 40¼ in., 102.2 cm

A medium-size mantle, two pieces, sewn together edge to edge, of solid-colored and geometric-, animal-, and bird-patterned stripes. There is a four-color, plain-weave tubular edge binding on all outer selvages. An unusual motif is rows of dancing figures in wide stripes, also women with huge skirts. The typical hooked motif appears along with people holding hands, a condor-bird man, horses, and horned animals. Varying shades of reds create a rich impression. See also cat. no. *59,* a large bag from Caupolín, in the Charazani region.

Origin: Bolivia, La Paz, Saavedra, Charazani
Linguistic Affiliation: Quechua/Aymara
Yarn Spin: Ground-, complementary-, and double-cloth warp spin, Z2S; weft, Z2S
Warp and Weft Count: 44 epi, 14 ppi
Provenance: La Paz, Bolivia, 6/80

1992.107.132

96. **Dancing tie or headband** *(wincha),*
late 19th century
Red, beige, and multicolored sheep's wool and camelid hair
Woven in two-color complementary-warp weave
Length: 23¼ in., 59.1 cm; width: ⅞ in., 2.2 cm

A medium-size, narrow band, one piece, of geometric-patterned stripes. There is an edge binding and fringe created by the wefts of the edge binding on all outer selvages. This textile was used as a strap on a bag from northern Potosí. The motifs are similar to those on textiles from Charazani region. Instead of beads on the outer selvages, this textile has a fringe. The weft is of S2Z-spun yarn, and it is finely woven with a dense warp count. See also cat. 94, another headband from Charazani.

Origin: Bolivia, La Paz, Saavedra, Charazani
Linguistic Affiliation: Quechua/Aymara
Yarn Spin: Complementary-warp spin, Z2S; weft, S2Z
Warp and Weft Count: 143 epi, 26 ppi
Provenance: La Paz, Bolivia, 4/80

1992.107.233

97. **Dancing tie or headband** *(wincha),*
late 19th century
Beige, red, and multicolored sheep's wool and camelid hair
Woven in two-color complementary-warp weave
Length: 22 in., 55.9 cm; width: 1 in., 2.5 cm

A medium-size, narrow band, two pieces, of geometric-patterned stripes and color changes where two pieces meet. There is an edge binding and multicolored fringe created by the edge binding wefts on all outer selvages and multicolored tassels at one end. Instead of beads on the outer selvages, this textile has a fringe. Iconography is similar to that of textiles from the Charazani region; see cat. no. 94 for comparison. It is not as tightly woven as is cat. no. 96, and the motifs are a little larger.

Origin: Bolivia, La Paz, Saavedra, Charazani
Linguistic Affiliation: Quechua/Aymara
Yarn Spin: Complementary-warp spin, Z2S; weft, S2Z
Warp and Weft Count: 100 epi, 20 ppi
Provenance: La Paz, Bolivia, 1/79

1992.107.234

98. Belt (*chumpi*), ca. 1940
See fig. 52, p. 53.
Tan, red, and multicolored sheep's wool
Woven in warp-faced plain and two-color
complementary-warp weaves
Length: 45½ in., 115.6 cm; width: 4 in.,
10.2 cm

A medium-size belt, one piece, with solid-colored and human-, floral-, geometric-, and animal-patterned stripes. There are eleven oblique, interlaced units and one long, interlaced tie on one end and remnants of a tie on other end. The provenance is questionable, as there are few weavers in the Yungas and only a few pieces like this came into La Paz. The images are clearly delineated; guitars, men and women with hands up and also holding hands, camelids, plants, and geometric outside borders. It may be of fine merino wool, for it has a silky hand. Frame (1986) identifies a braid, which is of a similar structure to this tie, that was found on a turban at the Paracas Necropolis and looks like two twisted strands.

Origin: Bolivia, La Paz, northern Yungas
Linguistic Affiliation: Quechua
Yarn Spin: Ground- and complementary-warp
spin, Z2S; weft, S2Z
Warp and Weft Count: 80 epi, 30 ppi
Provenance: La Paz, Bolivia, 2/79
Reference: Frame 1986, 71, fig. 15a

1992.107.197

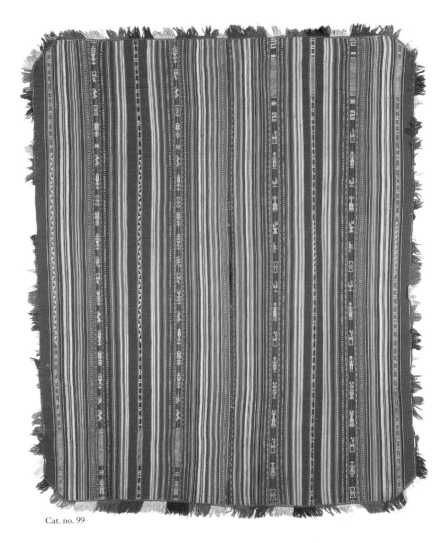

Cat. no. 99

99. Poncho (*poncho*), ca. 1940
Red and multicolored sheep's wool
Woven in warp-faced plain, two-color
complementary, and alternating float
weaves
Length: 53⅜ in., 135.6 cm; width: 44⅞ in.,
114 cm

A medium-size poncho, two pieces, of narrow, solid-colored and human-, geometric-, letter-, and bird-patterned stripes, joined edge to edge with a neck opening. There is a two-color edge binding sewn to all outer selvages, and the edge binding wefts create a multicolored fringe. The four corners are turned up and stitched. The color palette is similar to that of Lake Titicaca-style textiles. The poncho may be of merino wool. Letters are common design motifs even though many weavers do not read. Images are clearly delineated and also include hourglasses, llamas, guitars, men and women with hats, viscachas, birds, and a vase with flowers. Wells commented that the images may come from a game called *la lotería*. Rodman commented that the fringe and the poncho may be of commercial yarn, but it was respun and is very fine. A

synthetic dye palette. See also cat. no. *98* (fig. 52), a belt from northern Yungas.

Origin: Bolivia, La Paz, southern Yungas
Linguistic Affiliation: Quechua
Yarn Spin: Ground- and complementary-warp
spin, Z2S; weft, Z3S
Warp and Weft Count: 120 epi, 28 ppi
Provenance: La Paz, Bolivia, 3/79
References: Amy Oakland Rodman, Tim Wells,
personal communications, 1995

1992.107.99

100. Shawl (*chalina*), early 20th century
Shades of tan camelid hair
Woven in warp-faced plain weave
Length: 64 in., 162.6 cm; width: 30½ in.,
77.5 cm

A large shawl, one piece, with an interlaced decorative edge binding on outer three selvages with a knotted fringe. It has a soft, silky hand and is probably vicuña. The varying shades of the undyed yarn are from different parts of the animal's body. The interlaced decorative edge binding is an unusual feature.

Origin: Bolivia, La Paz, altiplano
Linguistic Affiliation: Spanish
Yarn Spin: Ground-warp spin, Z2S; weft, Z2S
Warp and Weft Count: 72 epi, 14 ppi
Provenance: La Paz, Bolivia, 6/80

1992.107.159

ORURO

101. Coca bag (*ch'uspa*), late 19th century
Multicolored camelid hair
Woven in warp-faced and two-color
complementary-warp weaves
Length: 10⅛ in., 25.7 cm; width: 12 in.,
30.5 cm

A medium-size bag, one piece, joined on the sides with a two-color, plain-weave tubular edge binding, which continues along top edges. It is of solid-colored and geometric-, animal-, and bird-patterned stripes. There is a multicolored strap and seventeen multicolored tassels along the bottom and sides. The strap could be a replacement for one that wore out. The blue and gold tassels are most likely sheep's wool; the white,

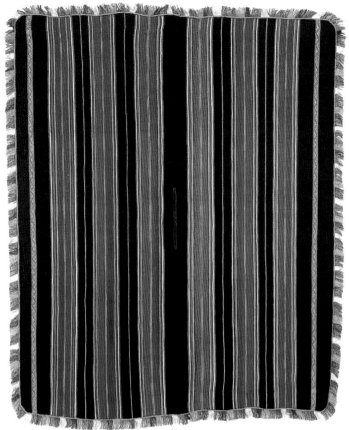

Cat. no. 105

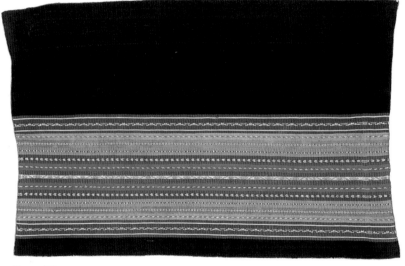

Cat. no. 106

edges and bottom. There are eleven tassels and a strap. Rowe (1977) locates a similar pattern in Chahuaytiri, Cuzco. Rodman commented that the strap is probably original. A natural dye palette. A great bag with strong designs and sun motifs in the central stripes.

Origin: Bolivia, Oruro, Avaroa
Linguistic Affiliation: Aymara
Yarn Spin: Ground- and complementary-warp spin, Z2S; weft, Z2S
Warp and Weft Count: 60 epi, 22 ppi
Provenance: La Paz, Bolivia, 3/78
References: Rowe 1977, 75, fig. 90; Amy Oakland Rodman, personal communication, 1995

1992.107.173

103. **Belt** *(chumpi),* late 19th century
Multicolored camelid hair
Woven in warp-faced and two-color complementary-warp weaves
Length: 65⅛ in., 165.4 cm; width: 2⅝ in., 6.7 cm

A long belt, one piece, with overall geometric and bird patterning. There are thirteen multicolored, oblique, interlaced units and a tassel on one end, and three multicolored, oblique, interlaced units and a tassel on the other end. Same sun motif as on cat. no. 102. Three-quarters of the belt design is a zigzag line within geometrics; the other quarter does not have zigzag and designs are of different motifs. Fine two-color designs in outside stripes with uniformity of design all over. A natural
dye palette.

Origin: Bolivia, Oruro, Avaroa
Linguistic Affiliation: Aymara
Yarn Spin: Ground- and complementary-warp spin, Z2S; weft, Z2S
Warp and Weft Count: 56 epi, 12 ppi
Provenance: Corrales, New Mexico, 9/92

1992.107.212

104. **Poncho** *(poncho),* late 19th century
Multicolored camelid hair
Woven in warp-faced plain weave
Length: 92¼ in., 234.3 cm; width: 89 in., 226.1 cm

A very large poncho, two pieces, sewn together edge to edge, with a neck opening and overall solid-colored stripes. There is
a plain-weave edge binding sewn to all selvages with a multicolored fringe created by the edge binding wefts. The four corners are turned back and stitched. These large ponchos are sometimes called horseman's ponchos, but this term is contested. Some researchers think that

pink, and purple tassels are probably alpaca. A fine hand and a natural dye palette.

Origin: Bolivia, Oruro, Avaroa
Linguistic Affiliation: Aymara
Yarn Spin: Ground- and complementary-warp spin, Z2S; weft, Z2S
Warp and Weft Count: 76 epi, 26 ppi
Provenance: Corrales, New Mexico, 8/85

1992.107.172

102. **Coca bag** *(ch'uspa),* mid- to late 19th century
Multicolored and *ch'imi* camelid hair
Woven in warp-faced plain and two-color complementary-warp weaves
Length: 10¼ in., 26 cm; width: 1½ in., 29.2 cm

A large bag, one piece, of solid-colored and geometric-patterned stripes. The sides are joined by a four-color tubular edge binding, which continues along the top

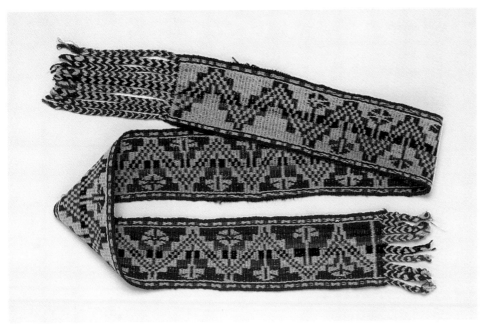

Cat. no. 107

they may have been woven by poor villagers as tribute to the *hacienda* owner, who may have worn them because they shed water. Others suggest that the *hilacata* or headman wore them. A natural dye palette.

Origin: Bolivia, Oruro, Avaroa
Linguistic Affiliation: Aymara
Yarn Spin: Ground-warp spin, Z2S; weft, Z2S
Warp and Weft Count: 68 epi, 12 ppi
Provenance: Corrales, New Mexico, 4/85
1992.107.1

105. **Poncho** *(poncho),* mid- to late 19th century
Red, black, and multicolored camelid hair
Woven in warp-faced plain and one-color supplementary-warp weaves
Length: 84 in., 213.4 cm; width: 71¾ in., 182.2 cm

A large poncho, two pieces, sewn together edge to edge, with a neck opening, which is bound with plain-weave cloth. It is of solid-colored and geometric-patterned stripes. There is a plain-weave edge binding. The four corners are turned up and stitched, with additional weft fringe on all four selvages. The supplementary-warp weave stripes are an unusual feature. Most of the other ponchos in the collection have overall striping or complementary-warp patterning. For a note on so-called horseman's ponchos, see comments for cat. no. 104, a poncho from this same province. A natural dye palette.

Origin: Bolivia, Oruro, Avaroa
Linguistic Affiliation: Aymara
Yarn Spin: Ground- and supplementary- warp spin, Z2S; weft, Z2S
Warp and Weft Count: 60 epi, 18 ppi
Provenance: San Francisco, California, 6/79
1992.107.112

106. **Woman's overskirt** *(aksu),* mid- to late 19th century
Black and multicolored camelid hair
Woven in warp-faced plain and two-color complementary weaves
Length: 49 in., 124.5 cm; width: 30⅝ in., 77.8 cm

A medium-size overskirt, two pieces, one narrow, one wide, joined together, of solid-colored and geometric-patterned stripes. There is a two-color, plain-weave tubular edge binding on three outer selvages. In the black stripes a less dense warp count results in the pink wefts showing through, giving subtle color variations—a lovely effect.

Origin: Bolivia, Oruro, Avaroa
Linguistic Affiliation: Aymara
Yarn Spin: Ground- and complementary-warp spin, Z2S; weft, Z2S
Warp and Weft Count: 84 epi, 22 ppi
Provenance: Corrales, New Mexico, 2/84
1992.107.147

107. **Belt** *(chumpi),* late 19th century
Multicolored and *ch'imi* camelid hair
Woven in warp-faced plain, two-color complementary, and alternating float weaves
Length: 45½ in., 115.5 cm; width: 2⅝ in., 6.7 cm

A medium-size belt, one piece, in overall geometric patterning with nine multi-colored, looped, oblique interlaced units on both ends. Design units are repeated uniformly in color instead of being presented randomly. A natural dye palette.

Origin: Bolivia, Oruro
Linguistic Affiliation: Quechua/Aymara
Yarn Spin: Ground- and complementary-warp spin, Z2S; weft, Z2S

Warp and Weft Count: 64 epi, 16 ppi
Provenance: La Paz, Bolivia, 5/80
1992.107.213

108. **Belt** *(chumpi),* early 20th century
Red-orange and multicolored camelid hair
Woven in warp-faced plain and two-color complementary-warp weaves in diagonal alignment
Length: 75 in., 190.5 cm; width: 1½ in., 3.8 cm

A very long narrow belt, one piece, in solid-colored and geometric-patterned stripes with eleven oblique, interlaced units on each end and seven on the other. Very finely woven. A mystery piece: no other examples, and not seen in use by anyone. Diagonal alignment produces a series of Vs, the dominant design motif in this belt. Varied color combination of warps in center band of complementary-warp weave gives the appearance of a more complex weave structure. Fine, silky hand; tightly spun yarn, densely warped. A synthetic dye palette.

Origin: Bolivia, Oruro
Linguistic Affiliation: Aymara
Yarn Spin: Ground- and complementary-warp spin, Z2S; weft, Z2S
Warp and Weft Count: 90 epi, 26 ppi
Provenance: La Paz, Bolivia, 5/84
1992.107.214

109. **Coca bag** *(ch'uspa),* late 19th century
Black, rose, and multicolored camelid hair
Woven in warp-faced plain and two-color complementary weaves with discontinuous warps dovetailed at bottom fold for color change
Length: 8 in., 20.3 cm, width: 10 in., 25.4 cm

A small bag, one piece, in solid-colored and geometric-patterned stripes, joined at the sides by a three-color tubular edge binding, continued along top edges. There is a strap, and seventeen multicolored tassels are added to the bottom and sides. Additional multicolored wrapped tassels were added to the first set of tassels. Because of the discontinuous warp technique, the front and back are different colors. Rowe (1977) discusses discontinuous warp technique. Iconographic elements are similar to those of a coca bag from the Bolívar region, cat. no. *12,* but smaller in dimensions. In this textile, the iconography of patterned stripes is balanced from side to side, but different on front and back. The tassel treatment is outstanding. No doubt a special or ceremonial piece. A natural dye palette, a real treasure.

Origin: Bolivia, Oruro
Linguistic Affiliation: Aymara
Yarn Spin: Ground-, complementary-warp spin, Z2S; weft, Z2S

Warp and Weft Count: 60 epi, 22 ppi
Provenance: Corrales, New Mexico, 4/86
Reference: Rowe 1977, 27–29, fig. 19

1992.107.178

110. **Coca bag** *(ch'uspa),* late 19th century
Multicolored and *ch'imi* camelid hair
Woven in warp-faced plain, two- and three-
color complementary, and warp-faced
double-cloth weaves
Length: 10½ in., 26.7 cm; width: 12 in.,
30.5 cm

A medium-size bag, one piece, in solid-
colored and geometric-, animal-, floral-,
and bird-patterned stripes, joined at sides by
a four-color tubular edge binding, which
continues along the top edges and partially
across the bottom. Along the bottom and
sides there are a fine strap and nine multicolored tassels. Two tassels are green yellow,
a color not used elsewhere in the bag.
Viscachas appear on the strap along with
stylized Indian motifs. Floral images may
relate to colonial influences. A frequent use
of *ch'imi* yarn adds to the color density of the
bag, and there is one narrow pink stripe of
S2Z-spun yarn. A very fine textile with
a natural dye palette.

Origin: Bolivia, Oruro
Linguistic Affiliation: Aymara
Yarn Spin: Ground-, complementary-, and
double-cloth warp spin, Z2S, S2Z; weft, Z2S
Warp and Weft Count: 72 epi, 18 ppi
Provenance: La Paz, Bolivia, 1/79

1992.107.179

111. **Hat, felt** *(montera),* 19th–20th century
Probably sheep's wool and vicuña
Felted technique
Length: 10 in., 25.4 cm; width at crown: 9⅜
in., 23.8 cm

One piece with a brim. This style also worn
by children. Width at brim is 15¾ inches,
40 cm

Origin: Bolivia, Oruro or Potosí
Linguistic Affiliation: Aymara/Spanish
Provenance: La Paz, Bolivia, 3/78

1992.107.236

112. **Woman's mantle** *(awayu),* late 19th century
Rose and multicolored camelid hair and silk
Woven in warp-faced plain and two-color
complementary-warp weaves
Length: 34½ in., 87.6 cm; width: 31 in.,
78.8 cm

A small mantle, two pieces, with narrow
solid-colored and geometric-patterned
bands sewn together edge to edge. Gold
warp selvages and figurative areas are
woven with traded silk yarn. Rose solid-
colored areas have *abrash* effect. There are

Cat. no. 108

Cat. no. 109

Cat. no. 115

similar, but older textiles with silk warps (dated after 1821) in the collection of the Museum für Völkerkunde in Vienna. A beautiful hand and a natural dye palette.

Origin: Bolivia, Oruro, Ladislao Cabrera, Lago Poopó, Pampa Aullagas
Linguistic Affiliation: Aymara
Yarn Spin: Ground- and complementary-warp spin, Z2S; weft, Z2S
Warp and Weft Count: 120 epi, 25 ppi
Provenance: La Paz, Bolivia, 3/78

1992.107.138

113. **Poncho** *(poncho),* mid 19th century
Dark blue and multicolored camelid hair
Woven in warp-faced plain and two-color complementary-warp weaves
Length: 71¼ in., 181 cm; width: 68¼ in., 173.3 cm

A very large poncho, two pieces, of solid-colored and narrow geometric-patterned stripes, joined edge to edge, with a neck opening, a multicolored edge binding, and fragments of multicolored fringe from the edge binding wefts. The four ends are turned up and stitched. S2Z-spun dark blue yarn in outer selvage stripes. According to Adelson and Tracht (1983), large ponchos were worn during the Independence period

by leaders of the Republican uprisings. This example, like the one from Achiri, Pacajes, La Paz, cat. no. *85* (fig. 54), may be a *challa-pata* woven for a chieftain. A natural dye palette.

Origin: Bolivia, Oruro
Linguistic Affiliation: Aymara
Yarn Spin: Ground- and complementary-warp spin, Z2S, S2Z; weft, Z2S
Warp and Weft Count: 68 epi, 16 ppi
Provenance: La Paz, Bolivia, 4/80
Reference: Adelson and Tracht 1983, 74

1992.108.108

114. **Saddlebags** *(alforja),* 18th–19th century
See fig. 40, p. 47.
Multicolored sheep's wool or camelid hair
Woven in warp-faced plain weave with knotted pile
Length (one bag): 13¼ in., 35.6 cm; width: 14 in., 35.6 cm; overall length of both bags including straps: 37 in., 94 cm

Two medium-size bags, joined by two multicolored pile straps; one side of the bags has brown and white stripes, the other is of multicolored pile. A checkerboard border is visible on both bags. There is a blue, plain-weave tubular edge binding on the sides and tops, and multicolored tassels of Z2S4Z-

spun yarn on both ends. Images include birds, hearts, lions, and geometrics. Lions and hearts are heraldic images used in the colonial period. There is a pre-Hispanic antecedent for this technique: The Middle Horizon four-pointed Huari hats are of knotted pile, but of a different structure; also there were pile textiles in the Tiwanaku area. Similar saddlebags are published in Adelson and Tracht (1983); the authors believe that, although colonial pile carpets are different from Asian carpets, this particular knotting technique may be of European origin. Rodman commented that Chipaya women in Oruro still make for themselves pile bags in which they keep clothing. The birds, which are looking up, are a familiar Late Intermediate period, pre-Columbian symbol from the coast. Franquemont commented that there are also pile structures from Huancavelica, Peru. A natural dye palette.

Origin: Bolivia, Oruro
Linguistic Affiliation: Aymara
Yarn Spin: Ground-warp spin, Z2S; weft, Z-spun singles
Warp and Weft Count: 26 epi, 12 ppi; 8 knots pi, 6 weft knots pi
Provenance: Corrales, New Mexico, 5/85
References: Adelson and Tracht 1983, 135; Amy

Cat. no. 118

Oakland Rodman, personal communication, 1995; Ed Franquemont, personal communication, 1996

1992.107.180

115. **Scarf** *(bufanda, ufanta)*, 19th century
Tan and multicolored camelid hair
Woven in warp-faced plain weave
Length: 64½ in., 163.8 cm; width: 7⅞ in., 20 cm

A long scarf with solid and multicolored stripes. A very silky hand. It resembles cat. no. 116, another scarf from this department. Meisch commented that scarves (*bufanda* is Spanish, *ufanta* is Aymarized Spanish) are worn by headmen or *hilacatas*.

Origin: Bolivia, Oruro (probably), altiplano
Linguistic Affiliation: Aymara
Yarn Spin: Ground-warp spin, Z2S; weft, Z2S
Warp and Weft Count: 96 epi, 22 ppi
Provenance: Santa Fe, New Mexico, 8/87
Reference: Lynn Meisch, personal communication, 1996

1992.107.156

116. **Scarf** *(bufanda, ufanta)*, 19th century
Tan and multicolored camelid hair
Woven in warp-faced plain weave
Length: 74½ in., 189.2 cm; width: 13 in., 33 cm

A very long scarf in solid and multicolored stripes with knotted fringes on both ends. Silky hand. The tan fiber may be vicuña. Fringes are of overspun fiber, Z2S4Z, and then knotted. The S2Z-spun yarn is in the outer selvage stripes, perhaps to allow the piece to lie flat. See cat. no. *115,* a similar scarf from this province.

Origin: Bolivia, Oruro (probably), altiplano
Linguistic Affiliation: Aymara
Yarn Spin: Ground-warp spin, Z2S, S2Z; weft, Z2S
Warp and Weft Count: 76 epi, 22 ppi
Provenance: Santa Fe, New Mexico, 8/85

1992.107.157

POTOSÍ

117. **Belt** *(chumpi)*, ca. 1960
Multicolored sheep's wool
Woven in warp-faced double cloth
Length: 33 in., 77.3 cm; width: 2¾ in., 7 cm

A medium-size belt, one piece, with overall bird, animal, geometric, and human patterning. There are eleven multicolored, oblique, interlaced units with a tie on one end and a tie with added fringe on the other end. Images include a man costumed for carnival, viscachas, rodents, condors, birds, and diagonal geometric motifs with checkerboard borders. A synthetic dye palette.

Origin: Bolivia, Potosí, Alonso Ibañez, Sacaca
Linguistic Affiliation: Quechua
Yarn Spin: Double-cloth warp spin, Z2S; weft, Z2S
Warp and Weft Count: 44 epi, 16 ppi
Provenance: La Paz, 1/76

1992.107.215

118. **Belt** *(chumpi)*, ca. 1950
Beige, dark brown, and multicolored sheep's wool
Woven in warp-faced double cloth
Length: 27½ in., 70 cm; width: ⅞ in., 2.3 cm

A narrow belt, with geometric patterning overall and a plain-weave tubular edge binding on warp selvages. There are eight oblique, interlaced units on one end and two- and four-color, crossed-warp weave ties on both ends tied to the belt. A regular repeat of designs. At one end, a few strands of pink yarn may be the weaver's mark. One tie spirals, the other lies flat. Unusual to have S2Z-spun yarn for weft. A synthetic dye palette.

Origin: Bolivia, Potosí, Chayanta, Macha
Linguistic Affiliation: Quechua
Yarn Spin: Double-cloth warp spin, Z2S; weft, S2Z
Warp and Weft Count: 76 epi, 30 ppi
Provenance: La Paz, Bolivia, 4/76

1992.107.220

119. **Hat** *(chullu)*, ca. 1950
See fig. 32, p. 41.
Beige and shades of brown sheep's wool
Knit: stockinette, garter stitches; color patterning, circular knitting on straight needles
Length: 11 in., 28 cm; width: 6⅝ in., 16.8 cm

A medium-size hat with geometric and floral patterning. There are ear flaps, which were knit separately and attached

Cat. no. 122

to the bottom with one oblique, interlaced unit and a tassel. This hat contains virtually every one of the Macha designs including the Burgos star. Most knitting yarn is Z2S; this is S2Z. Published in LeCount (1990). A beautiful specimen.

Origin: Bolivia, Potosí, Chayanta, Macha
Linguistic Affiliation: Quechua
Yarn Spin: Spin, S2Z
Gage: 22 spi
Provenance: Sucre, Bolivia, 6/80
Reference: LeCount 1990, 71, pl. 11; see also the patterns on p. 102, row 2, graph 16

1992.107.191

120. **Woman's skirt** *(aksu),* ca. 1950

Dark brown and multicolored sheep's wool
Woven in warp-faced plain, two- and three-color complementary, and warp-faced double-cloth weaves
Length: 38 in., 96.5 cm; width: 49½ in., 125.7 cm

A medium-size skirt, two pieces, with solid-colored and geometric-patterned stripes, joined edge to edge. There are double-cloth stripes on outer edges. A good example of different design patterns from this region. Patterning different on the two halves, a typical feature of *aksus.*

Origin: Bolivia, Potosí, Chayanta, Macha
Linguistic Affiliation: Quechua
Yarn Spin: Ground-, complementary-, and double-cloth warp spin, Z2S; weft, Z2S
Warp and Weft Count: 74 epi, 20 ppi
Provenance: San Francisco, California, 7/77

1992.107.134

121. **Little poncho** *(ponchito),* late 19th century

Red-brown and multicolored camelid hair
Woven in warp-faced plain and two-color complementary-warp weaves
Length: 38 in., 96.5 cm; width: 27 in., 68.6 cm

A small poncho, two pieces, in solid-colored and geometric-patterned stripes, sewn together edge to edge, with a neck opening trimmed in overcast stitch. There is a plain-weave edge binding and fringe created by the edge binding wefts on all outer selvages. The four corners are turned up and stitched. One inch from side selvages, S2Z- and Z2S-spun yarn aligned to create a herringbone effect. *Abrash* effect in solid-colored areas. Motifs, such as the hook, resemble those of Charazani weavings. A natural dye palette.

Origin: Bolivia, Potosí, Chayanta, Macha Cruz
Linguistic Affiliation: Quechua
Yarn Spin: Ground- and complementary-warp spin, Z2S, S2Z; weft, Z2S
Warp and Weft Count: 50 epi, 16 ppi
Provenance: La Paz, Bolivia, 6/80

1992.107.104

122. **Belt** *(chumpi),* ca. 1950

Multicolored sheep's wool
Woven in warp-faced double cloth
Length: 36 in., 91.4 cm; width: 1 in., 2.5 cm

A short belt in overall geometric, animal, and floral patterning with a two-color tubular edge binding on all outer selvages. The ends of the edge binding create a miniature tassel. At one end seven oblique, interlaced units are interlaced and woven together. Images include a double-headed llama, a frog within a frog, birds, condors, rodents, medallions, a woman on a horse, a snake, and large geometric motifs, which are in small patterned blocks. Motifs are not repeated. A synthetic dye palette.

Origin: Bolivia, Potosí, Chayanta, Pocoata
Linguistic Affiliation: Quechua
Yarn Spin: Double-cloth spin, Z2S; weft, S2Z
Warp and Weft Count: 88 epi, 11 ppi
Provenance: La Paz, Bolivia, 2/78

1992.107.221

123. **Pair of man's leggings** *(winchucas),* early 20th century

Beige and brown sheep's wool
Knit: diagonal stitch; circular knitting on straight needles
Length: 23 in., 58.4 cm; width: 11⅝ in., 29.5 cm

A long pair of diagonally knitted brown and beige leggings in zigzag patterns. LeCount (1990) commented that, for certain Bolivian fiestas, indigenous men wear patterned woolen leggings that women knit from handspun yarns. Those from the Pocoata area are longer and knit in light and dark natural tones of sheep's wool with red accents, often in the diagonal knitting technique.

Origin: Bolivia, Potosí, Chayanta, Pocoata
Linguistic Affiliation: Quechua
Yarn Spin: Spin, Z2S
Warp and Weft Count: 4 spi
Provenance: Corrales, New Mexico, 8/84
Reference: LeCount 1990, 35

1992.107.237

Cat. no. 123

124. **Belt** (*chumpi*), ca. 1950
Multicolored sheep's wool
Woven in warp-faced double cloth
Length: 53 in., 134.6 cm; width: 2¾ in., 7 cm

A long belt, one piece, in overall geometric, human, floral, and animal patterning with twenty oblique, interlaced units, tubular edge bindings on one end, and long ties on both ends, with a small tassel at the end of each tie. Images include condors, little birds, bovines, men on horses, and large geometric and floral designs on a striped background. Some asymmetrical arrangement of designs within pattern blocks. A synthetic dye palette.

Origin: Bolivia, Potosí, Bustillo, Chayanta
Linguistic Affiliation: Quechua/Aymara
Yarn Spin: Double-cloth warp spin, Z2S; weft, S2Z
Warp and Weft Count: 80 epi, 16 ppi
Provenance: La Paz, Bolivia, 4/79

1992.107.216

125. **Woman's mantle** (*awayu*), late 19th century
Black and multicolored camelid hair
Woven in warp-faced plain and two-color complementary weaves
Length: 48⅝ in., 123.5 cm; width: 45 in., 114.3 cm

A large mantle, two pieces, with solid-colored and geometric- and floral-patterned stripes joined edge to edge. There is a four-color tubular edge binding on all outer selvages. Stripes of S2Z-spun yarn on warp selvages. Within the complementary-warp weave stripes, there is a shift from geometric to abstract floral motifs in some rose beige stripes, a colonial-style influence. A silky hand, with a beautiful contrast of *pampas* and *pallays*. A natural dye palette.

Origin: Bolivia, Potosí, Bustillo, Chayanta
Linguistic Affiliation: Quechua/Aymara
Yarn Spin: Ground- and complementary-warp spin, Z2S, S2Z; weft, Z2S
Warp and Weft Count: 88 epi, 22 ppi
Provenance: La Paz, Bolivia, 3/78

1992.107.123

126. **Hatband, tie** (*t'isnu*), ca. 1970
See figs. 43, 44, p. 49.
Pink, green, beige, and yellow cotton
Woven in warp-faced double cloth
Length: 18¾ in., 47.6 cm; width: ½ in., 1.3 cm

A small hatband or tie, one piece, with overall animal and geometric patterning and a tassel and oblique interlaced units or ties on both ends. Five additional multi-colored tassels are attached to the ties. Images include condors, rodents, turkeys, other birds, four-legged animals, and

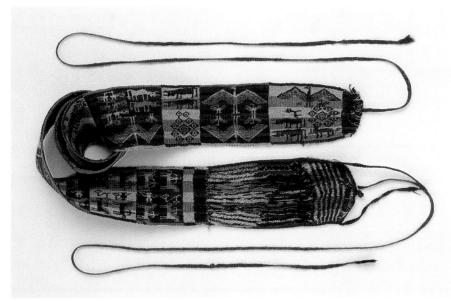

Cat. no. 124

geometric fillers. There are medallions hanging from condors' wings. It was probably woven on a special loom because of the fine yarn. A silky hand.

Origin: Bolivia, Potosí, Bustillo, Llallagua
Linguistic Affiliation: Quechua/Aymara
Yarn Spin: Double cloth warp spin, S2Z; weft, S2Z
Warp and Weft Count: 128 epi, 48 ppi
Provenance: Corrales, New Mexico, 1/82

1992.107.217

127. **Poncho** (*poncho*), ca. 1960
Maroon and multicolored sheep's wool
Woven in warp-faced and two-color complementary-warp weaves
Length: 68 in., 172.7 cm; width: 52½ in., 133.3 cm

A large poncho, two pieces, of narrow solid-colored and geometric-patterned stripes, joined edge to edge, with a neck opening. There is a plain-weave edge binding sewn to the textile on all outer selvages, and the edge binding wefts create a fringe. Rodman commented that the S design, similar to one in this textile, is a pre-Hispanic motif in warp-patterned weaves, to be found, notably, in Arica, Chile, and that there is a great range of color and fiber in the fringe. A synthetic dye palette.

Origin: Bolivia, Potosí, Linares, Caiza
Linguistic Affiliation: Quechua
Yarn Spin: Ground- and complementary-warp spin, Z2S; weft, Z2S
Warp and Weft Count: 74 epi, 20 ppi
Provenance: La Paz, Bolivia, 8/78
Reference: Amy Oakland Rodman, personal communication, 1995

1992.107.100

128. **Poncho** (*poncho*), ca. 1950
Maroon-and-black and maroon-and-beige *ikat* and multicolored sheep's wool
Woven in warp-faced and two- and three-color complementary-warp weaves with horizontal color changes
Length: 45 in., 114.3 cm; width: 53 in,. 134.5 cm

A large poncho, two pieces, joined edge to edge, with a neck opening, which has some additional orange stitching. It has *ikat,* solid-colored, and geometric-patterned stripes, with an edge binding stitched to all outer selvages. There are a few remnants of multicolored fringe. Inclusion of *ikat* stripes is a special feature of ponchos from this area. The two-color complementary-warp bands are very fine, and distinctly patterned. To achieve the rich maroon color, which gives an *abrash* effect, red and black fibers were combed together before they were spun. A synthetic dye palette.

Origin: Bolivia, Potosí, northern Chichas, Calcha
Linguistic Affiliation: Quechua
Yarn Spin: Ground- and complementary-warp spin, Z2S; weft, Z2S
Warp and Weft Count: 104 epi, 16 ppi
Provenance: La Paz, Bolivia, 1/76

1992.107.101

129. **Half overskirt** (*aksu*), ca. 1950
Black and multicolored sheep's wool or camelid hair
Woven in warp-faced and two-color complementary-warp weaves
Length: 49½ in., 125.7 cm; width: 27 in., 68.6 cm

A medium-size half skirt, one piece, with solid-colored areas and geometric-patterned stripes. There is an embroidered edge binding on one selvage with a narrow

Cat. no. 131

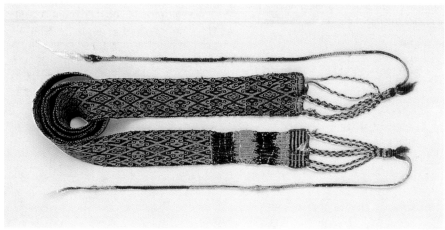

Cat. no. 133

complementary-warp weave band adjacent and remnants of an edge binding on one end. Images include the scroll and wave or hooked motifs. The complementary-warp weave designs are very fine. A lovely piece, with a synthetic dye palette.

Origin: Bolivia, Potosí, northern Chichas, Calcha
Linguistic Affiliation: Quechua
Yarn Spin: Ground- and complementary-warp spin, Z2S; weft, Z2S
Warp and Weft Count: 112 epi, 20 ppi
Provenance: La Paz, Bolivia, 1/77

1992.107.137

130. **Knit Bag** *(monedero),* ca. 1930s
Beige and multicolored sheep's wool or camelid hair
Knit: stockinette stitch; color patterning, circular knitting on straight needles
Length: 4½ in., 11.4 cm; width: 4 in., 10.2 cm

A small bag, one piece, with seven appendages knitted onto the bag and nine multicolored tassels. The eye, ear, and nose are embroidered. LeCount commented that the shape of bag, with four legs, head, udder, and tail, resembles a *llama.* It may be from southern La Paz, the Sicasica region in Aroma province.

Origin: Bolivia, northern Potosí
Linguistic Affiliation: Aymara
Yarn Spin: Spin, Z2S
Gage: 14 spi
Provenance: La Paz, Bolivia, 5/83
Reference: Cynthia LeCount, personal communication, October 1995

1992.107.181

131. **Knit Bag** *(monedero),* ca. 1950s
Multicolored sheep's wool or camelid hair
Knit: stockinette, garter, and scallop stitches; color patterning, circular knitting on straight needles
Length: 15 in., 38.1 cm; width: 6⅜ in., 16.2 cm

A large doll-shaped bag, a male figure, one piece, knit from top down, with human, bird, and animal images. The figure wears a hat, and its hair, eyes, mouth, fingers, and toes are clearly delineated. The feet and arms are stuffed with unspun fiber, and the fingers and toes are shaped with scallop or *pica pica* stitches. For another example, see LeCount (1990).

Origin: Bolivia, northern Potosí
Linguistic Affiliation: Aymara
Yarn Spin: Spin, Z2S
Gage: 11 spi
Provenance: Del Dios, California, 6/81
Reference: LeCount 1990, 70, pl. 9, no. 2

1992.107.182

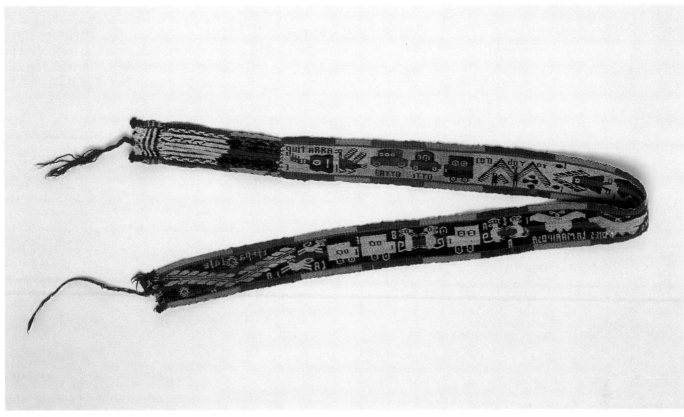

Cat. no. 134

132. Belt *(chumpi),* late 19th century
Rose, beige, and multicolored camelid hair
Woven in warp-faced plain and two- and
three-color complementary-warp weaves
Length: 60⅝ in., 154 cm; width: 2 in., 5 cm

A long belt, one piece, in overall geometric
patterning with nine looped, oblique, interlaced units sewn together at intervals at one
end, and remnants of a tie knotted to the
other end. Motifs are hooks, a shared
Andean motif. Finely woven. A natural dye
palette. See also cat. no. *133,* a similar belt.

Origin: Bolivia, northern Potosí
Linguistic Affiliation: Aymara
Yarn Spin: Ground- and complementary-warp
spin, Z2S; weft, S2Z
Warp and Weft Count: 90 epi, 24 ppi
Provenance: La Paz, Bolivia, 5/80

1992.107.218

133. Belt *(chumpi),* late 19th century
Beige and multicolored sheep's wool or
camelid hair
Woven in warp-faced plain and two-color
complementary-warp weaves
Length: 61¾ in., 156.8 cm; width: 1⅞ in.,
4.8 cm

A long belt, one piece, in overall geometric
patterning with nine oblique, interlaced
units sewn and woven together on one end
with additional units ending in a tassel and
long interlaced tie. On the other end there
also are long interlaced ties. Along with

other motifs, this belt has the same geometric hook designs as does a similar belt,
cat. no. 132. A natural dye palette.

Origin: Bolivia, northern Potosí
Linguistic Affiliation: Aymara
Yarn Spin: Ground- and complementary-warp
spin, Z2S; weft, S2Z
Warp and Weft Count: 104 epi, 16 ppi
Provenance: La Paz, Bolivia, 5/80

1992.107.219

134. Belt *(chumpi),* ca. 1940
Beige and multicolored sheep's wool
Woven in warp-faced double cloth
Length: 36 in., 91.4 cm; width: 1½ in.,
3.8 cm

A medium-size belt, one piece, in overall
patterning with nine oblique, interlaced
units sewn and woven together ending in
a looped interlaced tie. On the other end,
there is a tubular tie and two tassels on each
end. Animal and human images appear,
along with images of such objects as cars,
trucks, rodents, and an abstract human
form. There are woven words such as
guitarra, mariposa (butterfly), and condor
in association with the images they describe.
A charming and unusual piece. A synthetic
dye palette.

Origin: Bolivia, northern Potosí
Linguistic Affiliation: Aymara
Yarn Spin: Double-cloth warp spin, Z2S; weft,
S2Z
Warp and Weft Count: 64 epi, 18 ppi
Provenance: La Paz, Bolivia, 2/78

1992.107.222

135. Belt *(wak'a),* ca. 1950
Multicolored sheep's wool
Woven in warp-faced double cloth
Length: 37¼ in., 94.6 cm; width: 5⅞ in.,
14.9 cm

A medium-size, wide belt, one piece,
with overall geometric, bird, and animal
patterning. There are twenty-six oblique,
interlaced units sewn together at intervals
and ten rows of plain-weave finish at one
end. On the other end there are two
oblique, interlaced heading cords. A continuity of designs from side to side with
minimal color changes, a more formal
presentation, appears on a wide-scale layout.
Images include condors, horses, and hooked
geometrics. In the central diamonds, each
design is different. A synthetic dye palette.

Origin: Bolivia, northern Potosí
Linguistic Affiliation: Aymara
Yarn Spin: Double-cloth warp spin, Z2S; weft,
Z2S
Warp and Weft Count: 55 epi, 16 ppi
Provenance: La Paz, Bolivia, 1/77

1992.107.223

Cat. no. 140

136. Poncho *(poncho),* late 19th century
Purple, multicolored, and *ch'imi* sheep's
wool or camelid hair
Woven in warp-faced plain and two-color
complementary-warp weaves
Length: 41⅞ in., 106.4 cm; width: 40⅜ in.,
102.6 cm

A medium-size, square poncho, two pieces,
joined together edge to edge, with a neck
opening. It is of geometric-patterned and
solid-colored stripes, with a plain-weave
edge binding with multicolored fringe on
all outer selvages created by the edge
binding wefts. The use of *ch'imi* yarn adds
texture and depth. The termination areas
are in the center of both pieces, an unusual
placement. A visually satisfying piece of an
unusual purple color; a fine old textile of a
natural dye palette. It resembles cat. no. 25,
a large poncho from Challa, in design layout
and complementary-warp design.

Origin: Bolivia, northern Potosí
Linguistic Affiliation: Aymara
Yarn Spin: Ground- and complementary-warp
spin, Z2S; weft, Z2S
Warp and Weft Count: 56 epi, 20 ppi
Provenance: La Paz, Bolivia, 3/79

1992.107.103

137. Man's mantle *(llakuta),* 18th or 19th century
See fig. 57, p. 56.
Purple and black camelid hair
Woven in warp-faced plain weave
Length: 37½ in., 95.3 cm; width: 70 in.,
177.8 cm

A large mantle, two pieces, joined edge
to edge, with a three-color tubular edge
binding on all outer selvages. Possibly
woven in the eighteenth century, it has a
field of *abrash* and a shimmering pink effect
in the stripes created by different dye lots or

by dyeing the fleece before it was spun. This
garment is much wider than it is long, in
contrast to most other published examples.
There are S2Z-yarn stripes in the outer
edges. Adelson and Tracht (1983) wrote
that, from pre-Hispanic times through the
nineteenth century, a *llakuta* was a man's
mantle. Presently it is said to be worn by
women; men may wear it for weddings.

Origin: Bolivia, Potosí
Linguistic Affiliation: Aymara
Yarn Spin: Ground-warp spin, Z2S, S2Z; weft,
Z2S
Warp and Weft Count: 60 epi, 18 ppi
Provenance: La Paz, Bolivia, 4/81
Reference: Adelson and Tracht 1983, 84

1992.107.149

138. Woman's mantle *(awayu),*
18th–19th century
Purple, tan, multicolored, and silver-
wrapped camelid hair
Woven in warp-faced plain and two-color
complementary-warp weaves
Length: 39⅞ in., 101.3 cm; width: 37 in.,
94 cm

A large mantle, two pieces, of solid-colored
and geometric-patterned stripes joined edge
to edge. Remnants of a faded green silk
edge binding on all outer selvages. The
garment is in the colonial style and could
be from the city of Potosí, which in the
eighteenth century was the most populous
town in the Americas. Subtle coloring with
a natural dye palette. The metallic yarn
gives it a heavy hand. A unique piece.

Origin: Bolivia, Potosí
Linguistic Affiliation: Aymara
Yarn Spin: Ground- and complementary-warp
spin, Z2S; weft, Z2S
Warp and Weft Count: 112 epi, 26 ppi
Provenance: La Paz, Bolivia, 3/78

1992.107.139

139. Scarf *(bufanda, ufanta),* early 20th century
Tan camelid hair
Woven in warp-faced plain weave
Length: 58 in., 147.3 cm; width: 14½ in.,
36.8 cm

A long, wide scarf of shades of tan with a
crochet edge binding on the outer selvages.
Filé crochet patterned fringes are added,
along with single-strand fringes on both
ends, which are looped to patterned fringe.
Vicuña yarn is probably mixed with alpaca
and other fibers, as some of the fibers are
fuzzy. The varying shades of tan come from
different areas of the vicuña. A beautiful
cloth with a silky hand.

Origin: Bolivia, Potosí
Linguistic Affiliation: Aymara
Yarn Spin: Ground-warp spin, Z2S; weft, Z2S

Warp and Weft Count: 44 epi, 20 ppi
Provenance: La Paz, Bolivia, 4/80

1992.107.158

ALTIPLANO

140. **Hat, baby's** *(lluchu),* 20th century
Gray brown rabbit or viscacha spun with
alpaca
Knit: stockinette stitch; circular knitting on
straight needles
Length: 8 in., 20 cm; width: 7½ in., 19 cm

A medium-size hat, knitted in one piece
with ear flaps and a tie on the top. Very,
very soft, loose knit. Published in LeCount
(1990).

Origin: Bolivia, altiplano
Linguistic Affiliation: Aymara
Yarn Spin: Spin, Z2S
Gage: 10 spi
Provenance: La Paz, Bolivia, 3/78
Reference: LeCount 1990, 60, fig. 6.3

1992.107.187

Cat. no. 141

141. **Sling** *(honda),* 19th century
Multicolored sheep's wool or camelid hair
Woven in weft-faced plain and tapestry
weaves
Length: 56 in., 142.2 cm; width: 1 in., 2.5 cm

A medium-size sling, one piece, with a
small cradle. There is a multicolored fringe
on both sides of the cradle and three-
dimensional, three-color, four-strand twined
tubular structures with fringes on both
ends. One end is a loop. Finely twined cords
have a stiff hand because they are so tightly
constructed. Fringes may indicate ceremonial use.

Origin: Bolivia, altiplano
Linguistic Affiliation: Quechua/Aymara
Weft Count: 44 ppi
Provenance: Quito, Ecuador, 3/82

1992.107.230

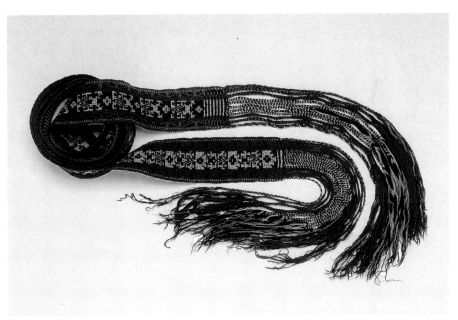

Cat. no. 143

CHILE
CAUTÍN

142. **Belt** *(trarihue),* early 20th century
Maroon, tan, and multicolored sheep's wool
or camelid hair
Woven in warp-faced plain, two-color
complementary, one-color supplementary,
and alternating float weaves
Length: 128 in., 325.1 cm; width: 3¼ in.,
8.3 cm

A long belt, one piece, patterned overall
with geometric motifs. There are sixteen
oblique, interlaced units with two rows of
twining at each end. Sixty percent of the
belt is in one pattern, forty percent in

another. Mapuche (Araucanian) belts are
discussed in Rowe (1977). Moraga commented that Cautín now is known as the
ninth Araucanian region, and there are
several Mapuche reservations in the
Temuco area. See also cat. no. *143.*

Origin: Chile, Cautín, Temuco, Quepe
Linguistic Affiliation: Mapuche
Yarn Spin: Ground-, complementary-, and supple-
mentary-warp spin, Z2S; weft, Z2S
Warp and Weft Count: 56 epi, 10 ppi
Provenance: Temuco, Chile, 3/79
References: Rowe 1977, 40, fig, 39; Vanessa
Moraga, personal communication, July 1996

1992.107.17

143. **Belt** *(trarihue),* 20th century
Beige, red, black, and multicolored sheep's
wool or camelid hair

Woven in warp-faced plain, two-color
complementary, and alternating float
weaves
Length: 125¼ in., 318.1 cm; width: 2⅝ in.,
6.7 cm

A long belt, one piece, patterned overall
with geometric motifs. There are sixteen
oblique, interlaced units at one end and
eleven at the other. Some of the interlacing
has come loose and creates a fringe. The
patterning alternates with a plain-weave
section. See also cat. no. 39, another belt
from the same location.

Origin: Chile, Cautín, Temuco, Quepe
Linguistic Affiliation: Mapuche
Yarn Spin: Ground- and complementary-warp
spin, Z2S; weft, Z2S
Warp and Weft Count: 64 epi, 10 ppi
Provenance: Temuco, Chile

1992.107.18

Cat. no. 145

144. **Woman's mantle** *(ikulla, kepam)*, early 20th century
Black sheep's wool
Woven in warp-faced plain weave
Length: 61 in., 155 cm; *width:* 46¾ in., 118.7 cm

A large shoulder cloth, one piece, with a tassel at three corners; one is missing. A beautifully woven piece; the termination area is not visible. Moraga commented that the Mapuche adopted the Inca style of dress, called locally the *ikulla,* and the *kepam* or *chamal.* The *ikulla* is a mantle that resembles the *chamal* and was worn like a cape. Garments were differentiated only by color; women's textiles were dyed a deeply saturated shade of indigo, which appeared almost black. They were woven of the highest quality wool, which had the greatest luster, elasticity, and sheen. They were dyed after being woven. This piece has a subtle scalloped selvage, created, Franquemont suggested, when weavers use two wefts, one going from one side, one from the other.

Dye may be synthetic, as green shading appears in black wefts.

Origin: Chile, Cautín, Temuco, Quepe
Linguistic Affiliation: Mapuche
Yarn Spin: Ground-warp spin, Z2S; weft, Z2S
Warp and Weft Count: 44 epi, 16 ppi
Provenance: Temuco, Chile, 3/79
References: Ed Franquemont, personal communication, January 1996; Vanessa Moraga, personal communications, December 1995 and July 1996

1992.107.2

ECUADOR
AZUAY

145. **Shawl** *(paño),* ca. 1890
White and blue *ikat* cotton
Woven in warp-faced plain weave
Length: 123 in., 312.4 cm; *width:* 35⅝ in., 90.5 cm

A long, woman's shawl, one piece, in geometric *ikat* patterns with two warp macramé sections and warp fringe at both

ends. It was purchased from a family who said they had had it since the 1880s; it is probably a wedding shawl. Macramé words are *como el boton della rosa* (like the bud of a rose), *del corazon* (from the heart), *que te adora* (how he adores thee), and *eres Bella hermosa* (you are beautiful). Cloth feels like silk, it is so fine. Meisch commented that Spanish-speakers knot the fringe of these textiles in a macramé overhand knot, adding extra yarn to the unwoven warp yarns as they knot. Blue dye is indigo, stiffened with cornstarch. The knotters, who are usually different from the weavers, trim the ends with a knife when the textile is finished. There also is an image of the Great Seal of Ecuador in macramé section. Miller (1996 [1991]) has discussed the shawls from the Gualaceo region.

Origin: Ecuador, Azuay, Gualacco
Linguistic Affiliation: Spanish
Yarn Spin: Ground-warp spin, Z2S; weft, Z2S
Warp and Weft Count: 124 epi, 26 ppi
Provenance: Cuenca, Ecuador, n.d.
References: Miller (1996 [1991]); Lynn Meisch, personal communication, January 1996

1992.107.21

CHIMBORAZO

146. **Poncho** *(poncho),* early 20th century
White and blue-and-white *ikat* cotton
Woven in warp-faced plain weave
Length: 56¾ in., 144.1 cm; *width:* 56¼ in., 142.9 cm

A very large poncho, two pieces, sewn together edge to edge, with a neck opening and a plain-weave edge binding with fringe created on all outer selvages by the edge binding wefts. The termination areas are at the same ends, whereas in some other Andean textiles, the terminaation areas are on opposite ends. The *ikat*-patterned bands are beautifully balanced across the piece; a lovely cloth. The blue dye is probably indigo. Meisch commented that it was woven on a backstrap loom, as there are no staked looms in Ecuador. There are eleven Cacha communities in this area.

Origin: Ecuador, Chimborazo, Riobamba, Cacha, Obraje
Linguistic Affiliation: Quichua
Yarn Spin: Ground-warp spin, Z2S; weft, Z2S
Warp and Weft Count: 100 epi, 14 ppi
Provenance: Austin, Texas, 2/87
Reference: Lynn Meisch, personal communication, January 1996

1992.107.22

Cat. no. 146

Cat. no. 148

147. **Poncho** *(poncho)*, ca. 1960
Rose, multicolored, and *ikat* sheep's wool
Woven in warp-faced plain weave
Length: 51 in., 129.5 cm; width: 49⅛ in.,
124.8 cm

A large poncho, two pieces, sewn together
edge to edge, with a neck opening, of *ikat*
geometric-patterned and solid-colored
stripes. There is a plain-weave edge binding
on all outer selvages. See also cat. no. *146,*
another poncho from the same location.
Meisch said that weavers may combine
natural and aniline dyes to achieve the
desired effect.

Origin: Ecuador, Chimborazo, Riobamba, Cacha
Obraje
Linguistic Affiliation: Quichua
Yarn Spin: Ground-warp spin, S2Z, Z2S; weft,
S2Z
Warp and Weft Count: 52 epi, 16 ppi
Provenance: Quito, Ecuador, 1/78
Reference: Lynn Meisch, personal communication,
January 1996.

1992.107.23

CAÑAR

148. **Belt** *(chumbi)*, 1956
Reddish orange, beige, and multicolored
sheep's wool
Woven in warp-faced plain and two-color
complementary-warp weaves with horizontal color changes
Length: 112 in., 284.5 cm; width: 2 in.,
5.1 cm

A very long belt, one piece, with overall
patterning with an oblique interlaced warp
fringe on one end and pieces of bias tape
on the other end. This belt came from the
same family that had the shawl, cat. no. *145.*
It is of dyed and hand-spun yarn. Images
include an anchor, deer, birds, cars, a couple,
a crucifix, a church, stars, other geometrics,
and words: *7 Julio de 1956 esta faja es tejido
de Manuel Jesus Camas; JHS los venados del
Camas, indio boracia a la mujer.* Meisch
commented that the words could be
describing adjacent images. She translated:

"July 7 of 1956, this belt was woven by
Manuel Jesus Camas; JHS [Jesus Christ] the
deer of Camas, Indian [translation uncertain, greedy?] to the woman." Rowe (1977)
discussed a belt from this location.

Origin: Ecuador, Cañar, Cañar
Linguistic Affiliation: Quichua
Yarn Spin: Ground- and complementary-warp
spin, Z2S; weft, Z2S
Warp and Weft Count: 56 epi, 26 ppi
(complementary-warp weave)
Provenance: Cuenca, Ecuador, 1/78
References: Rowe 1977, 73, fig. 86; Lynn Meisch,
personal communication, January 1996

1992.107.5

IMBABURA

149. **Mask** *(Aya Uma,* or *Diablo Uma)*, ca. 1950
Commercial cloth; inner hat felted
Length: 26 in., 66 cm; width: 10½ in.,
26.7 cm

A long helmet-style mask, with embroidered images and tubular stuffed, decorated
appendages attached at the head, ear, and
nose areas. There are openings for the
mouth and eyes, and the sides are open.
The iconography, which includes a human
wearing a similar mask, animals, birds,
a snake, a crucifix, and other geometric
motifs, is different on the front and back of
the mask. The rest of the costume is made
of cardboard and foil. Meisch commented
that the indigenous people do not like to use
the term *devil,* and call these masks *Aya
Uma,* a nature spirit. The mask is worn in
the areas around Cayambe, in Pichincha
province, and throughout Imbabura
province for the San Juan and San Pedro
festivals only. Men also wear chaps of sheep-
skin or goatskin.

Origin: Ecuador, Imbabura, Otavalo
Linguistic Affiliation: Quichua
Provenance: Quito, Ecuador, 5/79
Reference: Lynn Meisch, personal communication,
February 1996

1992.107.20

PERU
APURÍMAC

150. **Hair tie** *(wata, watana)*, mid-20th century
Multicolored sheep's wool or camelid hair,
white cotton
Woven in warp-faced plain weave and two-
color complementary-warp weave, with
horizontal color changes
Length: 52½ in., 130.8 cm; width: ¼ in.,
0.6 cm

A very narrow patterned band with finely
delineated images of birds and geometric
forms and a fringe on one end. The complementary-warp patterning creates the
"pebbled" look.

Origin: Peru, Apurímac, Andahuaylas,
Vilcabamba,
Linguistic Affiliation: Quechua
Yarn Spin: Ground-warp spin: Z2S; complemen-
tary-warp spin, S2Z; weft, Z2S
Warp and Weft Count: 200 epi, 28 ppi
Provenance: Cuzco, Peru, 1/79

1992.107.16

151. **Belt** *(chumpi)*, ca. 1950
Multicolored sheep's wool and camelid hair
Woven in warp-faced plain weave, two- and
three-color complementary-warp weave in
alternate and diagonal alignment with horizontal color changes
Length: 58½ in., 148.6 cm; width: 3¼ in.,
8.3 cm

A medium-size belt, densely patterned
throughout with geometric and bird motifs
and oblique interlaced units at one end,
which are sewn together. Appleby questioned a woman on the plaza in Cuzco, who
was selling these belts; she translated some
of the symbols as potato and wheat seeds,
the Inca road, tower, stairway or pass,
terrace, a seed warehouse, a cultivated field,
a *kero* (a wooden drinking vessel), a crown,
potatoes, young plantings, stars, a river,
corn, the four sections of a community
(Q. *suyus*), flowers, a hoe for digging fields,
and a vine plant. This kind of information is
probably subjective, her opinion, and would
have to be verified in the community. The
weft is camelid hair and of S2Z-spun yarn.
Ed Franquemont commented that this belt
style, with its repeating motifs, is very
similar to those woven in Challwahuacho,
Cotabambas; this piece may in fact be from
that town. Rowe (1977) also commented on
these belts. For a similar belt, see cat. no. *152*
(fig. 33).

Origin: Peru, Apurímac, Cotabambas, Challa
Wacho
Linguistic Affiliation: Quechua
Yarn Spin: Complementary-warp spin, Z2S; weft,
S2Z
Warp and Weft Count: 78 epi, 10 ppi
Provenance: Cuzco, Peru, 1/78

Cat. no. 149

Cat. no. 153

Cat. no. 154

References: Rowe 1977, fig. 103; Ed Franquemont, in Schevill 1986, 95; Jeffrey Appleby, personal communication, April 1996

1992.107.51

152. **Belt** *(chumpi),* ca. 1950
See fig. 33, p. 42.
Multicolored sheep's wool and camelid hair
Woven in warp-faced plain weave, two- and three-color complementary-warp weave in alternate and diagonal alignment with horizontal color changes
Length: 62½ in, 158.8 cm; width: 2½ in., 6.4 cm

A medium-size belt, densely patterned throughout with geometric motifs. At one end are oblique interlaced units, which are sewn and drawn together, and there is some colored commercial binding on both ends. For a similar belt, see cat. no. 151.

Origin: Peru, Apurímac, Cotabambas, Challa Wacho
Linguistic Affiliation: Quechua
Yarn Spin: Complementary-warp spin, Z2S; weft, S2Z
Warp and Weft Count: 96 epi, 14 ppi
Provenance: Cuzco, Peru, 5/78

1992.107.52

153. **Poncho** *(poncho),* 18th–19th century
Dark blue and multicolored sheep's wool or camelid hair
Woven in warp-faced plain and two-color complementary-warp weaves
Length: 70 in., 177.9 cm; width: 39½ in., 100.3 cm

A very long poncho of two pieces, sewn together edge to edge. The neck opening is trimmed with a plain-weave band. Solid-colored stripes alternate with patterned ones with *ch'unchus* or jungle figures similar to those in Q'ero textiles from the Ocongate region. Other images include flowers, possibly corn and insects, and two human figures wearing hats and holding hands. Different tones of dark blue, probably an indigo dye, create an *abrash* effect. Reds probably are synthetic dyes.

Origin: Peru, Apurímac, Cotabambas or Abancay
Linguistic Affiliation: Quechua
Yarn Spin: Warp and weft spin, Z2S
Warp and Weft Count: 40 epi, 20 ppi
Provenance: Cuzco, 5/80

1992.107.76

154. **Woman's mantle** *(llijlla),* 19th century
Purple and multicolored sheep's wool or camelid hair
Woven in warp-faced plain weave, two- and three-color complementary weave, and two-color supplementary-warp weave

Length: 38¼ in., 97.2 cm; width: 31 in., 78.7 cm

A medium-size mantle, two pieces, with solid-colored and floral- and geometric-patterned stripes that are joined by a metallic and fiber belt, which may be from an older piece. Because of this unusual feature, the textile may have been used in a religious context. The floral iconography indicates colonial influence. The purple and red solid-colored areas have *abrash* effects.

Origin: Peru, Apurímac, Apurímac Valley
Linguistic Affiliation: Quechua
Yarn Spin: Ground- and complementary-warp spin, Z2S; supplementary-warp spin, Z2S4Z
Warp and Weft Count: 44 epi, 18 ppi
Provenance: Cuzco, Peru, 4/83

1992.107.87

155. **Poncho** *(poncho),* 1830
See fig. 39, p. 45.
Multicolors, probably camelid hair
Woven in warp-faced plain and two-color complementary-warp weaves
Length: 64½ in., 163.8 cm; width: 70 in., 177.8 cm

A large poncho, seven pieces sewn together, of solid-colored and animal-, human-, floral-, and geometric-patterned stripes. There is a neck opening created by discontinuous wefts trimmed with silk ribbon and a plain-weave edge binding on all outer selvages. The fringe is created by the edge binding wefts, and the four corners are turned up and stitched. An impressive piece, this is the only example in the collection made up of seven pieces with complex warp striping. Alberto Miori commented that, in 1830, Apurímac was still part of the department of Cuzco; the date was obtained from family records. The poncho was handed down from woman to woman and never worn by men, even for ceremonial functions. It was woven for Colonel Humberto Cruz, an officer in the War of Independence and later in the army of the Bolivian-Peruvian Confederation (1835). The presence of the Bolivian national colors in the accessory stripes may be a confirmation of this. It includes several known colonial motifs such as double-headed eagles and mermaids (sirens). Woven into one of the stripes is an inscription: *Ia se cabo mi placer mi gloria se dehizo que el quien perdido lo que quiso no tiene mas que perder ahi no se que hacer.* Miori configured the poem, and my translation is: "My pleasure is finished, my glory is destroyed, as he who lost what he desired, Ay! I do not know what to do." Images also include finely delineated humans with hats, lizards, frogs, birds, and abstract flowers. A natural dye palette.

Cat. no. 156

Origin: Peru, Apurímac, Grau, Oropeza, Mamara
Linguistic Affiliation: Quechua
Yarn Spin: Ground- and complementary-warp spin, Z2S; weft, Z2S
Warp and Weft Count: 103 epi, 20 ppi
Provenance: Cuzco, Peru, 4/82
Reference: Alberto Miori, personal communication, April 1982

L96.120.1

CUZCO

156. **Coca bag** *(ch'uspa),* ca. 1970
Red, beige, and multicolored sheep's wool or camelid hair
Woven in warp-faced plain and two- and three-color complementary-warp weaves
Length: 7¼ in., 18.4 cm; width: 6 in., 15.2 cm

A medium-size bag, two pieces, sewn together at the bottom, with narrow solid-colored and wide geometric-, animal-, and human-patterned warp stripes. The sides are joined by a tubular edge binding that continues along the top, and there are large bunches of warp fringe of re-plied yarn on the bottom. Two pockets with inside openings were created by longer warps and are trimmed with a tubular edge binding, and there is a fine narrow strap tied to the inside corners. Franquemont commented that the design near the selvage band is called *sakas,* and that people are still making these bags.

Cat. no. 158

Cat. no. 159

Origin: Peru, Cuzco, Calca, Ccachin, Ampares
Linguistic Affiliation: Quechua
Yarn Spin: Ground- and complementary-warp spin, Z2S; weft, Z2S
Warp and Weft Count: 88 epi, 28 ppi
Provenance: Cuzco, Peru, 5/78
Reference: Ed Franquemont, personal communication, January 1996

1992.107.42

157. **Coca bag** *(ch'uspa),* 19th century
Beige, red, and multicolored sheep's wool or camelid hair
Woven in warp-faced plain and one-color supplementary-warp weaves
Length: 5½ in., 14 cm; width: 5½ in., 14 cm

A small bag, one piece, joined by a tubular edge binding of plain weave with supplementary-warp inserts, which continues along top edges. The fringe was added and is of plied and re-plied yarn, and there is a strap of two pieces. There is some S2Z-spun yarn in the center stripes. A natural dye palette. For similar bags, see cat. no. 181, *182.*

Origin: Peru, Cuzco, Calca, Ccachin
Linguistic Affiliation: Quechua
Yarn Spin: Ground- and supplementary-warp spin, Z2S, S2Z; weft, Z2S
Warp and Weft Count: 72 epi, 20 ppi
Provenance: Cuzco, Peru, 1/79

1992.107.34

158. **Poncho** *(poncho),* ca. 1960
Red, beige, and multicolored sheep's wool or camelid hair
Woven in warp-faced plain and one-color supplementary-warp weaves
Length: 43¼ in., 109.9 cm; width: 43½ in., 110.5 cm

A medium-size poncho, two pieces, of narrow solid-colored and wide geometric-patterned stripes, sewn together edge to edge. There is a neck opening with edge binding and remnants of fringe, and another edge binding sewn onto all selvages with remnants of fringe created by the edge binding wefts. Franquemont commented that the termination area is not visible, and that the weaving is excellent.

Origin: Peru, Cuzco, Calca, Chahuaytiri, Pisac
Linguistic Affiliation: Quechua
Yarn Spin: Ground- and supplementary-warp spin, Z2S, S2Z; weft, Z2S
Warp and Weft Count: 44 epi, 14 ppi
Provenance: Pisac, Peru, 1/79
Reference: Ed Franquemont, personal communication, January 1996

1992.107.89

159. **Coca bag** *(ch'uspa),* ca. 1950
Red and multicolored sheep's wool or camelid hair
Woven in warp-faced plain and one-color supplementary-warp weaves
Length: 4 in., 10.2 cm; width: 7½ in., 19.1 cm

A small bag, two pieces, sewn together at the bottom and joined on the sides by a tubular edge binding, which continues along the top edges. The bag is of narrow, solid-colored and wide geometric-patterned stripes. There are two pockets with inside openings created by longer warps, one main strap joined on the outside corners, and additional straps of intersecting warps. Long fringes of re-plied yarn decorate the straps, pockets, and the bottom of the bag. This special bag is for a fiesta dance. No termination area is visible. The strap structure resembles hair ties with bands of intersecting warps. Two red tassels on each side may be the weaver's identification marks. For a similar bag, see cat. no. 165.

Origin: Peru, Cuzco, Calca, Chahuaytiri
Linguistic Affiliation: Quechua
Yarn Spin: Ground- and supplementary-warp spin, Z2S; weft, Z2S
Warp and Weft Count: 80 epi, 26 ppi
Provenance: Pisac, Peru, 1/78

1992.107.40

160. **Woman's mantle** *(llijlla),* ca. 1960
Red and multicolored sheep's wool or camelid hair
Woven in warp-faced plain and two- and three-color complementary-warp weaves
Length: 41 in., 104.1 cm; width: 45 in., 114.3 cm

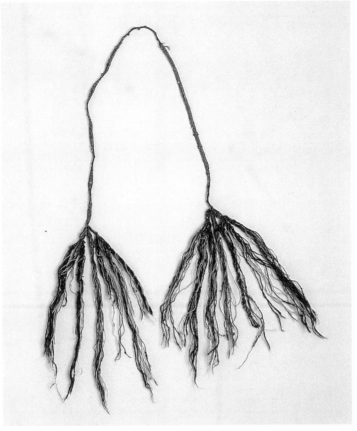

Cat. no. 161

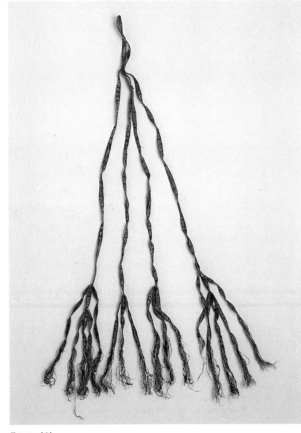

Cat. no. 164

A large mantle, two pieces, joined edge to edge, of solid-colored and human-, animal-, and geometric-patterned stripes, with a three-color tubular edge binding on all four sides. A fringe is created by six oblique interlaced units. Images include large diamonds, horses ridden by men holding flags, and single human figures. Seibold (1992) has written on textiles from this town.

Origin: Peru, Cuzco, Calca, Lares, Choquecancha
Linguistic Affiliation: Quechua
Yarn Spin: Ground- and complementary-warp spin, Z2S; weft, Z2S
Warp and Weft Count: 44 epi, 20 ppi
Provenance: Cuzco, Peru, 4/78
Reference: Seibold 1992

1992.107.55

161. **Hair tie** *(wata, watana),* mid-20th century
Multicolored sheep's wool or camelid hair and horsehair with beads
Woven in warp-faced plain and two-color complementary-warp weaves
Length: 30 in., 76.2 cm; width: ⅛ in., 0.3 cm

A very narrow, geometric-patterned band with additional bands created by intersecting transverse warps. There are beads woven into the main band. Loose warps create fringes. The use of beads threaded onto the wefts in the weaving process adds another dimension to this lovely hair tie; on

one side they are placed in eye of diamond, on the other side between diamonds on the weft. Ed Franquemont (1986b), noting that *watas* were largely ignored in the literature, commented that hair ties, with their intersecting transverse warps, are ingenious in design and technology. Sacaca suggested the origin. For other hair ties, see cat. no. 162–64, 167, 168.

Origin: Peru, Cuzco, Calca, Colquepata
Linguistic Affiliation: Quechua
Yarn Spin: Ground- and complementary-warp spin, Z2S; weft, Z2S
Warp and Weft Count: 128 epi, 20 ppi
Provenance: Cuzco, Peru, 5/78
References: Franquemont 1986b, 89; Timoteo Ccarita Sacaca, personal communication, April 1996

1992.107.8

162. **Hair tie** *(wata, watana),* early 20th century
Multicolored sheep's wool or camelid hair
Woven in warp-faced plain and two-color complementary-warp weaves
Length: 49 in., 124.5 cm; width: ¼ in., 0.6 cm

A very narrow, geometric-patterned band, with additional bands created by transverse warps. Some loose warps create fringe, others are worn away. Very fine weaving and tightly spun yarn creates a light hand. Added bands are of geometric designs, and the primary band has abstract animal and

floral designs. Franquemont suggested the origin. For comments on hair ties, see cat. no. 161. For other hair ties, see cat. no. 163, *164,* 167, 168.

Origin: Peru, Cuzco, Calca, Lares
Linguistic Affiliation: Quechua
Yarn Spin: Ground- and complementary-warp spin, Z2S, S2Z; weft, Z2S
Warp and Weft Count: 112 epi, 48 ppi
Provenance: Cuzco, Peru, 1/79
Reference: Ed Franquemont, personal communication, January 1996

1992.107.11

163. **Hair tie** *(wata, watana),* early to mid-20th century
See figs. 47, 48, p. 51.
Multicolored sheep's wool or camelid hair
Woven in warp-faced plain, two- and three-color complementary, and alternating float weaves
Length: 52 in., 132.1 cm; width: ¼ in., 0.6 cm

A very narrow, geometric-patterned band with three added bands of intersecting transverse warps at each end, which create additional bands. Loose warps create fringes. In the main band there are two different sets of colors, perhaps a discontinuous warp structure. The hair tie is very finely woven of tightly spun and plied yarn. Added bands are in sets with similar iconography and colors on each end.

Cat. no. 169

Franquemont suggested the origin, and commented that these ties are extraordinary pieces of weaving; it is worth taking time to study them. See also cat. no. *161, 162, 164,* 167, 168.

Origin: Peru, Cuzco, Calca, Lares
Linguistic Affiliation: Quechua
Yarn Spin: Ground- and complementary-warp spin, Z2S, S2Z; weft, Z2S
Warp and Weft Count: 112 epi, 40 ppi
Provenance: Cuzco, Peru, 1/79
Reference: Ed Franquemont, personal communication, January 1996

1992.107.12

164. **Hair tie, double** *(wata, watana),* mid-20th century
See fig. 45, p. 50.
Multicolored sheep's wool or camelid hair
Woven in warp-faced plain and two-color complementary-warp weaves
Length: 25¼ in., 64.2 cm; width: ¼ in., 0.6 cm

Four narrow, geometric-patterned bands with two additional bands of intersecting transverse warps added to the outside and inside band. Loose warps create fringe. The two bands are sewn together in two areas near the top. Very tightly woven. Franquemont suggested the origin. See also cat. no. *161-63,* 167, 168.

Origin: Peru, Cuzco, Calca, Lares
Linguistic Affiliation: Quechua
Yarn Spin: Ground- and complementary-warp spin, S2Z; weft, Z2S
Warp and Weft Count: 112 epi, 32 ppi
Provenance: Cuzco, Peru, 5/80
Reference: Ed Franquemont, personal communication, January 1996

1992.107.14

165. **Coca bag** *(ch'uspa),* 1960
Red, beige, and multicolored sheep's wool or camelid hair
Woven in warp-faced plain and one-color supplementary-warp weaves
Length: 8¼ in., 21 cm; width: 5⅛ in., 13 cm

A medium-size bag, one piece, with solid-colored and geometric-patterned stripes. The sides are joined with a three-color tubular edge binding, which continues along the top edges. A fringe of re-plied yarn was added to the bottom, and a narrow strap is attached to the inside corners of the bag. The tan yarn may be vicuña. No termination area is visible. The multicolored stripes are of Z2S-spun yarn; the tan stripe is of S2Z-spun yarn. Franquemont suggested the origin.

Origin: Peru, Cuzco, Calca, Lauramarca
Linguistic Affiliation: Quechua
Yarn Spin: Ground- and supplementary-warp spin, Z2S, S2Z; weft, Z2S
Warp and Weft Count: 72 epi, 30 ppi
Provenance: Pisac, Peru, 2/79
Reference: Ed Franquemont, personal communication, January 1996

1992.107.41

166. **Woman's mantle** *(llijlla),* early 20th century
Green and multicolored sheep's wool or camelid hair
Woven in warp-faced plain, three-color complementary, and one-and two-color supplementary weaves
Length: 27 in., 68.6 cm; width: 29 in., 73.7 cm

A small mantle, two pieces, sewn together edge to edge, of solid-colored and geometric-patterned stripes. Not many of this style survived. Women separated them and gave halves to their daughters. The S2Z-spun yarn at the outer selvages helps the piece lie flat. The black weft is visible and creates a sheen. The red orange is not a solid color and gives an *abrash* effect. A synthetic dye palette.

Origin: Peru, Cuzco, Calca
Linguistic Affiliation: Quechua
Yarn Spin: Ground-, complementary-, and supplementary-warp spin, Z2S, S2Z; weft, Z2S
Warp and Weft Count: 60 epi, 24 ppi
Provenance: Cuzco, Peru, 1/79

1992.107.80

167. **Hair tie** *(wata, watana),* mid-20th century
Red, green, and multicolored sheep's wool or camelid hair, horsehair, and beads
Woven in warp-faced plain and two-color complementary-warp weaves
Length: 51 in., 129.5 cm; width: ⅛ in., 0.3 cm

Three narrow, geometric-patterned bands with additional bands created by intersecting transverse warps that have beads woven into them. Loose warp ends of re-plied yarn create fringe of varying thickness. A festival hair tie made and worn in the highlands of Calca from Ollantaytambo to Lares. A complex and wonderful piece. See also cat. no. *161-64,* 167, 168.

Origin: Peru, Cuzco, Calca
Linguistic Affiliation: Quechua
Yarn Spin: Ground- and complementary-warp spin, Z2S; weft, Z2S
Warp and Weft Count: 112 epi, 32 ppi
Provenance: Cuzco, Peru, n.d.

1992.107.9

168. **Hair tie** *(wata, watana),* late 19th century
Maroon, beige, and multicolored sheep's wool or camelid hair
Woven in warp-faced plain and two-color complementary-warp weave in alternate and diagonal alignment
Length: 50 in., 127 cm; width: ½ in., 1.3 cm

A narrow, geometric-patterned band with additional bands of intersecting transverse warps added to each end. Loose warps create fringes on ends of each band. Heavier hand and thicker yarn than some of the other hair ties, such as cat. no. 162, 163. Complementary warps in diagonal alignment create a series of Vs. For comments on hair ties, see cat. no. *164,* 167.

Origin: Peru, Cuzco, Calca
Linguistic Affiliation: Quechua
Yarn Spin: Ground- and complementary-warp spin, Z2S, S2Z; weft, Z2S
Warp and Weft Count: 80 epi, 28 ppi
Provenance: Calca, Peru, n.d.

1992.107.13

169. **Woman's mantle** *(llijlla),* 19th century
Black and multicolored alpaca hair
Woven in warp-faced plain, two-color complementary-, and one-color supplementary-warp weaves
Length: 33½ in., 85.1 cm; width: 42½ in., 108 cm

A large mantle, two pieces, with large solid-colored and geometric-patterned stripes, joined edge to edge. The S2Z-spun yarn is in the outside stripes and in the center stripes, creating a herringbone effect. Basting stitches on outer selvages suggest that there was a fringe at one time. The complementary warps of green and gold create a raised texture with narrow olive stripes flanking the patterned stripe. Sacaca suggested this origin.

Origin: Peru, Cuzco, Canchis, Checacupe, Collonoma
Linguistic Affiliation: Quechua
Yarn Spin: Ground-, complementary-, and supplementary-warp spin, Z2S, S2Z; weft, Z2S
Warp and Weft Count: 96 epi, 16 ppi
Provenance: Pisac, Peru, 1/79
Reference: Timoteo Ccarita Sacaca, personal communication, April 1996

1992.107.92

170. **Ceremonial carrying cloth** *(t'iqulla),* ca. 1950
Multicolored sheep's wool or camelid hair
Woven in warp-faced plain, one-color supplementary, and alternating float weaves with discontinuous warps dovetailed at the center
Length: 36 in., 91.4 cm; width: 36 in., 91.4 cm

Cat. no. 170

A medium-size carrying cloth, two pieces, joined at the center, of solid-colored and geometric-patterned stripes. The discontinuous warps dovetailed at the center create color changes, beige to dark brown and tan to gray. Similar features, such as alternating float edging, iconography, and stripes of tan and gray, also are found in a woman's mantle from this region, cat. no. 171. This cloth on which coca leaves are cast may be used for divination. Rowe (1977) discussed the discontinuous warp changes, a pre-Columbian technique that has survived in the Cuzco area. Franquemont commented that discontinuous warp weaving is done on a scaffolding. The technique is documented in John Cohen's film *Peruvian Weaving: A Continuous Warp for 5,000 Years* (1980). Sacaca said that the four sections represent the four *suyus* or communities.

Origin: Peru, Cuzco, Canchis, Checacupe
Linguistic Affiliation: Quechua
Yarn Spin: Ground- and supplementary-warp spin, Z2S, S2Z; weft, Z2S
Warp and Weft Count: 72 epi, 20 ppi
Provenance: Cuzco, Peru, 2/78
References: Rowe 1977, 27–29, fig. 19; Ed Franquemont, personal communication, January 1996; Timoteo Ccarita Sacaca, personal communication, April 1996

1992.107.81

171. **Woman's mantle** *(llijlla),* ca. 1940
Multicolored sheep's wool or camelid hair
Woven in warp-faced plain, one-color supplementary, and alternating float weaves
Length: 37 in., 94 cm; width: 35 in., 89 cm

A large mantle, two pieces, of solid-colored and geometric-patterned stripes, joined edge to edge. The weft is visible in parts of the gray area, giving a speckled effect. The alternating float weave creates borders on the side selvages. The patterning is similar to that of the ceremonial cloth from this region (cat. no. *170*). Franquemont commented that this cloth and another mantle, cat. no. 172, are made on staked looms, whereas a third mantle from this province, cat. no. 186, was woven on a body-tension or backstrap loom. With the latter loom, patterns migrate to side selvages; weavers working on staked looms can put patterns wherever they want.

Origin: Peru, Cuzco, Canchis, Checacupe
Linguistic Affiliation: Quechua
Yarn Spin: Ground- and supplementary-warp spin, Z2S, S2Z; weft, Z2S
Warp and Weft Count: 40 epi, 14 ppi
Provenance: Cuzco, Peru, 3/82
Reference: Ed Franquemont, personal communication, January 1996

1992.107.79

Cat. no. 174

172. **Woman's mantle** *(llijlla),* 19th century
Beige and multicolored sheep's wool or camelid hair
Woven in warp-faced plain, two-color complementary-, and one-color supplementary-warp weaves.
Length: 38 in., 96.5 cm; width: 37½ in., 95.3 cm

A medium-size mantle, two pieces, joined edge to edge, of geometric-patterned and solid-colored stripes with a tubular edge binding on all outer selvages. Textiles with predominantly beige background and similar colors and patterns are often associated with Tinta, in Canchis. Checacupe is nearby.

Origin: Peru, Cuzco, Canchis, Checacupe
Linguistic Affiliation: Quechua
Yarn Spin: Ground-, complementary-, and supplementary-warp spin, Z2S; weft, Z2S
Warp and Weft Count: 63 epi, 14 ppi
Provenance: Cuzco, Peru, 5/80

1992.107.97

173. **Hat** *(chullu),* ca. 1950
Multicolored sheep's wool or camelid hair
Knit: stockinette, garter, scallop stitches; intarsia patterning, circular knitting on straight needles
Length: 17¾ in., 45.1 cm; width: 8½ in., 21.6 cm

A medium-size hat, one piece, with a very elongated top and ear flaps, both with tassels. The ear flaps are trimmed with scalloped edging, and the top tassel is in three parts. Some motifs are floral-like, and may show colonial influence. Unusually long top with horizontal band motifs and a diamond shape on the bottom. Very fine knitting with complex color changes. LeCount commented that the scalloped edge is knit separately and hand-stitched onto the ear flap. The tube-shaped tassel construction is a mystery. The color patterning is knit-purl intarsia, and the surface appears singed because fuzz obscures the design. It is knit from the bottom up.

Origin: Peru, Cuzco, Canchis, Chilca
Linguistic Affiliation: Quechua
Yarn Spin: Spin, Z2S
Gage: 18 spi
Provenance: Cuzco, Peru, 5/80
Reference: Cynthia LeCount, personal communication, October 1995

1992.107.32

174. **Woman's mantle** *(llijlla),* ca. 1950
Multicolored sheep's wool or camelid hair
Woven in warp-faced plain, one-color supplementary, and alternating float weaves
Length: 41 in., 104.1 cm; width: 37½ in., 95.1 cm

A medium-size mantle, two pieces, of solid-colored and geometric-patterned stripes, joined edge to edge. There are alternating float weave stripes on side selvages. Color palette is varied and intense; the piece is vibrant. The patterning in a poncho from the same region, cat. no. 175, is similar.

Origin: Peru, Cuzco, Canchis, Chilca
Linguistic Affiliation: Quechua
Yarn Spin: Ground- and supplementary-warp spin, Z2S; weft, Z2S
Warp and Weft Count: 48 epi, 16 ppi
Provenance: Cuzco, Peru, 3/81

1992.107.77

175. **Poncho** *(poncho),* ca. 1970
Beige and multicolored sheep's wool or camelid hair
Woven in warp-faced plain, two-color complementary-, and one-color supplementary-warp weaves
Length: 46 in., 116.8 cm; width: 32¾ in., 83.2 cm

A medium-size poncho, two pieces, joined edge to edge, with a neck opening. There is a plain-weave edge binding sewn to all outer selvages, with a fringe of added yarn and edge binding wefts. The four corners are turned up and stitched. A wide range of colors. Patterning resembles that in a mantle from the same region, cat. no. *174.*

Origin: Peru, Cuzco, Canchis, Chilca
Linguistic Affiliation: Quechua
Yarn Spin: Ground-, complementary-, and supplementary-warp spin, Z2S, S2Z; weft, Z2S
Warp and Weft Count: 55 epi, 16 ppi
Provenance: Cuzco, Peru, 5/78

1992.107.91

176. **Woman's mantle** *(llijlla),* mid-19th century
Purple and multicolored sheep's wool or camelid hair
Woven in warp-faced plain, two-color complementary-, and one-color supplementary-warp weaves
Length: 35½ in., 90.2 cm; width: 27½ in., 69.9 cm

A small shoulder cloth, two pieces, joined in the center, with solid-colored and geometric-, floral-, and bird-patterned stripes. Black wefts visible in patterned areas create a color contrast. Color palette unusual. In color, layout, and patterns, this mantle resembles cat. no. *154,* a mantle from the Apurímac valley.

Origin: Peru, Cuzco, Canchis, Combapata
Linguistic Affiliation: Quechua
Yarn Spin: Ground-, complementary-, and supplementary-warp spin, Z2S, S2Z; weft, Z2S
Warp and Weft Count: 64 epi, 18 ppi
Provenance: Pisac, Peru, 1/79

1992.107.9

177. **Poncho** *(poncho),* 19th century
Beige and multicolored sheep's wool or camelid hair
Woven in warp-faced plain and one-color supplementary-warp weaves
Length: 60½ in., 153.7 cm; width: 45½ in., 115.6 cm

A large poncho, two pieces, of solid-colored and geometric-, bird-, and floral-patterned stripes, joined edge to edge, with a neck opening trimmed with plain-weave edge binding and remnants of fringe. A similar edge binding is sewn onto all outer selvages, also with remnants of fringe created by the edge binding wefts. The four corners are turned up and stitched. Narrow blue and beige stripes, a combination of Z2S- and S2Z-spun yarn, are positioned at side selvages. Beige background similar to textiles from Checacupe or Tinta; see cat. no. 172 and 185. A successful design, beautifully woven. Sacaca suggested the origin.

Origin: Peru, Cuzco, Canchis, Combapata or Tinta
Linguistic Affiliation: Quechua
Yarn Spin: Ground- and supplementary-warp spin, Z2S, S2Z; weft: Z2S
Warp and Weft Count: 52 epi, 16 ppi
Provenance: Cuzco, Peru, 5/78
Reference: Timoteo Ccarita Sacaca, personal communication, April 1996

1992.107.72

178. **Saddle blanket** *(frazada),* 19th century
Multicolored camelid hair
Woven in weft-faced tapestry plain weave with dovetailed color changes
Length: 29½ in., 74.9 cm; width: 19 cm, 48.3 cm

A medium-size blanket, one piece, in overall diamond patterning. Diamond forms are outlined in contrasting colors with eccentric weft technique. A very soft textile. Franquemont commented that the same technique appears in cat. no. *191,* a tunic from Apurímac. Also, he doubted that it was a saddle blanket, but could not identify it for certain. Sacaca said that the textile could be two hundred years old and that the blue was indigo dye.

Origin: Peru, Cuzco, Canchis, Lake Sabinacocha, Finaya
Linguistic Affiliation: Quechua
Yarn Spin: Weft spin, Z2S, warp; Z2S
Warp and Weft Count: 9 epi, 32 ppi
Provenance: Pitumarca, Peru, 5/83
References: Ed Franquemont, personal communication, January 1996; Timoteo Ccarita Sacaca, personal communication, May 1996

1992.107.3

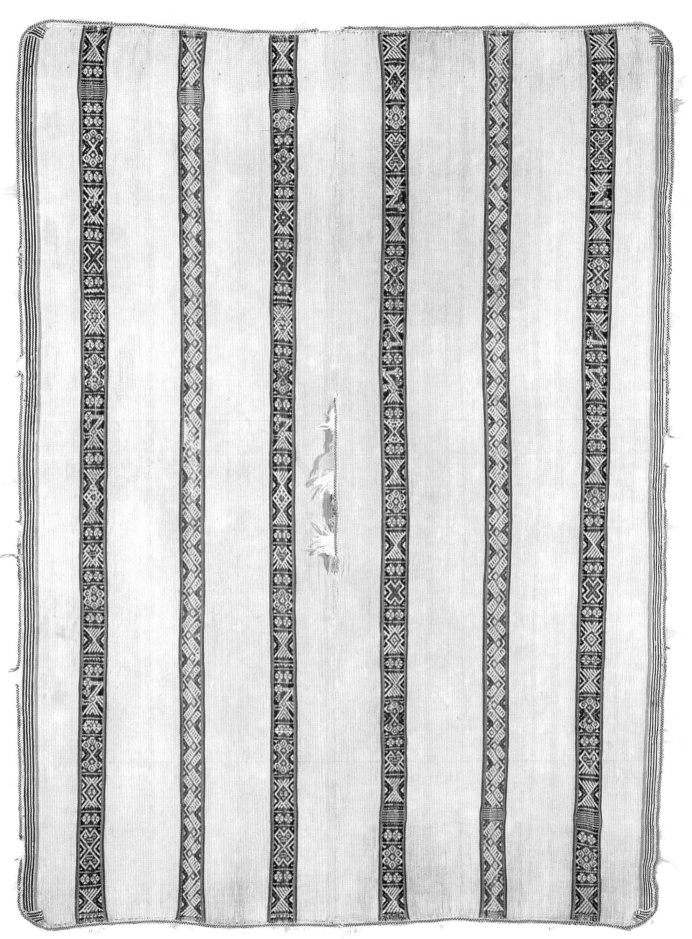

Cat. no. 177

Cat. no. 178

Cat. no. 182

179. Hat (chullu), ca. 1950

Maroon and multicolored sheep's wool or camelid hair

Knit: stockinette, garter, scallop stitches; color patterning, circular knitting on straight needles

Length: 19 in., 48.3 cm; width: 8¾ in., 22.2 cm

A medium-size hat, one piece, in overall geometric patterning with ear flaps and a scalloped edging on the bottom of the hat and on the ear flaps. There is one tassel on the elongated top. Very fine work. Ear flap construction is a variation of an ear flap discussed by LeCount (1990). LeCount commented that this hat was made of hand-spun yarn with some natural brown; some rows have four colors carried all the way around. The double wave design is typical of Pitumarca.

Origin: Peru, Cuzco, Canchis, Pitumarca
Linguistic Affiliation: Quechua
Yarn Spin: Spin, Z2S
Warp and Weft Count: 22 spi
Provenance: Cuzco, Peru, 5/78
References: LeCount 1990, 84, no. 10; Cynthia LeCount, personal communication, October 1995

1992.107.33

180. Woman's mantle (llijlla), mid-20th century

See fig. 23, p. 30.

Black and multicolored sheep's wool or camelid hair

Woven in warp-faced plain and two-color complementary-warp weaves

Length: 37 in., 93.9 cm; width: 34 in., 68.4 cm

A medium-size mantle, two pieces, of solid-colored and geometric-, floral-, and

human-patterned stripes, joined edge to edge, with a twill tape trim sewn onto all outer selvages. According to Wilson (1996 [1991]), the large abstract human image, the *ch'unchu,* represents a jungle inhabitant as distinct from the highlander. Franquemont commented that the *chilli* pattern in green and yellow means "things that are raggedy and frayed." Origin suggested by Timoteo Ccarita Sacaca.

Origin: Peru, Cuzco, Canchis, Pitumarca
Linguistic Affiliation: Quechua
Yarn Spin: Ground- and complementary-warp spin, Z2S; weft, Z2S
Warp and Weft Count: 64 epi, 18 ppi
Provenance: Lima, Peru, 4/80
References: Wilson 1996 (1991), 216; Ed Franquemont, personal communication, January 1996; Timoteo Ccarita Sacaca, personal communication, April 1996

1992.107.83

181. Coca bag (ch'uspa), early 20th century

Multicolored sheep's wool or camelid hair

Woven in warp-faced plain and one- and two-color supplementary-warp weaves

Length: 5 in., 12.7 cm; width: 5 in., 12.7 cm

A small bag, one piece, of geometric- and floral-patterned stripes. The sides are joined with a two-color tubular edge binding, which continues along top edges, and there is a long fringe of re-plied yarn. Some of the geometric motifs resemble abstract butter-flies. In patterning, size, and layout, this bag is similar to other examples, see cat. no. 157, *182.*

Origin: Peru, Cuzco, Canchis, Tinta
Linguistic Affiliation: Quechua
Yarn Spin: Ground- and supplementary-warp spin, Z2S, S2Z; weft, Z2S

Warp and Weft Count: 72 epi, 28 ppi
Provenance: Cuzco, Peru, 1/79

1992.107.35

182. Coca bag (ch'uspa), early 20th century

Multicolored camelid hair

Woven in warp-faced plain and two-color supplementary-warp weaves

Length: 6 in., 15.2 cm; width: 6 in., 15.2 cm

A small bag, one piece, of geometric-patterned stripes, joined by a three-color tubular edge binding, which continues along top edges. There is a long fringe of re-plied yarn. Some of the geometric motifs resemble abstract butterflies. Both Z2S- and S2Z-spun yarn in the supplementary warp. In patterning, size, and layout, this bag is similar to other examples, see cat. no. 157, 181.

Origin: Peru, Cuzco, Canchis, Tinta
Linguistic Affiliation: Quechua
Yarn Spin: Ground- and supplementary-warp spin, Z2S, S2Z; weft, Z2S
Warp and Weft Count: 80 epi, 28 ppi
Provenance: Cuzco, Peru, 5/78

1992.107.36

183. Hat (chullu), ca. 1960

Beige and multicolored sheep's wool or camelid hair

Knit: stockinette and popcorn stitches; intarsia patterning, circular knitting on straight needles

Length: 7 in., 17.8 cm; width: 10 in., 25.4 cm

A medium-size hat, one piece, with overall diamond-shaped patterning and ear flaps, which have scalloped borders and fringe. There are four tassels near the top and one

Cat. no. 184

are carried along. A unique shape. This hat is published in LeCount (1990).

Origin: Peru, Cuzco, Canchis, Tinta
Linguistic Affiliation: Quechua
Yarn Spin: Spin, Z2S
Gage: 10 spi
Provenance: Cuzco, Peru, 2/79
Reference: LeCount 1990, 29, fig. 3.11

1992.107.31

185. Poncho *(poncho),* 20th century
Beige and multicolored sheep's wool or camelid hair
Woven in warp-faced plain and one-color supplementary-warp weaves
Length: 58½ in., 148.6 cm; width: 45½ in., 115.6 cm

A large poncho, two pieces, of solid-colored and geometric-patterned stripes, joined edge to edge, with a small neck opening. There is a plain-weave edge binding sewn to all outer selvages with a fringe created by the edge binding wefts. The four corners are turned up and stitched. The weave construction is similar to that of other Tinta pieces. This, with its beige background and layout, resembles another poncho, cat. no. *177,* and a mantle, cat. no. 172. Franquemont commented that the poncho may have been woven in Checacupe, as one of a family of styles.

Origin: Peru, Cuzco, Canchis, Tinta
Linguistic Affiliation: Quechua
Yarn Spin: Ground- and supplementary-warp spin, Z2S; weft, Z2S
Warp and Weft Count: 60 epi, 14 ppi
Provenance: Cuzco, Peru, 5/78
Reference: Ed Franquemont, personal communication, January 1996

1992.107.73

186. Woman's mantle *(llijlla),* early 20th century
Black and multicolored sheep's wool or camelid hair
Woven in warp-faced plain, two-color complementary-, and one-color supplementary-warp weaves
Length: 35½ in., 90.2 cm; width: 34 in., 87.4 cm

A medium-size, woman's mantle, two pieces, of wide solid-colored areas and geometric- and animal-patterned stripes, joined edge to edge. One of the images is a double-headed cat, a pre-Columbian motif. Remnants of basting stitches near selvages suggest that there was a cloth binding or finish on all sides. This textile has Aymara features, such as the black *pampas* and fine motifs, but in Quechua colors. One *pampa* area is of S2Z-spun yarn and the other side is of Z2S. One rose stripe on the outer area is a combination of S2Z and Z2S, giving

on the top. S2Z-spun green yarn is in only one small area. The other green yarn is Z2S spun. Some of the yarn is commercial, some is handspun. This hat was published in LeCount (1990).

Origin: Peru, Cuzco, Canchis, Tinta
Linguistic Affiliation: Quechua
Yarn Spin: Spin, Z2S, S2Z
Gage: 14 spi
Provenance: Cuzco, Peru, 1/79
Reference: LeCount 1990, 68, pl. 6

1992.107.30

184. Hat *(chullu),* ca. 1970
Green, pink, and multicolored sheep's wool or camelid hair
Knit: stockinette, popcorn, garter, and scallop stitches; color patterning, circular knitting on straight needles
Length: 7½ in., 19.1 cm; width: 7½ in., 19.1 cm

A small hat, one piece, in overall geometric patterning, with ear flaps. There is a scallop-stitch trim on the ear flaps and along the bottom edges, and two elongated tops with tassels. The elongated tops are divided and knitted separately. The lower quarter is a finer knit; the upper area is more elastic because fewer colored yarns

a herringbone effect. The weft is visible in some parts of the cloth, which affects the pattern. Origin may have been Melgar, in Puno.

Origin: Peru, Cuzco, Canchis
Linguistic Affiliation: Quechua
Yarn Spin: Ground-, complementary-, and supplementary-warp spin, Z2S, S2Z; weft, Z2S
Warp and Weft Count: 64 epi, 16 ppi
Provenance: Cuzco, Peru, 1/79

1992.107.82

187. Woman's mantle *(llijlla),* ca. 1960

Multicolored sheep's wool or camelid hair
Woven in warp-faced plain and two-color complementary-warp weaves
Length: 42½ in., 108 cm; width: 49 in., 124.5 cm

A large mantle, two pieces, of solid-colored and geometric- and animal-patterned stripes joined edge to edge. Images include large diamond shapes or *chaskas* (Q. star), and mirror horse images on one side; on the other side, two single horses. Purple stripes give *abrash* effect. Designs smaller than in another mantle from the same province, cat. no. 189.

Origin: Peru, Cuzco, Chumbivilcas, Santo Tomás
Linguistic Affiliation: Quechua
Yarn Spin: Ground- and complementary-warp spin, Z2S; weft, Z2S
Warp and Weft Count: 44 epi, 20 ppi
Provenance: Cuzco, Peru, 3/81

1992.107.57

188. Belt *(chumpi),* ca. 1950

Maroon, beige, and multicolored sheep's wool or camelid hair
Woven in warp-faced plain and two-color complementary-warp weaves
Length: 51 in., 129.5 cm; width: 4¾ in., 12.1 cm

A long belt, one piece, in narrow solid-colored and human-, animal-, bird-, and geometric-patterned stripes, with twelve oblique, interlaced units at one end. Images include figures on horseback—some holding birds—long necked and long-bodied animals—probably llamas—and rayed diamonds or *chaskas,* common motifs in the Cuzco area. Contemporary style no longer has several small horses but single large ones. Iconography and colors are suggestive of a belt from Ayaviri, Puno, Peru, published in Schevill (1986). Meisch commented that, in Tarabuco, Bolivia, images of humans on horses indicate carnival. In Peru, they sometimes represent a general who fought in the war with Chile, or the Spanish horsemen who drew and quartered the Inca, Tupac Amaru.

Cat. no. 187

Origin: Peru, Cuzco, Chumbivilcas
Linguistic Affiliation: Quechua
Yarn Spin: Ground- and complementary-warp spin, Z2S; weft, Z2S
Warp and Weft Count: 58 epi, 12 ppi
Provenance: Cuzco, Peru, 5/78
References: Schevill 1986, 105, cat. no. 318; Lynn Meisch, personal communication, January 1996

1992.107.53

189. Woman's mantle *(llijlla),* ca. 1950

Red and multicolored sheep's wool or camelid hair
Woven in warp-faced plain and two-color complementary-warp weaves
Length: 35¾ in., 90.8 cm; width: 43 in., 109.2 cm

A small shoulder cloth, two pieces, of solid-colored and human-, geometric-, and animal-patterned stripes, joined edge to edge. Images include figures on horses and radiating stars or *chaskas.* Pattern warps are overspun and create a highly textured surface. The textile was probably finished with a fringe, as some tufts of yarn and some basting stitches are still present. Franquemont commented on the excellent use of color striping and the work in pick-up. Long termination areas indicate that it was woven on a staked loom. Colors and patterning are similar to those in another mantle from this province, cat. no. *187.*

Origin: Peru, Cuzco, Chumbivilcas
Linguistic Affiliation: Quechua

Yarn Spin: Ground- and complementary-warp spin, Z2S; weft, Z2S
Warp and Weft Count: 56 epi, 18 ppi
Provenance: Cuzco, Peru, 4/83
References: Ed Franquemont, personal communication, January 1996

1992.107.50

190. Poncho *(poncho),* 17th–18th century

Multicolored camelid hair
Woven in warp-faced plain and two- and three-color alternating float weaves
Length: 71¼ in., 181 cm; width: 64 in., 162.6 cm

A large poncho, four pieces, sewn together, with a neck opening; solid-colored stripes and animal and floral patterning in one edge binding. There are two separate edge bindings—one is complementary-warp weave, the other is plain weave—sewn to all outer selvages, with fringe created by the edge binding wefts. The four corners are turned up and stitched. A pieced poncho with two edge bindings creates a unique textile. There is an *abrash* effect in the rose stripes. Appleby commented that the local people thought that this poncho came from the mountains outside Tinta. A natural dye palette. A lovely and fragile piece.

Origin: Peru, Cuzco, Chumbivilcas
Linguistic Affiliation: Quechua
Yarn Spin: Ground-warp spin, Z2S; weft, Z2S

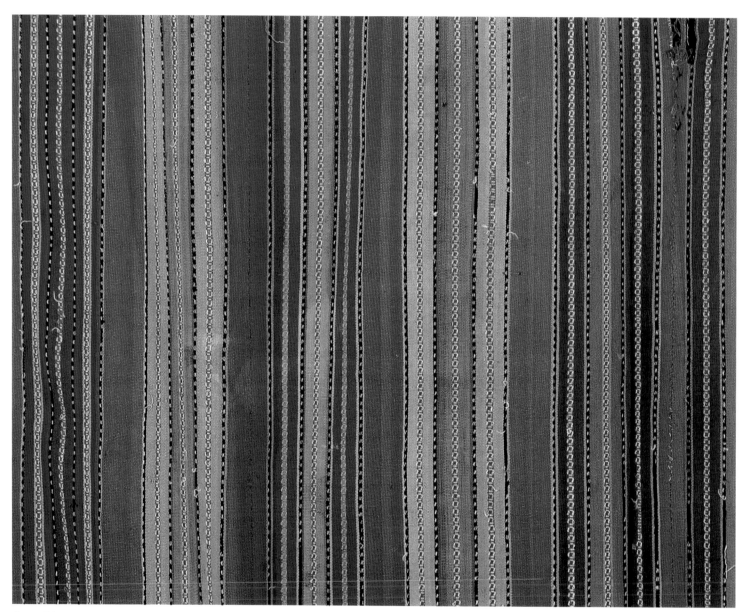

Cat. no. 190

Provenance: Cuzco, Peru, 3/81
Reference: Jeffrey Appleby, personal communication, August 1996

L96.120.2

191. **Festival tunic** *(unku),* 20th century
Brown and multicolored camelid hair
Woven in weft-faced plain and tapestry weaves
Length: 32¼ in., 81.9 cm; width: 24 in., 61 cm

A brown tunic, two pieces, with neck and sleeve openings, of a solid-colored background with birds, pyramids, and geometric motifs on the front. It is seamed on the sides, and the motifs are in eccentric tapestry weave. There are double warps at sides. A tunic for dances. Franquemont commented that the piece was woven on a backstrap loom and is made of two four-selvage cloths, and that these tapestry techniques are present in Navajo and European tapestries. Sacaca commented that it is a traditional young man's tunic because of the two birds facing each other—the joining of two people; the zigzag on the bottom could mean "a good road" in life. It might have been a replica of a tunic or special *unku* from the past, or perhaps an older piece was used for a model. Heckman commented that almost all the good examples of Inca tunics have a zigzag in some form on or near the bottom.

Origin: Peru, Cuzco, Chumbivilcas
Linguistic Affiliation: Quechua
Yarn Spin: Ground-warp spin, Z2S; weft, Z2S
Warp and Weft Count: 10 epi, 40 ppi
Provenance: Cuzco, Peru, 5/80
Reference: Ed Franquemont, personal communication, January 1996; Timoteo Ccarita Sacaca and Andrea Heckman, personal communications, May 1996

1992.107.69

192. **Coca bag** *(ch'uspa),* late 16th–17th century
See fig. 22, p. 29.
Multicolored camelid hair
Woven in weft-faced eccentric tapestry weave
Length: 13¼ in., 33.6 cm; width: 6¼ in., 15.9 cm

A small bag, one piece, side seams not joined, ends finished with buttonhole stitch, in overall patterning. Images reflect colonial influences and include feathered birds in detail, abstract birds' heads, abstract flowers, animals, and geometrics. The bag was woven in the Cuzco area when Bolivia was part of the viceroyalty of Peru, and Cuzco was a well-known weaving center. A lovely textile. A similar bag was published in

Cat. no. 191

Adelson and Tracht (1983), who wrote that tapestry-woven textiles have a long and important history in the Lake Titicaca basin plateau; the tradition survived until the early Spanish Colonial period. Sometimes Spanish iconography, such as heraldic images, was used on indigenous textiles such as *ch'uspas.*

Origin: Peru, Cuzco, Cuzco
Linguistic Affiliation: Quechua
Yarn Spin: Ground-warp spin, Z2S; weft, Z2S
Warp and Weft Count: 48 epi, 44 ppi
Provenance: La Paz, Bolivia, 3/76
Reference: Adelson and Tracht 1983, 124 and pl. 50

L96.120.3

193. **Copper fringe,** 19th century
See fig. 41, pp. 46–47.
Yellow-green cotton or camelid hair, flat strips of copper
Lacework
Length: 26½ in., 67.3 cm; width: 1⅛ in., 2.6 cm

A band of copper-wrapped lacework, one piece, of flat copper strips embellished with copper scallops. Perhaps this piece functioned as part of religious paraphernalia for sacred ceremonies. Appleby suggested that this fringe was used on dresses. A unique textile.

Origin: Peru, Cuzco, Cuzco
Linguistic Affiliation: Spanish
Yarn Spin: Spin, Z2S
Provenance: Cuzco, Peru, 12/76
Reference: Jeffrey Appleby, personal communication, July 1995

1992.107.7

194. **Hat** *(chullu),* early 20th century
Vicuña and multicolored sheep's wool
Knit: stockinette, eyelet, and scallop stitches; color patterning, circular knitting on straight needles
Length: 6⅛ in., 15.6 cm; width: 6¾ in., 17.1 cm

A small knitted hat for a child. One piece, of solid-colored areas with floral patterns. The ear flaps are trimmed with a scallop edge and there is one tassel at the top of the hat. The eyelet stitches create triangular and diamond shapes in the cap. Published in LeCount (1990), who wrote that vicuña was popular among the upper-class women of the Cuzco, La Paz, and Potosí areas. The animal is now protected. LeCount also commented that the eyelet stitch is still used for almost identical baby caps in acrylic or cotton.

Origin: Peru, Cuzco, Cuzco
Linguistic Affiliation: Quechua
Gage: 11 spi
Provenance: Cuzco, Peru, 3/82
References: LeCount 1990, 60, fig. 6.4; Cynthia LeCount, personal communication, October 1995

1992.107.24

195. **Hat, lappeted,** 18th century
Natural linen and maroon camelid hair; unbleached linen cloth
Embroidery: fillers, French knots, scallop, other stitches, including raised work
Length: 31½ in., 80.2 cm, overall; width: 7½ in., 19 cm, at crown

A shaped head covering with long flaps, two pieces, joined edge to edge for the crown, with overall dense embroidery. The crown length is 11 inches, and the flaps are 20½ inches by 3⅝ inches. There are two ties at the ends of the flaps and a scalloped edge binding for shaping gathered cloth. There is an additional knotted piece on top of the hat at the joining of the two pieces. Images suggest colonial influences and include aristocratic figures in short tunics and wigs, two angels in short, full pants, baskets and fruits as rendered in paintings from the Cuzco school, and wooden drinking vessels, or *keros,* of this period. Unlike another lappeted hat, cat. no. *196* (fig. 42), this one is not padded on top. Green (1970) wrote that, by the 1770s, lappeted caps were no longer stylish in Europe, and probably died out much earlier in Spain. She adds that the hats are not pictured or described as part of Peruvian garb so it is hard to say when they ceased being worn. They may have been part of a dance or ceremonial costume still worn by the Indians long after they had been part of colonial dress. Another example, in the

Cat. no. 199

Cat. no. 200

collections of the Brooklyn Museum (41.1275.103), is discussed by Phipps (1996), who suggested that the hat may be an interpretation of a European judicial wig and may have been worn by the *caciques* of the villages near Cuzco, during the Inquisition, when they presided at court. Each village had a different design.

Origin: Peru, Cuzco, Cuzco or Lima
Linguistic Affiliation: Quechua/Spanish
Provenance: Santa Barbara, California, 3/80
References: Green 1970, 5–6; Phipps 1996, fn. 187

1992.107.43

196. Hat, lappeted, 18th century
See fig. 42, p. 47.
Natural linen and dark rose camelid hair; unbleached linen cloth
Embroidery: fillers, French knots, scallop, and other stitches, including raised work
Length: 31¾ in. overall, 80.6 cm; width: 5¾ in. at crown, 14.6 cm

A shaped head covering with long flaps, three pieces, joined at the back of the head, with overall dense embroidery. There are two gussets and gathered areas in the crown portion for shaping, and scalloped stitching

on the outer edges. A knotted headpiece is joined to the head covering. In addition to the Hapsburg double-headed eagle, there are floral, faunal, human, and geometric designs. This hat was published in Green (1970): Mr. Miguel Valle of Miraflores, Peru, kindly supplied information and a photograph of [a cap] formerly in his own collection. In shape, design, and visible technique, the cap is almost exactly like the Metropolitan example, though with a different scene on the lappets. The Hapsburg eagle graces the back of this one as well, and numerous floral and bird motifs are present. On one embroidered flap a forest is depicted with cartoonlike flowers, trees, and birds. Indians of the *montaña* are pictured, attired in high feather headdresses similar to those shown on the *ḳeros* and carrying bows and arrows. The waist-length hair and knee-length tunic correspond to the representations of *montaña* Indians on *ḳeros* as well. . . . possibly middle- or lower-class non-Indian women wore these linen and wool caps in the eighteenth century, . . . embroidered for them by Indian women, incorporating Inca and Spanish motifs [5–6]. See also cat. no. 195, another lappeted hat.

Origin: Peru, Cuzco, Cuzco
Linguistic Affiliation: Quechua/Spanish
Provenance: Cuzco, Peru, 2/79
Reference: Green 1970, 5–6

1992.107.44

197. Woman's mantle *(llijlla),* 17th–18th century
See fig. 17, p. 24.
Dark brown and multicolored camelid hair, silk, and metallic yarn
Woven in warp-faced plain, two-color complementary-, and one-color supplementary-warp weaves
Length: 39½ in., 100.3 cm; width: 31 in., 78.7 cm

A medium-size mantle, two pieces, with solid-colored *pampas* and bird-, human-, and geometric-patterned stripes, joined edge to edge. There is S2Z-spun yarn on the outer edges and next to the metallic supplementary-warp patterning, and very narrow stripes of gold silk complementary-warp patterning at center and outer edges. The high warp count creates a tightly packed cloth with a fine hand. A fringe probably was present as two rows of stitching are visible. The use of metallic and silk yarn

TRADITIONAL TEXTILES OF THE ANDES

suggests a special function. In the hierarchy of *indígenas*, the upper class and mestizos would wear a garment like this one. Franquemont suggested that its origin may have been northwest Cuzco, between Anta and Vilcabamba.

Origin: Peru, Cuzco, Cuzco
Linguistic Affiliation: Quechua
Yarn Spin: Ground-, complementary-, and supplementary-warp spin, Z2S, S2Z; weft, Z2S
Warp and Weft Count: 96 epi, 14 ppi
Provenance: Lima, Peru, 4/78
Reference: Ed Franquemont, personal communication, January 1996

1992.107.88

198. **Coca bag** *(ch'uspa)*, ca. 1950
Multicolored sheep's wool and camelid hair
Woven in warp-face plain and three-color complementary-warp weaves
Length: 5¼ in., 13.3 cm; width: 6¼ in., 15.9 cm

A small bag, one piece, sewn together along the sides, of solid-colored and human- and geometric-patterned stripes with a herringbone twill cloth binding added to sides and top edges. A long warp fringe on the bottom is of Z3S and re-plied yarn. Z2S- and S2Z-spun yarns, which may be vicuña in tan stripes, create a herringbone effect. The termination areas have been doubled back and hidden inside the warp fringes, creating four layers of cloth along the bottom seam. Figures may be *ch'unchus* or wild *indígenas* from the jungle, as discussed by Wilson (1996 [1991]). See cat. no. *199*, a similar bag.

Origin: Peru, Cuzco, Paucartambo, Ocongate, Q'ero
Linguistic Affiliation: Quechua
Yarn Spin: Ground- and complementary-warp spin, Z2S, S2Z; weft, Z2S
Warp and Weft Count: 100 epi, 32 ppi
Provenance: Cuzco, Peru, 3/82
Reference: Wilson 1996 (1991), 216

1992.107.48

199. **Coca bag** *(ch'uspa)*, ca. 1940
Multicolored sheep's wool or camelid hair
Woven in warp-faced plain, three-color complementary-, and one-color supplementary-warp weaves
Length: 7½ in., 19.1 cm; width: 6¼ in., 115.9 cm

A small bag, one piece, sewn together on the sides, of narrow solid-colored and human- and geometric-patterned stripes. There are three small pockets created by longer warps tensioned separately with exterior flaps, which open from the inside, and fringe added to the bottom. The edge binding is similar to that on another bag, cat. no. 198, and there is a long strap of three pieces sewn

to the bag at the corners. The larger section of the bag is for coca leaves; the small pockets are for rocks of lime to be used with the leaves. Human figures may be *ch'unchus*, who represent jungle inhabitants as distinct from highlanders; see Wilson (1996 [1991]).

Origin: Peru, Cuzco, Paucartambo, Ocongate, Q'ero
Linguistic Affiliation: Quechua
Yarn Spin: Ground-, complementary-, and supplementary-warp spin, Z2S, S2Z; weft, Z2S
Warp and Weft Count: 80 epi, 36 ppi
Provenance: Cuzco, Peru, 2/79
Reference: Wilson 1996 (1991), 216

1992.107.49

200. **Woman's mantle** *(llijlla)*, early 20th century
Black and multicolored sheep's wool or camelid hair
Woven in warp-faced and three-color complementary-warp weaves
Length: 36½ in., 92.7 cm; width: 33 in., 88.8 cm

A small mantle, two pieces, joined edge to edge, of large solid-colored areas and geometric- and human-patterned warp stripes. The *ch'unchu* or human figure also appears. S2Z-spun yarn aligned with the Z2S-spun yarn creates a herringbone effect in plain-weave sections and also on the edges, allowing the piece to lie flat. Termination areas very small. A fine cloth, soft to the hand.

Origin: Peru, Cuzco, Paucartambo, Ocongate, Q'ero
Linguistic Affiliation: Quechua
Yarn Spin: Ground- and complementary-warp spin, Z2S, S2Z; weft, Z2S
Warp and Weft Count: 96 epi, 24 ppi
Provenance: Cuzco, Peru, 3/81

1992.107.59

201. **Poncho** *(poncho)*, ca. 1970
Pink, dark blue, and multicolored sheep's wool or camelid hair
Woven in warp-faced plain and three-color complementary-warp weaves
Length: 57 in., 144.8 cm; width: 27¾ in., 70.5 cm

A large poncho, two pieces, in narrow solid-colored and wide geometric- and human-patterned stripes, joined edge to edge, with a neck opening. There is a complementary-warp weave edge binding sewn to all outer selvages, with an added fringe of re-plied yarn. The four corners are turned up and stitched. Ponchos always are coarser than mantles; compare, for instance, the warp sett in cat. no. *200*. A beautifully lined up piece. See also cat. no. *198*, on which the *ch'unchu* or jungle dweller also appears.

Cat. no. 201

Origin: Peru, Cuzco, Paucartambo, Ocongate, Q'ero
Linguistic Affiliation: Quechua
Yarn Spin: Ground- and complementary-warp spin, Z2S, S2Z; weft, Z2S
Warp and Weft Count: 44 epi, 24 ppi
Provenance: Q'ero, Peru, 1/79

1992.107.90

202. **Scarf or shawl** *(chalina)*, early 20th century
Tan and multicolored sheep's wool or camelid hair
Woven in warp-faced plain weave
Length: 59 in., 149.9 cm; width: 5¼ in., 13.3 cm

A long scarf, one piece, with wide and narrow solid-colored stripes. The tan yarn may be vicuña. The S2Z- and Z2S-spun yarn is warped in 1/16-inch stripes, which creates a herringbone effect. A light textile with a fine hand. Franquemont commented that the combination of S2Z- and Z2S-spun yarn recalls Q'ero weaving, but scarves are not part of Indian clothing there.

Origin: Peru, Cuzco, Paucartambo, Ocongate, Q'ero
Linguistic Affiliation: Quechua
Yarn Spin: Ground-warp spin, Z2S, S2Z; weft, Z2S

Cat. no. 205

Cat. no. 206

Warp and Weft Count: 88 epi, 30 ppi
Provenance: Cuzco, Peru, 5/84
Reference: Ed Franquemont, personal communication, January 1996

1992.107.4

203. **Bag** *(ch'uspa),* ca. 1960
Multicolored sheep's wool or camelid hair
Knit: stockinette, garter, scallop stitches;
intarsia patterning, circular knitting on
straight needles
Length: 4⅞ in., 12.3 cm; width: 2½ in.,
6.4 cm

A small knitted bag, one piece, bottle-
shaped with two fringed pockets that open
on the inside. A triangular flap is added on
one side. There are fringes of re-plied yarn
on the bottom and sides and a strap attached
to the flap. On the other end, transverse
warps create another band as in the hair ties.
The pockets are called *unillas.* LeCount calls
these purses or *monederos.* The bag is tightly
knitted, and the iconography is diamonds
within diamonds, typical of the Cuzco area.
A labor-intensive bag, beautifully knitted
and finished, although the strap is well
worn. LeCount commented that the tie was
not original, the yarn was handspun, and
the fringe alpaca. This style of bag is not
used anymore, but is still made for sale.
Pockets are created by picking up stitches
on finished bag, knitting them as separate
units, which have no opening to interior
of bags.

Origin: Peru, Cuzco, Paucartambo
Linguistic Affiliation: Quechua
Yarn Spin: Spin, Z2S
Gage: 15 spi
Provenance: Cuzco, Peru, 2/78
Reference: Cynthia LeCount, personal communication, October 1995

1992.107.47

204. **Coca bag** *(ch'uspa),* early 20th century
Brown and multicolored sheep's wool or
camelid hair
Woven in warp-faced plain and two-color
complementary-warp weaves
Length: 9½ in., 24.1 cm; width: 10¼ in.,
26 cm

A medium-size bag, one piece, of solid-
colored and geometric-patterned stripes.
The sides are joined by a tubular edge
binding, which continues along top edges,
and, on the bottom, there is an attached
fringe of re-plied yarn. A strap with fringe
is sewn to the bag. The strap is unique,
not found in other bags, and the surface is
decorated with a running stitch in four-
color zigzags on both sides. Franquemont
commented that the complementary-warp
bands are the same structure as used for

Cat. no. 207

hair ties in Chinchero, thus confirming the
origin. The motifs are called *mayu k'inku*
(Q. meandering river) and *haykakusisan-
sisan* (Q.), a stage of fruit development.

Origin: Peru, Cuzco, Urubamba, Chinchero
Linguistic Affiliation: Quechua
Yarn Spin: Ground- and complementary-warp
spin, Z2S, S2Z; weft, Z2S
Warp and Weft Count: 56 epi, 18 ppi
Provenance: Cuzco, Peru, 2/79
Reference: Ed Franquemont, personal communication, January 1996

1992.107.39

205. **Bag** *(ch'uspa),* early 20th century
Multicolored sheep's wool or camelid hair
Knit: stockinette stitch, color patterning,
circular knitting on straight needles
Length: 13¼ in., 33.7 cm; width: 5⅜ in.,
13.7 cm

A medium-size bag, one piece, in overall
bird, animal, and geometric patterning.
There is a long tie sewn onto the bag near
the bottom and two tassels, one on the top
and the other two inches from the top. The
images include the letter M interspersed
with little dogs or cats, birds, deer, and
geometric motifs. LeCount commented that
it was knit in two-color patterning with
three colors in zigzag rows. Because it was
knit from top to bottom, the motifs appear
upside down. Franquemont questioned the
origin.

Origin: Peru, Cuzco, Urubamba, Chinchero
Linguistic Affiliation: Quechua
Yarn Spin: Spin, Z2S
Gage: 16 epi
Provenance: Cuzco, Peru, 5/78
References: Cynthia LeCount, personal communication, October 1995; Ed Franquemont, personal communication, January 1996

1992.107.45

206. Bag *(ch'uspa),* ca. 1950

Multicolored sheep's wool or camelid hair
Knit: stockinette, garter, scallop stitches;
color patterning, circular knitting on
straight needles
Length: 9 in., 22.9 cm; width: 4¼ in.,
10.8 cm

A medium-size bag, one piece, with two
elongated sleevelike appendages extending
from bottom of bag, which is in overall
animal, bird, and geometric patterning.
There is a strap, a seven-color tubular structure, attached to the inside corners, and
fringes on both appendages. Iconography
includes double-headed birds, long-beaked
birds with floral designs in their beaks,
probably hummingbirds, long-tailed two-
legged birds, ducks, and geometric motifs.
When the bag, which in shape resembles
a pair of pants, is viewed with the strap on
top, the images are upside down. LeCount
commented that graphs of some of these
designs appear in her book (1990). The bag
was knit from top to bottom, and three
colors were brought around in every row.
Franquemont noted that there are eight
different kinds of birds. He also commented
that this piece may be a hat because of way
the images are viewed; not useful for a bag.
The yarn is handspun. A unique artifact.

Origin: Peru, Cuzco, Urubamba, Chinchero
Linguistic Affiliation: Quechua
Yarn Spin: Spin, Z2S
Gage: 13 spi
Provenance: Pisac, Peru, 1/78
References: LeCount 1990, 89; Cynthia LeCount,
personal communication, October 1995; Ed
Franquemont, personal communication, January
1996

1992.107.46

207. Hat *(chullu),* ca. 1960

Multicolored sheep's wool or camelid hair
Knit: stockinette, garter, scallop stitches;
crochet; color patterning, circular knitting
on straight needles
Length: 17 in., 43.2 cm; width: 9 in., 22.9 cm

A medium-size hat, one piece, in overall
geometric and bird patterning with an elongated top. There are ear flaps, both with
tassels, which have a scalloped edging, and
two straps attached to the edging. This hat
was published in LeCount (1990); she wrote
that rounded caps with long tails and deeply
scalloped edge are no longer made, and calls
the elongated top a "tail." She commented
that the ear flaps are knit from picked-up
stitches at side edges, a typical use in
Chinchero of relatively coarsely handspun
yarn and natural dyes. The lower edge of
the hat is a row of finger-chained scalloping,
and from there, it is knitted up. The inter-

Cat. no. 208

Cat. no. 210

Cat. no. 211

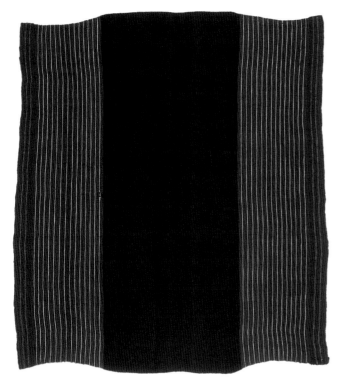

Cat. no. 212

Cat. no. 213

locking **S** curve and bird are typical for Chinchero.

Origin: Peru, Cuzco, Urubamba, Chinchero
Linguistic Affiliation: Quechua
Yarn Spin: Spin, Z2S
Gage: 10 spi
Provenance: Cuzco, Peru, 5/77
Reference: LeCount 1990, 52; Cynthia LeCount, personal communication, October 1995

1992.107.29

208. **Hair tie** *(wata, watana),* mid-20th century
Multicolored and *ch'imi* sheep's wool or camelid hair
Woven in warp-faced plain and two-color complementary-warp weaves
Length: 34 in., 86.4 cm; width: ⅜ in., 1 cm

A narrow band, one piece, in overall geometric patterning with a fringe of re-plied yarn at one end. A lovely little band; the consistency in images shows the weaver's fine control. An unusual feature is S2Z-spun yarn for the warp and *ch'imi* yarn for the weft. For comments on hair ties, see cat. no. *161.*

Origin: Peru, Cuzco, Urubamba, Chinchero
Linguistic Affiliation: Quechua
Yarn Spin: Ground- and complementary-warp spin, S2Z; weft, Z2S
Warp and Weft Count: 112 epi, 24 ppi
Provenance: Cuzco, Peru, 1/79

1992.107.10

209. **Hair tie** *(wata, watana),* mid-20th century
Multicolored sheep's wool or camelid hair
Woven in warp-faced plain and two-color complementary-warp weaves
Length: 51 in., 129.5 cm; width: ⅜ in., 1 cm

A narrow band, with bands of intersecting transverse warps added to the main band and, again, to added bands, in overall geometric patterning. Each end has a warp fringe of re-plied yarn. The woven bands are of tightly spun yarn, which results in their twisting in circular forms. Franquemont suggested the origin. For comments on hair ties, see cat. no. *161.*

Origin: Peru, Cuzco, Urubamba, Ollantaytambo, Patacancha
Linguistic Affiliation: Quechua
Yarn Spin: Ground- and complementary-warp spin, Z2S; weft, Z2S
Warp and Weft Count: 84 epi, 24 ppi
Provenance: Pisac, Peru, 1/79
Reference: Ed Franquemont, personal communication, January 1996

1992.107.15

HUÁNUCO

210. **Poncho** *(poncho),* 20th century
Shades of tan and brown sheep's wool
Woven in warp-faced plain weave
Length: 64½ in., 163.8 cm; width: 54 in., 137.2 cm

A large poncho, two pieces, of solid-colored stripes joined edge to edge, with a neck

opening bound with hand-woven edge binding, which also is machine-stitched to all outer selvages. One of the dyes may be *nogal* or walnut. These ponchos are woven by Serrano men on the backstrap loom. Bird and Losack (1986) discussed these textiles and their production. A beautiful piece, subtle changes in striping; in some stripes, two shades make for alternating stripes within stripes. Unusually large and of tightly packed warps. Franquemont commented that pieces are cut from a long, single warp.

Origin: Peru, Huánuco, Punchao
Linguistic Affiliation: Quechua
Yarn Spin: Ground-warp spin, Z2S; weft, Z2S
Warp and Weft Count: 136 epi, 20 ppi
Provenance: Pisac, Peru, 4/78
References: Bird and Losack 1986, 344–46, fig. 14, 18; Ed Franquemont, personal communication, January 1996

1992.107.75

JUNÍN

211. **Woman's mantle** *(llijlla),* 1945
Multicolored sheep's wool or camelid hair
Woven in weft-faced and interlocking tapestry weaves
Length: 25¾ in., 65.4 cm; width: 31⅝ in., 80.4 cm

A small mantle, one piece, in solid-colored and patterned stripes. A fuzzy textured edge binding is machine sewn to all outer selvages with ten rows of top stitching.

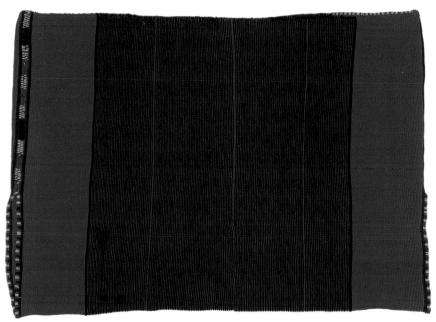

Cat. no. 214

Images include the Peruvian coat of arms with the date May 10, 1945, large butterflies, geometrics, and florals. An unusual piece, as weft-faced patterning is not found in many other areas. In Ayacucho, this technique is used for weavings in natural dyes for the tourist market. Franquemont commented that the piece is treadle loomed with tapestry technique and that the butterfly motifs are unusual.

Origin: Peru, Junín, Huancayo
Linguistic Affiliation: Quechua
Yarn Spin: Ground-warp spin, S2Z; weft, S2Z
Warp and Weft Count: 12 epi, 56 ppi
Provenance: New York City, New York, 9/81
Reference: Ed Franquemont, personal communication, January 1996

1992.107.78

MOQUEGUA

212. **Man's mantle** *(llakuta),* 18th–19th century
Black, multicolored, and *ch'imi* sheep's wool or camelid hair
Woven in warp-faced plain and alternating float weaves
Length: 44¼ in., 112.4 cm; width: 40¼ in., 102.2 cm

A large mantle, one piece, with large solid-colored areas or *pampas* and narrow warp stripes on both sides. There are narrow yellow strips of warp striping near the weft selvages. A rare old textile, it resembles a *llakuta* from the department of Potosí,

Bolivia. Adelson and Tracht (1983) stated that this type of *llakuta* is among the oldest textile heirlooms found in Bolivia today, and probably dates from the post-conquest or early colonial period.

Origin: Peru, Moquegua, Ubinas
Linguistic Affiliation: Quechua/Aymara
Yarn Spin: Ground-warp spin, Z2S, S2Z; weft, Z2S
Warp and Weft Count: 96 epi, 18 ppi
Provenance: Cuzco, Peru, 3/82
Reference: Adelson and Tracht 1983, 86, pl, 23

1992.107.64

213. **Man's mantle** *(llakuta),* 18th–19th century
Brown, multicolored, and *ch'imi* sheep's wool or camelid hair
Woven in warp-faced plain and alternating float weaves
Length: 45¼ in., 115 cm; width: 43 in., 109.2 cm

A large mantle, two pieces, joined at the center, with large solid-colored areas or *pampas* and narrow warp stripes. There are narrow yellow stripes on weft selvages. Variation in spin, thickness, and the color of single ply in *ch'imi* two-ply yarn creates a richness and depth of color. See also another *llakuta,* cat. no. *212.*

Origin: Peru, Moquegua, Ubinas
Linguistic Affiliation: Quechua/Aymara
Yarn Spin: Ground-warp spin, Z2S; weft, Z2S
Warp and Weft Count: 80 epi, 18 ppi
Provenance: Corrales, New Mexico, 10/85

1992.107.65

214. **Man's tunic,** *(khawa),* 18th–19th century
Red rose and multicolored sheep's wool
Woven in warp-faced plain weave
Length: 20¼ in., 51.5 cm; width: 29 in., 75 cm

A small tunic, one piece, of solid-colored areas or *pampas* and warp stripes, with a neck opening. The side seams are joined with decorative stitching, and the sleeve openings and part of the bottom selvage are also trimmed with decorative stitching. The S2Z-spun yarn alternates with Z2S-spun yarn in the *pampas* and in the stripes. Red is Z2S spun and dark blue, S2Z spun, creating a herringbone effect. Fine feel of cloth, a rare old piece. Similar to a colonial-period *khawa* from the department of Potosí, published in Adelson and Tracht (1983), but with different colors. Also see cat. no. 91, another *khawa* from the department of Potosí, in Bolivia. Franquemont commented that the yarn was sheep's wool with cochineal-dyed reds; it is part of a costume no longer known.

Origin: Peru, Moquegua, Ubinas
Linguistic Affiliation: Aymara/Quechua
Yarn Spin: Ground-warp spin, Z2S, S2Z; weft, Z2S
Warp and Weft Count: 80 epi, 16 ppi
Provenance: Cuzco, Peru, 3/81
References: Adelson and Tracht, 1983, 58, pl. 3; Ed Franquemont, personal communication, January 1996

1992.107.74

PUNO

215. **Woman's mantle** *(awayu),* 19th century
Rose, dark blue, and multicolored sheep's wool or camelid hair
Woven in warp-faced and two and three-color complementary-warp weaves
Length: 33¾ in., 85.7 cm; width: 38¼ in., 97.2 cm

A small mantle, one piece, of solid-colored and narrow geometric-patterned stripes, with a three-color tubular edge binding on all outer selvages. The alternating three colors in warps on both weft selvages create a pebble effect. Long termination areas. A natural dye palette.

Origin: Peru, Puno, Azángaro
Linguistic Affiliation: Aymara
Yarn Spin: Ground- and complementary-warp spin, Z2S; weft, Z2S
Warp and Weft Count: 52 epi, 12 ppi
Provenance: Cuzco, Peru, 3/81

1992.107.85

216. **Belt** *(wak'a),* 19th century
Dark blue, beige, and multicolored camelid hair
Woven in warp-faced plain and two-color complementary-warp weaves
Length: 36 in., 91.5 cm; width: 4½ in., 11.4 cm

A medium-size belt, one piece, with geometric-, animal-, and bird-patterned and solid-colored stripes. On one end twelve oblique, interlaced units are divided into two groups; remnants of ties on the other end. Termination areas lead into oblique interlaced units. May be for *luto* or mourning; a unique textile. Rodman commented that this textile has the typical imagery of early Aymara weavings from Lake Titicaca area, and that the belt is of camelid yarn with a natural dye palette.

Origin: Peru, Puno, Chucuito, Juli
Linguistic Affiliation: Quechua/Aymara
Yarn Spin: Ground- and complementary-warp spin, Z2S; weft, Z2S
Warp and Weft Count: 72 epi, 24 ppi
Provenance: Juli, Peru, 7/78
Reference: Amy Oakland Rodman, personal communication, 1995

1992.107.54

217. **Coca or ceremonial cloth** *(inkuña),*
mid- to late 19th century
Dark rose, multicolored, and *ch'imi* sheep's wool or camelid hair
Woven in warp-faced plain and two-color complementary-warp weaves
Length: 38¼ in., 97.2 cm; width: 37¼ in., 94.6 cm

A medium-size cloth, one piece, with geometric-patterned and solid-colored stripes. The slight visibility of brown and pink wefts changes the surface color in some areas. S2Z-spun yarn is not only found at side selvages, but also outlines complementary-warp weave stripes in some areas. The combination of Z2S and S2Z yarn in outer areas allows the piece to lie flat. Yorke (1986) identified a local Juli style prevalent along the western and southern shores of Lake Titicaca and stated that many Juli pieces, particularly ceremonial *inkuñas* like this one, have a succession of colored stripes centering on a very narrow figured band.

Origin: Peru, Puno, Chucuito, Juli
Linguistic Affiliation: Quechua/Aymara
Yarn Spin: Ground- and complementary-warp spin, Z2S, S2Z; weft, Z2S
Warp and Weft Count: 80 epi, 20 ppi
Provenance: Del Dios, California, 2/81
Reference: Yorke 1980, 14

1992.107.62

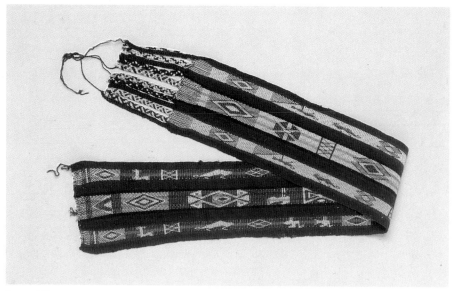

Cat. no. 216

218. **Woman's cloth** *(fullu),* 19th century
Purple and multicolored sheep's wool or camelid hair
Woven in warp-faced plain and two-color complementary-warp weaves
Length: 35 in., 89 cm; width: 20 in., 50.8 cm

A small cloth, one piece, with solid-colored areas or *pampas* and geometric-patterned stripes. The varying shades of purple give an *abrash* effect, and the S2Z-spun yarn in purple is a shade lighter than the other warps. The rose and gold wefts give different hues of color in the ground. Long termination areas. A fine piece, lovely soft hand; rare, old textile. Yorke (1980), writing about head cloths from Juli, said that small shoulder cloths lack the fine stripe series but retain the characteristic figured stripe. Franquemont commented that this cloth could be half of a larger piece. See also cat. no. *219, 220.*

Origin: Peru, Puno, Chucuito, Juli
Linguistic Affiliation: Quechua/Aymara
Yarn Spin: Ground- and complementary-warp spin, Z2S, S2Z; weft. Z2S
Warp and Weft Count: 80 epi, 32 ppi
Provenance: Corrales, New Mexico, 3/85
References: Yorke 1980, 14; Ed Franquemont, personal communication, January 1996

1992.107.60

219. **Woman's cloth** *(fullu),* 19th century
Black and multicolored sheep's wool or camelid hair
Woven in warp-faced plain and two-color complementary-warp weaves
Length: 40½ in., 102.0 cm; width: 26½ in., 67.3 cm

A small cloth, one piece, with large solid-colored areas or *pampas* and geometric-patterned stripes. There is a plain weave tubular edge binding on all outer selvages.

S2Z- and Z2S-spun yarn in outer sections create a herringbone effect. This textile resembles a *fullu* from Ilave, made in the 1900s and published in Schevill (1986); in 1985, Gale Hoskins commented that women wear this style of cloth on their heads or over their shoulders during periods of mourning, and that the pink wefts have special significance. For other headcloths from this region, see cat. no. 218, 220.

Origin: Peru, Puno, Chucuito, Juli
Linguistic Affiliation: Quechua/Aymara
Yarn Spin: Ground- and complementary-warp spin, Z2S; weft, Z2S
Warp and Weft Count: 80 epi, 24 ppi
Provenance: Juli, Peru, 7/78
Reference: Schevill 1986, 318

1992.107.61

220. **Woman's cloth** *(fullu),* 19th century
Black sheep's wool or camelid hair
Woven in warp-faced plain weave
Length: 39 in., 99.1 cm; width: 29 in., 73.7 cm

A medium-size cloth, two pieces, sewn together edge to edge, with a plain-weave tubular edge binding on outer selvages. These cloths are sometimes worn over hats. The pink wefts create a shimmering effect and modify the color of the ground. In 1985, the women in nearby Taquile were wearing a solid-colored black headcloth, also with pink wefts, like this example. For other headcloths from this region, see cat. no. 218, *219.*

Origin: Peru, Puno, Chucuito, Juli
Linguistic Affiliation: Quechua/Aymara
Yarn Spin: Ground-warp spin, Z2S, S2Z; weft, Z2S
Warp and Weft Count: 96 epi, 32 ppi
Provenance: Juli, Peru, 3/81

1992.107.63

Cat. no. 217

Cat. no. 219

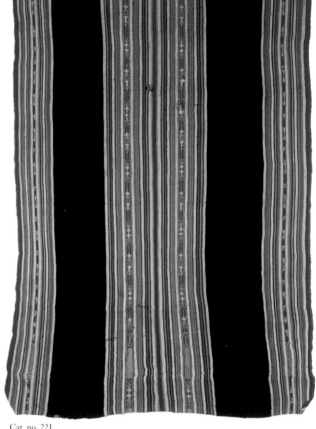

Cat. no. 221

221. **Woman's mantle** *(awayu),* late 19th century
Black and multicolored sheep's wool or camelid hair
Woven in warp-faced plain and two-color complementary-warp weaves
Length: 39½ in., 100.3 cm; width: 27¾ in., 70.5 cm

A medium-size mantle, one piece, with solid-colored stripes and areas or *pampas* and geometric-patterned stripes. May be half of a larger cloth. An extremely fine piece.

Origin: Peru, Puno, Chucuito, Juli
Linguistic Affiliation: Quechua/Aymara
Yarn Spin: Ground- and complementary-warp spin, Z2S; weft, Z2S
Warp and Weft Count: 80 epi, 24 ppi
Provenance: Juli, Peru, 7/78

1992.107.86

222. **Poncho** *(poncho),* late 19th century
Red, black-purple and multicolored sheep's wool or camelid hair
Woven in warp-faced and two-color complementary-warp weaves
Length: 54 in., 137.2 cm; width: 49¼ in., 125.1 cm

A large poncho, two pieces, of solid-colored and only two geometric-, bird-, and animal-patterned stripes, joined edge to edge, with

a neck opening. Images include double-headed eagles and llamas. There is an alternating float weave edge binding and fringe created by extra edge binding wefts sewn onto all outer selvages. The four corners are turned up and stitched. The pink wefts give the black-purple stripes a speckled effect. An extremely fine piece. The complementary-warp weave stripes are near the outer edges, perhaps indicating that it was woven on the backstrap loom. Franquemont commented that it does not look like a piece from Lake Titicaca.

Origin: Peru, Puno, Chucuito, Juli
Linguistic Affiliation: Quechua/Aymara
Yarn Spin: Ground- and complementary-warp spin, Z2S; weft, Z2S
Warp and Weft Count: 80 epi, 28 ppi
Provenance: New York City, New York, 5/85
Reference: Ed Franquemont, personal communication, January 1996

1992.107.68

223. **Poncho** *(poncho),* late 19th century
Black-purple and multicolored sheep's wool or camelid hair
Woven in warp-face plain weave
Length: 57¼ in., 145.4 cm; width: 50¾ in., 128.9 cm

A large poncho, two pieces, of a solid-colored background joined edge to edge,

with a neck opening, which is trimmed with a three-color tubular edge binding. There are two edge bindings on the outer selvages: One is a narrow warp, geometric-patterned band, the other a plain-weave binding with a fringe created by extra wefts along with the regular wefts. The four corners are turned up and stitched. Unlike the binding on the outer selvages, the tubular edge binding at the neck was done after the two pieces were sewn together.

Origin: Peru, Puno, Chucuito, Juli
Linguistic Affiliation: Quechua/Aymara
Yarn Spin: Ground-warp spin, Z2S; weft, Z2S
Warp and Weft Count: 72 epi, 17 ppi
Provenance: La Paz, Bolivia, 5/84

1992.107.70

224. **Coca bag** *(ch'uspa),* 19th century
Red, multicolored, and *ch'imi* camelid hair
Woven in warp-faced plain, two-color complementary, and alternating float weaves
Length: 8¼ in., 21 cm; width: 11½ in., 29.2 cm

A medium-size bag, one piece, of solid-colored and bird- and geometric-patterned stripes. The sides are joined by a four-strand, warp-twined edge binding, and there are six tassels on the sides and bottom.

A wide strap is attached to the corners of the bag. Rodman commented that this textile, of alpaca with a natural dye palette, is in the Lake Titicaca regional style. Rowe (1977) described the twined technique used on the side selvages. Franquemont commented on the edge binding and suggested that this bag was an early Taquile piece.

Origin: Peru, Puno, Huancané
Linguistic Affiliation: Quechua/Aymara
Yarn Spin: Ground- and complementary-warp spin, Z2S; weft, Z2S
Warp and Weft Count: 96 epi, 26 ppi
Provenance: Corrales, New Mexico, 8/84
References: Rowe 1977, 106, construction 15; Amy Oakland Rodman, personal communication, 1995; Ed Franquemont, personal communication, January 1996

1992.107.37

225. **Coca or ceremonial cloth** *(inkuña),*
19th century
Red and multicolored camelid hair
Woven in warp-faced plain and two-color complementary-warp weaves
Length: 40 in., 101.6 cm; width: 37 in., 94 cm

A medium-size cloth, one piece, with solid-colored and geometric-patterned stripes. There is a mix of S2Z- and Z2S-spun yarns in the ground and complementary-warp weaves. Particularly large termination areas are only on one side. The brown weft visible in plain-weave areas affects the surface color of the red *pampas*. Rodman suggested that the fiber may be camelid with a natural dye palette.

Origin: Peru, Puno, Huancané
Linguistic Affiliation: Quechua/Aymara
Yarn Spin: Ground- and complementary-warp spin, Z2S, S2Z; weft, Z2S
Warp and Weft Count: 44 epi, 20 ppi
Provenance: La Paz, Bolivia, 1/79
Reference: Amy Oakland Rodman, personal communication, 1995.

1992.107.84

226. **Woman's mantle** *(llijlla),* 19th century
Black and multicolored sheep's wool or camelid hair
Woven in warp-faced plain and two-color complementary-warp weaves.
Length: 38 in., 96.5 cm; width: 40 in., 101.6 cm

A large shoulder cloth, two pieces, with solid-colored areas or *pampas* and geometric-, bird-, animal-, and floral-patterned stripes, joined edge to edge. Pink yarn basting in various parts of the outer selvages may have held a commercial cloth fringe in place. Soft, subtle coloring.

Origin: Peru, Puno, Melgar, Ayaviri
Linguistic Affiliation: Quechua/Aymara
Yarn Spin: Ground- and complementary-warp

Cat. no. 222

Cat. no. 225

Cat. no. 228

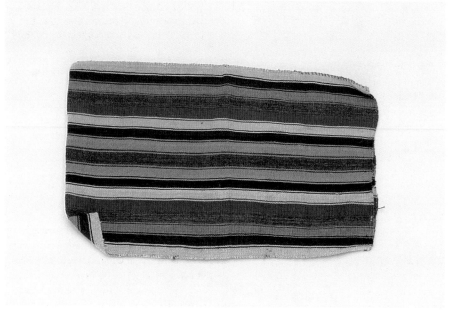

Cat. no. 230

spin, Z2S; weft, Z2S
Warp and Weft Count: 72 epi, 16 ppi
Provenance: Cuzco, Peru, 1/79

1992.107.93

227. **Coca cloth** *(inkuña),* 19th century
Multicolored and *ch'imi* sheep's wool or
camelid hair
Woven in warp-faced plain weave
Length: 21 in., 53.3 cm; width: 22 in.,
55.9 cm

A small cloth, one piece, of solid-colored
stripes with a tubular edge binding on all
outer selvages. This is a smaller version of
a larger coca cloth also from the mountain
region above Acora, see cat. no. *229* (fig. 12).
Beautifully woven piece; subtle changes in
striping, narrow and wide stripes.

Origin: Peru, Puno, Puno, Acora
Linguistic Affiliation: Quechua/Aymara
Yarn Spin: Ground-warp spin, Z2S; weft, Z2S
Warp and Weft Count: 64 epi, 16 ppi
Provenance: La Paz, Bolivia, 5/80

1992.107.66

228. **Woman's mantle** *(wayllas),* 19th century
Black and multicolored sheep's wool or
camelid hair
Woven in warp-faced plain weave
Length: 53⅝ in., 135.6 cm; width: 43½ in.,
110.5 cm

A large, woman's mantle, one piece, with
solid-colored areas or *pampas* and narrow
solid-colored stripes. The striping system is
in a style found in the Acora area near Lake
Titicaca and also on early Taquile pieces.
There are narrow blue stripes on the weft
selvages, and the black *pampas* are a combination of S2Z- and Z2S-spun yarn. This
mantle resembles a *wayllas* published in
Adelson and Tracht (1983) and said to be
used for marriage ceremonies. A similar
wayllas, also with blue stripes on the weft
selvages, is published in Siegel (1991).
Franquemont suggested that this is a
Bolivian textile: The striping is unusual for
Peruvian cloth.

Origin: Peru, Puno, Puno, Acora or Chucuito
Linguistic Affiliation: Quechua/Aymara
Yarn Spin: Ground-warp spin, Z2S, S2Z; weft,
Z2S
Warp and Weft Count: 72 epi, 18 ppi
Provenance: Corrales, New Mexico, 8/84
References: Adelson and Tracht 1983, 90, pl. 25;
Siegel 1991, 84; Ed Franquemont, personal
communication, January 1996

1992.107.95

229. Woman's mantle *(wayllas),* 19th century
See fig. 12, p. 21.
Multicolored and *ch'imi* sheep's wool or
camelid hair
Woven in warp-faced plain weave
Length: 43¼ in., 109.9 cm; width: 44½ in.,
113 cm

A large, woman's mantle, two pieces, of
solid-colored stripes joined edge to edge,
with a three-color tubular edge binding on
all outer selvages. Roger Yorke collected
similar textiles in Acora and established a
geographic classification (1980) for these
striped ones, which were woven in mountains above Acora. Gold yarn, which has a
mottled effect like blue and white *ch'imi,* is
made up of dark yellow and light brown.
Brown and black stripes are S2Z- and Z2S-
spun yarn, creating a herringbone effect.
Tubular edge binding very fine. A soft
hand. Rodman commented that the striping
was reminiscent of pre-Hispanic textiles.
This textile is a larger version of another
inkuña from this region, cat. no. 227.

Origin: Peru, Puno, Puno, Acora, pampa
Linguistic Affiliation: Quechua/Aymara
Yarn Spin: Ground-warp spin, Z2S, S2Z; weft,
Z2S
Warp and Weft Count: 80 epi, 21 ppi
Provenance: Corrales, New Mexico, 1/85
References: Yorke 1980; Amy Oakland Rodman,
personal communication, 1995

1992.107.96

230. Coca bag *(ch'uspa),* 20th century
Multicolored and *ch'imi* camelid hair
Woven in warp-faced plain weave
Length: 13½ in., 34.3 cm; width: 8 in.,
20.3 cm

A medium-size bag, one piece, of solid-
colored stripes, with handsewn sides. It may
be a grain or seed holder, a *wayaka,* from the
altiplano of Puno. The stripes, a combination of wide and narrow stripes, with the
center stripe called the heart (Cereceda
1986), are bilaterally symmetrical from the
center to the weft selvages. (Cereceda has
written extensively on striped Andean
textiles; see also cat. no. 227, 229.) Rodman
commented that the fiber was alpaca in
natural colors.

Origin: Peru, Puno, Puno
Linguistic Affiliation: Quechua/Aymara
Yarn Spin: Ground-warp spin, Z2S; weft, Z2S
Warp and Weft Count: 80 epi, 28 ppi
Provenance: Cuzco, Peru, 1/79
References: Cereceda 1986; Amy Oakland
Rodman, personal communication, 1995

1992.107.38

Cat. no. 231

231. Woman's mantle *(awayu),*
early 20th century
Multicolored sheep's wool or camelid hair
Woven in warp-faced plain and two-color
complementary-warp weaves
Length: 45½ in., 115.6 cm; width: 44½ in.,
113 cm

A large, woman's mantle, two pieces, joined
at the center, of solid-colored and narrow
bird- and geometric-patterned stripes. The
iconography, which includes double-headed
eagles, is similar to that of textiles from the
Juli area. Some of the narrow stripes have
color changes in each warp pair, which
contrast with the solid-colored ones. There
are long termination areas in the complementary-warp weave stripes and an *abrash*
effect in the green and in some brown areas.
A soft hand. Gisbert, Arze, and Cajias
comment on the iconography, mentioning
that images similar to those in this textile
appear in the Baroque architecture of the
zone (1992, photo 173). Franquemont commented that the motifs were similar to other
designs from Lake Titicaca.

Origin: Peru, Puno, Puno
Linguistic Affiliation: Quechua/Aymara
Yarn Spin: Ground- and complementary-warp
spin, Z2S; weft, Z2S
Warp and Weft Count: 60 epi, 16 ppi
Provenance: Cuzco, Peru, 3/81
References: Gisbert, Arze, and Cajias 1992; Ed
Franquemont, personal communication, January
1996

1992.107.56

232. Woman's mantle *(awayu),* 19th century
Purple and multicolored camelid hair
Woven in warp-faced and two-color
complementary-warp weaves
Length: 22 in., 55.9 cm; width: 44½ in.,
113 cm

A large, woman's mantle, two pieces, joined
at the center, of large solid-colored areas or
pampas and narrow geometric-patterned
and solid-colored stripes. There is a tubular
edge binding on all outer selvages and one
red tassel attached to the weft selvage center.
Rodman commented that the textile was
very carefully woven, the yarn evenly spun,
of camelid hair, with a natural dye palette.

Origin: Peru, Puno-Moquegua border
Linguistic Affiliation: Quechua/Aymara
Yarn Spin: Ground- and complementary-warp
spin, Z2S; weft, Z2S
Warp and Weft Count: 80 epi, 28 ppi
Provenance: Corrales, New Mexico, 10/85
Reference: Amy Oakland Rodman, personal
communication, 1995

1992.107.98

233. Sling *(honda),* ca. 1950
Multicolored sheep's wool or camelid hair
Woven in weft-faced tapestry weave
Length: 76½ in., 194.3 cm; width: 2 in.,
5.1 cm

A medium-size sling, one piece, with a
fringed geometric-patterned cradle in the
center and pompoms, and two long, gradu-
ated tubular structures with pompoms, one
with a loop and a pompom at the end,
and the other with a pompom. Men make
these slings, starting with the narrow unit,
building up to the cradle, and tapering
down to the other end. Franquemont
commented that the tubular structures are
three-dimensional, the result of three-color,
four-strand twining, and that the sling is
ceremonial. A similar sling is published in
Cahlander (1980).

Origin: Peru, Puno, Puno
Linguistic Affiliation: Quechua/Aymara
Yarn Spin: Ground-warp spin, Z2S; weft, Z2S
Warp and Weft Count: 12 epi at cradle, 36 ppi
Provenance: Cuzco, Peru, 5/80
References: Cahlander 1980, 11, pl. 1.8; Ed
Franquemont, personal communication,
January 1996

1992.107.6

234. Hat, man's *(chullu),* ca. 1960
Red, blue, and multicolored sheep's wool
Knit: stockinette and garter stitches; color
patterning and intarsia, circular knitting on
straight needles
Length: 16⅜ in., 41.6 cm; width: 9¾ in.,
24.8 cm

A large hat, one piece, in overall floral, bird,
and geometric patterning. There is a knitted
edging on the bottom and a long tassel at
the top. Bands of birds and geometrics alternate with floral and diagonal geometric
motifs, typical of Taquile. An unusual
feature is the absence of ear flaps. Finely
knit. LeCount commented that there is
some zigzag intarsia for color accents, and
the floats are woven in at back. A synthetic
dye palette.

Origin: Peru, Puno, Puno, Lake Titicaca, Taquile
Linguistic Affiliation: Quechua
Yarn Spin: Z2S
Gage: 17 spi
Provenance: Puno, Peru, 2/78

Cat. no. 232

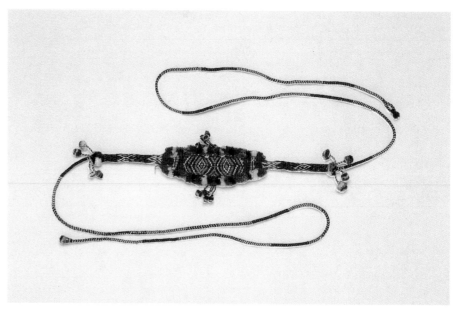

Cat. no. 233

Cat. no. 234

Cat. no. 235

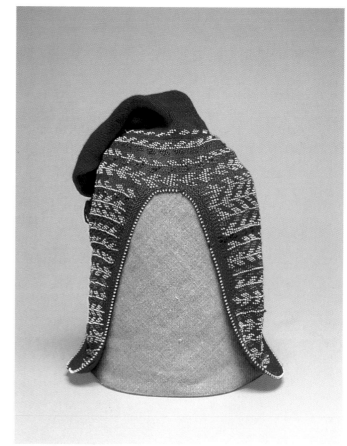

Cat. no. 237

Reference: Cynthia LeCount, personal communication, October 1995

235. Hat, woman's *(chullu)*, ca. 1960

Beige sheep's wool or camelid hair
Knit: stockinette, garter stitches; color patterning and intarsia, circular knitting on straight needles
Length: 13¼ in., 33.7 cm; width: 9 in., 22.9 cm

A large hat, one piece, with a solid-colored area and floral-, bird-, and geometric-patterned stripes. There is a ribbed ruffle on the bottom, with a neck opening, and one tassel on the top. Horizontal bands of floral and diagonal geometrics alternating with bands of birds and other geometric motifs are typical of Taquile. LeCount commented that zigzag intarsia is used for color accents. The ruffle protects the wearer from the sun and is knitted from picked-up stitches at base of hat. All designs have meaning; for example, the hexagonal shape represents the six *suyus* or parts of the island. For a man's hat from Taquile, see cat. no. *234*.

Origin: Peru, Puno, Puno, Lake Titicaca, Taquile
Linguistic Affiliation: Quechua
Yarn Spin: Spin, Z2S
Gage: 15 epi
Provenance: Puno, Peru, 2/78
Reference: Cynthia LeCount, personal communication, October 1995

236. Woman's mantle *(llijlla)*, ca. 1930

Multicolored sheep's wool or camelid hair
Woven in warp-faced plain and two-color complementary-warp weaves
Length: 40 in., 101.6 cm; width: 37¼ in., 94.6 cm

A medium-size mantle, two pieces, of bird- and geometric-patterned and solid-colored stripes, joined edge to edge. Shades of red from dark maroon to red orange and shades of purple and green give a mottled effect. Other colors are bright and vivid.

Origin: Peru, Puno, Puno, Lake Titicaca, Taquile
Linguistic Affiliation: Quechua
Yarn Spin: Ground- and complementary-warp spin, Z2S; weft, Z2S
Warp and Weft Count: 50 epi, 17 ppi
Provenance: Puno, Peru, 2/78

237. Hat *(chullu)*, early 20th century

Dark magenta sheep's wool or camelid hair, multicolored beads
Knit: stockinette, garter stitches; bead knitting; circular knitting on straight needles
Length: 8 in., 20.3 cm; width: 5 in., 12.7 cm

A small hat, one piece, with geometric patterns created by glass seed beads. There are long ear flaps, also edged with glass seed beads, and one tassel stitched onto the hat. The glass seed beads are white and shades of blue, yellow, and green, and show through to the reverse side. An unusual shape. Also see another beaded hat, cat. no. *238*. LeCount, writing about this style of hat (1990), said that beaded hats are worn by women for fiestas and other special occasions; examples like this are rare. She also commented that the edges may have been beaded and, because of dye spots, the hat was possibly dyed or redyed after it was knitted. Similar hats are worn down into the southern Lake Titicaca area in Bolivia.

Origin: Peru, Puno, Puno, Lake Titicaca
Linguistic Affiliation: Quechua/Aymara
Yarn Spin: Spin, Z2S
Gage: 9½ spi
Provenance: Cuzco, Peru, 5/78
References: LeCount 1990, 54; Cynthia LeCount, personal communication, October 1995

Cat. no. 238

Cat. no. 239

238. **Hat** *(chullu),* early 20th century
Green and multicolored sheep's wool or camelid hair, multicolored glass beads
Knit: stockinette and garter stitches; bead knitting; circular knitting on straight needles
Length: 11¼ in., 28.6 cm; width: 8⅝ in., 21.8 cm

A medium-size hat, one piece, with elongated ear flaps, in a rounded-bottom shape edged with glass seed beads and with one tassel at the top. There is a solid-colored area, and the white glass seed beads create images of llamas, birds, and humans. At the top, decreases create ridges. For another beaded hat and comments on this style, see cat. no. 237. LeCount commented that the iconography, which includes a man with an umbrella who is holding hands with a woman with a purse, two llamas and a baby llama, bulls, and lake ducks, is charming. There is an interesting variation on every other duck's wings. This style is no longer made. This example was published in LeCount (1990) and also in *Vogue Knitting* (1989).

Origin: Peru, Puno, Puno, Lake Titicaca
Linguistic Affiliation: Quechua/Aymara
Yarn Spin, Z2S
Gage: 10½ spi
Provenance: Cuzco, Peru, 1/79
References: Erlich 1989, 6; LeCount 1990, 69, pl. 8, bottom row; Cynthia LeCount, personal communication, 1995

1992.107.26

239. **Poncho** *(poncho),* 19th–20th century
Black and beige sheep's wool
Woven in warp-faced plain weave
Length: 60½ in., 153.7 cm; width: 53 in., 134.6 cm

A large poncho, two pieces, in overall stripes, joined edge to edge, with a neck opening. The four corners are turned up and stitched. This style of poncho from Lake Titicaca is illustrated in old photographs and, with only black and beige stripes, is unusual. Two areas of narrow stripes contrast with uniform striping elsewhere.

Origin: Peru, Puno, Puno, Lake Titicaca
Linguistic Affiliation: Quechua/Aymara
Yarn Spin: Ground-warp spin, Z2S; weft, Z2S
Warp and Weft Count: 76 epi, 18 ppi
Provenance: La Paz, Bolivia, 5/84

1992.107.71

240. **Coca or ceremonial cloth** *(inkuña),* 19th century
Multicolored sheep's wool or camelid hair
Woven in warp-faced plain weave
Length: 30¾ in., 78.1 cm; width: 34¼ in., 87 cm

A medium-size cloth, one piece, with large striped areas or *pampas* and narrow, solid-colored stripes. The dotted effect or so-called chain weave is created by the sequencing of colored warps. The cloth has a fine hand.

Origin: Peru, Puno, Puno, Lake Titicaca
Linguistic Affiliation: Quechua
Yarn Spin: Ground-warp spin, Z2S; weft, Z2S
Warp and Weft Count: 80 epi, 20 ppi
Provenance: San Francisco, California, 7/85

1992.107.67

GLOSSARY OF FOREIGN WORDS

Textiles listed in the catalogue raisonné occasionally have names that contradict the definitions listed below. This is inevitable, given the number of hands a textile may have passed through on its way to its home in the museum. For example, a Spanish-speaking store owner in La Paz, Bolivia, may have bought textiles from an Aymara or Quechua speaker without inquiring about the local names and uses of the pieces. When these textiles were sold to an English speaker, they may have been named according to their appearance. Something like this may be the case for the textile listed as cat. no. 48, which is regarded as an Aymara textile, but is identified by the Spanish word, *chalina,* usually meaning scarf, but here meaning little shawl. We do not know the Aymara name for the textile (if it had one), nor whether it was used as a scarf or a shawl or both.

A.: Aymara; C.: Chipaya; Q.: Quechua (Quichua in Ecuador); M.: Mapuche; S.: Spanish; ?: etymology uncertain

abrash (Arabic): Mottled.

agllana (Q.): In Ecuador, to select or choose; a textile technique whereby certain yarns are picked up to create a pattern. The root is the same as that of *akllakuna,* below.

akllakuna (Q.): Chosen women; women who were selected by the Inca state to spin and weave for the Sun and the state, and who were given as wives to nobility, taken as secondary wives by the Inca, or sometimes sacrificed.

aksu (Q.): In Inca times, a rectangular cotton or camelid-fiber garment, usually made from two four-selvage pieces sewn together and worn by a female wrapped round her body, held up by a stickpin at each shoulder, and tied shut by a belt at her waist. Today, especially in Bolivia, the *aksu* is much smaller, made of sheep's wool or synthetic or camelid fiber, and does not entirely cover the body, but is worn over an *almilla.*

alforja (S.): Saddlebag.

ali pacha (Q.): Good cloth, referring to finely spun and well-woven textiles.

allwi masi (Q.): Warping partners.

almilla (S.): Tailored dress adopted by indigenous women after the Spanish conquest and usually made from bayeta.

altiplano (S.): High plain; the Lake Titicaca basin and high plains in Bolivia.

anaku (Q.): The term used for *aksu* in Ecuador where *anakus,* worn by most younger women, are not full-body coverings, but wrap skirts or tubular skirts worn over a blouse, sweater, T-shirt, or blouse-and-slip combination.

awayu (A.): Woman's square or rectangular mantle, usually made from two four-selvage pieces sewn together, although some *awayus* from the Lake Titicaca area are made from three pieces and some from one. *Awayu* is derived from *awa-,* the Quechua root for weave. *Awayus* are sometimes used by women to haul bundles on their backs.

Aya Uma (Q.): Name of a native spirit; refers to a two-faced cloth mask (spirit head) worn in Imbabura and Pichincha provinces, Ecuador, for the fiestas of San Juan and San Pedro.

baita (S.): Derived from *bayeta;* in Ecuador, refers to a woman's mantle made from a rectangular piece of cloth.

bayeta (S.): Plain-weave wool yardage woven on the treadle loom.

bufanda (S.): Scarf; this term has been borrowed by Aymara speakers as *ufanta*.

Callawaya (Q.) or **Qollahuaya** (A.): Itinerant healers from the Charazani region of Bolivia.

capacho (S.): A medium-sized woven bag, usually used to hold food.

capote (S.): Cloak.

chalina (S.): Little shawl.

chamal or chemal (M.): Rectangular woven cloth worn by men wrapped around the body from the chest or waist down, and secured with a belt.

chapuna (Q.): A small wooden tool used in the Tarabuco region of Bolivia to help change sheds during weaving. The term is derived from the Aymara verb, *chapuña,* meaning to hit someone with great force, usually in the chest.

chaska (Q.): Star.

chemal (M.): See *chamal.*

chilli (Q.): Something frayed and ragged.

ch'imi (A.): Two or more yarns, each a different color, plied together to create a shimmering effect.

chullu (Q.): Knit hat.

chumpi (Q.): Belt, usually with four selvages; *chumbi* in Quichua.

ch'unchus (Q.): Jungle-dwelling *indígenas;* a highland term with connotations of disparagement; a people regarded by the highlanders as, unlike themselves, uncivilized savages.

ch'uspa (Q.): Small, four-selvage bag used to hold coca leaves.

fachalina (Q.): Woman's mantle (see *awayu*). In Ecuador, fachalinas are often made from one piece of treadle-loom woven or commercially manufactured cloth.

frazada (S.): Blanket.

fullu (A.): Blanket; but also refers to a man's or perhaps a woman's mantle worn over the usual mantle as an extra covering (see *llakuta*).

guantes (S.): Gloves.

hacienda (S.): Large agricultural landholding; a term usually used of property owned by non-*indígenas.*

haykakusisan-sisan (Q.): A stage in the development of a fruit.

hilacata (A.): Headman.

honda (S.): Sling.

ikat (Malay): A dyeing technique whereby the warp or weft yarns are wrapped with a resist and dyed before the textile is woven.

ikulla (M.) or **kepam** (M.): A long, rectangular woven cloth tied over one shoulder; worn by women.

indígena (S.): Indigenous person, native South American.

inkuña (A., Q.): Small, four-selvage cloth used to hold coca leaves or food; used in ritual offerings to the earth or other deities.

intarsia: A flat-knitting technique in which separate color sections are knit in a single row.

ira (C.): Tunic worn by men of the Chipaya ethnic group in Bolivia (see *kushma*).

isallu or **iskallu** (A.): Woman's mantle (see *awayu*).

iskallu (A.): See *isallu.*

iskayu (A.): Alternative spelling of *iskallu.*

kancha (Q.): Courtyard.

kepam (M.): See *ikulla.*

kero (Q.): Wooden drinking vessel.

khawa (A.): Man's tunic (see *kushma*).

kipu (Q.): Knotted cords used by the Incas as mnemonic devices to keep records.

kushma (Q.): Man's tunic made of one four-selvage piece of cloth with a slit woven for the neck hole, then folded in half and sewn partway up the sides, with slits left for armholes. Some *kushmas* are made of two strips of cloth, joined edge to edge, rather than from one piece. In highland Ecuador, the *kushma* is wrapped with a belt and, in some communities, does not have side seams.

lipi (A.): Extremely fine double-faced cloth.

llakuta (Q.): Man's mantle, usually made of one large, rectangular, four-selvage piece of cloth. The *llakuta* and *unku* were outlawed by the Spanish after the great Andean uprisings in the 1780s.

llautu (Q.): In Inca times, a man's headdress consisting of a woven band or braid wound around the head; outlawed by the Spanish as a sign of Inca nationalism after the colonial uprisings.

llijlla (Q.): Woman's mantle (see *awayu*).

lluchu 1. (Q.): Skinned, naked, unclothed; used by *indígenas* in Ecuador to refer to whites and mestizos who do not wear traditional indigenous dress. 2. (A.): Knit hat; a reversal of the syllables of *chullu* (Q.): knit hat.

lluq'i (Q.): Backward-spun yarn.

luto (S.): Mourning.

mayu k'inku (Q.): Meandering river.

mesa (S.): Table; also refers to an offering placed on a cloth.

monedero (S.): Knit coin purse.

montera (S.): Felted brimmed hat; in Tarabuco, Bolivia, *montera* refers to leather helmets probably copied from those worn by Basque shepherds.

ñawi (Q.): Eye.

nogal (S.): Walnut.

pallay (Q.): See *agllana.*

pampa (Q.): Plains or level ground; this often refers to the plain-weave sections of four-selvage cloth.

paño (S.): *Ikat* shawl with macramé fringe made and worn in Azuay, Ecuador.

pica pica (S.): Pike, referring to knitted scallops.

ponchito (S.): Little poncho.

poncho (?, possibly Mapuche): A man's garment usually made of two four-selvage pieces of cloth joined together and with a slit left for the head. Strip ponchos are made of a number of narrow strips of cloth sewn together.

poncho capote (S.): Festival poncho.

q'ara (Q.): Naked, uncultured, uncivilized; used by *indígenas* in Peru to refer to whites and mestizos who do not wear traditional indigenous dress.

Qollahuaya (A.): See *Callawaya*.

qumpi (Q.): In Inca times, the highest grade of cloth, usually weft-faced tapestry weave, but also possibly fine, double-faced cloth.

santo (S.): Saint.

Sendero Luminoso (S.): Shining Path; Peruvian Maoist guerilla group.

suyu (Q.): Sector; Tawantinsuyu, the Four Sectors, was the name the Incas gave their empire.

tari (A.): See *inkuña*.

tinku (Q.): Encounter; often refers to ritual battles between two moieties or halves of a community.

t'iqulla (Q.): Ceremonial carrying cloth.

t'isnu (A.): Small band, braid tie.

trarihue (M.): Belt.

traruchiripa (M.): Belt.

tulma (Q., A.): Tassel, braid tie.

tupu (Q.): Stickpin, used to pin a woman's mantle across her chest.

ufanta (A.): See *bufanda*.

unilla (Q.): Small pockets on knitted purses. This term is related to the Quichua word *uñita,* which refers to little woven pockets on coca bags from the Tarabuco region, in Bolivia. *Una* means a nursing baby animal or human, and the little pockets are considered the babies of the bag to which they are attached.

unku (Q.): Man's tunic (see *kushma*). In Tarabuco, Bolivia, the *unku,* with no side seams, has been reduced in size so that it covers only the upper chest.

unkuña (Q.): See *inkuña*.

urku (A., Q.): A four selvage skirt gathered at the waist and worn by women. *Urku* is the Quechua word for mountain, and these skirts look like small mountains.

wak'a (A.): Woman's belt, usually four-selvage.

wallas or **wayllas** (A.): In earlier eras, a man's mantle. It is an archaic garment today worn only for weddings in a few communities. In some communities the word also refers to a woman's one-piece mantle.

wara (Q.): Loincloth; outlawed by the Spanish after the colonial uprisings.

waraka (Q.): Sling.

wata or **watana** (Q.): Tie, braid tie.

wayallas (A.): See *wallas*.

wayaka (A.): Small, striped, four-selvage bag used to hold seeds.

wichi wichi (A.): Decorative sling or cords with tassels; used in dances.

wincha (A.): Headband.

winchucas (?): Man's knitted leggings.

REFERENCES AND WORKS CONSULTED

Ackerman, Raquel. 1996 [1991]. "Clothes and Identity in the Central Andes: Province of Abancay, Peru." In *Textile Traditions of Mesoamerica and the Andes: An Anthology,* edited by Margot Blum Schevill, Janet Catherine Berlo, and Edward B. Dwyer, 231–60. Austin, Tex.: University of Texas Press.

Adelson, Laurie, and Bruce Takami. 1978. *Weaving Traditions of Highland Bolivia.* Los Angeles: Craft and Folk Art Museum.

Adelson, Laurie, and Arthur Tracht. 1983. *Aymara Weavings: Ceremonial Textiles of Colonial and 19th Century Bolivia.* Washington, D.C.: Smithsonian Institution.

Arriaga, Pablo José de. 1968 [1621]. *The Extirpation of Idolatry in Peru.* Translated and edited by L. Clark Keating. Lexington, Ky.: University of Kentucky Press.

Bastien, Joseph W. 1985 [1978]. *Mountain of the Condor: Metaphor and Ritual in an Andean Ayllu.* Prospect Heights, Ill.: Waveland Press.

Berenguer, José, and Percy Dauelsberg. 1989. "El norte grande en la orbita de Tiwanaku." In *Culturas de Chile, Prehistoria, Desde sus origenes hasta los albores de la conquista.* Edited by J. Hidalgo L., V. Schiappacasse F., H. Niemeyer F., C. Aldunate del S., and I. Solimano R., 129–80. Santiago, Chile: Editorial Andres Bello.

Bertonio, Ludovico. 1984 [1612]. *Vocabvlario de la lengva Aymara.* Facsimile edition. Cochabamba, Bolivia: Ediciones CERES.

Bird, Junius. 1946. "The Cultural Sequence of the Northern Chilean Coast." In *Handbook of South American Indians.* Edited by Julian Steward. Vol. 2: 587–94. Washington, D.C.: Smithsonian Institution, Bureau of American Ethnology.

Bird, Junius, John Hyslop, and Milica Skinner. 1985. "The Preceramic Excavations at the Huaca Prieta, Chicama Valley, Peru." *Anthropological Papers* (New York: American Museum of Natural History) 62, no. 1: 260–93.

Bird, Junius, and Joy Mahler. 1952. "America's Oldest Cotton Fabrics." *American Fabrics,* no. 20 (Winter 1951–1952): 73–79.

Birren, Faber. 1961. *Creative Color.* New York: Van Nostrand Reinhold.

Bordieu, Pierre. 1977. *Outline of a Theory of Practice.* Cambridge: Cambridge University Press.

Bruce, Susan Lee. 1986. "Textile Miniatures from Pacatnamú, Peru." In *The Junius B. Bird Conference on Andean Textiles.* Edited by Ann Pollard Rowe, 183–204. Washington, D.C.: The Textile Museum.

Cahlander, Adele, Marjorie Cason, and Ann Houston. 1978. *Bolivian Tubular Edging and Crossed-Warp Techniques.* Monograph 1. Boulder, Colo.: The Weaver's Journal.

Cahlander, Adele, Elayne Zorn, and Ann Pollard Rowe. 1980. *Sling Braiding of the Andes.* Boulder, Colo.: Colorado Fiber Center.

Carpenter, Lawrence K. 1982. Ecuadorian Quichua: Descriptive Sketch and Variation. Ph.D. diss. University of Florida, Gainesville.

Cason, Marjorie, and Adele Cahlander. 1976. *The Art of Bolivian Highland Weaving.* New York: Watson-Guptill.

Cereceda, Veronica. 1986. "The Semiology of Andean Textiles: The Talegas of Isluga." In *The Anthropological History of Andean Polities.* Edited by John Murra, Nathan Wachtel, and Jacques Revel, 149–73. Cambridge, Mass.: Cambridge University Press.

Clark, Niki R. 1993. The Estuquiña Textile Tradition: Cultural Patterning in Late Prehistoric Fabrics, Moquegua, Far Southern Peru. Ph.D. diss. Washington University, St. Louis.

Clark, Niki R., and Amy Oakland Rodman. 1995. "Ancient Andean Headgear: Medium and Measure of Cultural Identity." In *Contact, Crossover, and Continuity: Proceedings of the Fourth Biennial Symposium of the Textile Society of America,* 293–304. Los Angeles, Calif.: Textile Society of America.

Cobo, Father Bernabe. 1979 [1653]. *History of the Inca Empire.* Translated and edited by Roland Hamilton. Austin, Tex.: University of Texas Press.

Cohen, John. 1980. *Peruvian Weaving: A Continuous Warp for 5,000 Years.* VHS. 25 min. Center for Media and Independent Learning, Berkeley, Calif.

Collier, George A., Rosa Mendoza de Rick, and Steve Berger. 1981. "Aymara Weavings from Highland Bolivia." Stanford, Calif.: Stanford University Museum of Art. Unpublished.

Dauelsberg, Percy. 1963. "Complejo Faldas del Morro." In *Actas del Encuentro Internacional de Arquelogia de San Pedro de Atacama,* 33–50. Antofagasta, Chile: Universdad del Norte.

_____. 1974. "Excavaciones arqueológicas en Quiani." *Revista Chungara* (Arica, Chile) no. 4: 7–38.

_____. 1985. "Faldas del Morro: fase cultural agro-alfarera temprana." *Revista Chungara* (Arica, Chile) no. 14: 7–44.

De Lucca D., Manuel. 1983. *Diccionario Aymara-Castellano, Castellano-Aymara.* La Paz, Bolivia: Comisión de Alfabetización y Literatura en Aymara (CALA).

Desrosiers, Sophie. 1986. "An Interpretation of Technical Weaving Data Found in an Early 17th-Century Chronicle." In *The Junius B. Bird Conference on Andean Textiles.* Edited by Ann Pollard Rowe, 219–41. Washington, D.C.: The Textile Museum.

Doyon-Bernard, Suzette. 1990. "From Twining to Triple Cloth: Experimentation and Innovation in Ancient Peruvian Weaving (ca. 5000–400 B.C.)." *American Antiquity* 55: 68–87.

Dransart, Penny. 1991. "Llamas, herders and the exploitation of raw materials in the Atacama Desert." *World Archaeology* 22, no. 3: 304–19.

Emery, Irene. 1966. *The Primary Structure of Fabrics: An Illustrated Classification.* Washington, D.C.: The Textile Museum.

Femenias, Blenda. 1987. Introduction to *Andean Aesthetics: Textiles of Peru and Bolivia.* Edited by Blenda Femenias, 1–8. Madison, Wisc.: University of Wisconsin-Madison, Elvehjem Museum of Art.

_____. 1995. "Ethnic Artists and the Appropriation of Fashion: Embroidery and Identity in the Colca Valley, Peru." In *Contact, Crossover, and Continuity: Proceedings of the Fourth Biennial Symposium of the Textile Society of America,* 331–42. Los Angeles, Calif.: Textile Society of America.

Flores Huatta, Alejandro, and Paula Quispe Cruz. 1994. "Preserving Our Culture." In *All Roads Are Good: Native Voices on Life and Culture.* Edited by Terence Winch, 166–75. Washington, D.C.: Smithsonian Institution Press; National Museum of the American Indian.

Frame, Mary. 1986. "The Visual Images of Fabric Structures in Ancient Peruvian Art." In *The Junius B. Bird Conference on Andean Textiles.* Edited by Ann Pollard Rowe, 47–80. Washington, D.C.: The Textile Museum.

Franquemont, Christine R. 1986. "Chinchero Pallays: An Ethnic Code." In *The Junius B. Bird Conference on Andean Textiles.* Edited by Ann Pollard Rowe, 331–38. Washington, D. C.: The Textile Museum.

Franquemont, Christine, and Edward Franquemont. 1978. "Report on Textile Production in the Vicinity of Lircay, Huancavelica, Peru." Study for Cia. de Minas Buenaventura, Lima, Peru.

_____. 1988. "Learning to Weave in Chinchero." *The Textile Museum Journal* 26: 55–78.

Franquemont, Edward M. 1986a. "Cloth Production Rates in Chinchero, Peru." In *The Junius B. Bird Conference on Andean Textiles.* Edited by Ann Pollard Rowe, 309–30. Washington, D.C.: The Textile Musuem.

_____. 1986b. "Threads of Time: Andean Cloth and Costume." In *Costume as Communication,* by Margot Blum Schevill, 81–91. Bristol, R.I.: Brown University, Haffenreffer Museum of Anthropology.

Girault, Louis. 1969. *Textiles Boliviens: Région de Charazani.* Paris: Catalogues du Musée de L'Homme.

Gisbert, Teresa, Silvia Arze, and Martha Cajias. 1992. *Arte textil y mundo andino.* Buenos Aires, Argentina: Tipográfica editora Argentina.

Goodell, Grace. 1968. "A Study of Andean Spinning in the Cuzco Region." *The Textile Museum Journal* 2, no. 3: 2–8.

Green, Judith S. 1970. *Peruvian Embroidery.* Ethnic Technology Notes, no. 5. San Diego, Calif.: San Diego Museum of Man.

Karp, Ivan, and Steven D. Lavine, ed. 1991. *Exhibiting Cultures: The Poetics and Politics of Museum Display.* Washington, D.C.: Smithsonian Institution Press.

Karp, Ivan, Christine Mullen Kreamer, and Steven D. Lavine, ed. 1992. *Museums and Communities: The Politics of Public Culture.* Washington, D.C.: Smithsonian Institution Press.

King, Mary Elizabeth. 1978. "Analytical Methods and Prehistoric Textiles." *American Antiquity* 43: 89–96.

LeCount, Cynthia Gravelle. 1990. *Andean Folk Knitting: Traditions and Techniques from Peru and Bolivia.* Saint Paul, Minn.: Dos Tejedoras Fiber Arts Publications.

Mannheim, Bruce. 1991. *The Language of the Inka Since the European Invasion.* Austin, Tex.: University of Texas Press.

_____. 1992. "The Inka Language in the Colonial World." *Colonial Latin American Review* 1, no. 1–2: 79–107.

Medlin, Mary Ann. 1996 [1991]. "Ethnic Dress and Calcha Festivals, Bolivia." In *Textile Traditions of Mesoamerica and the Andes: An Anthology.* Edited by Margot Blum Schevill, Janet Catherine Berlo, and Edward B. Dwyer, 261–79. Austin, Tex.: University of Texas Press.

Meisch, Lynn. 1980a. "The Cañari People: Their Costume and Weaving." *El Palacio (Museum of New Mexico Quarterly)* 86, no. 3 (Fall): 15–26.

_____. 1980b. "Spinning in Ecuador." *Spin Off* 4: 24–29.

_____. 1981. "Costume and Weaving in Saraguro, Ecuador." *The Textile Museum Journal* 19–20 (1980–1981): 55–64.

_____. 1986a. "Spinning in Bolivia." *Spin Off* X, no. 1 (Spring): 25–29.

_____. 1986b. "Weaving Styles in Tarabuco, Bolivia." In *The Junius B. Bird Conference on Andean Textiles.* Edited by Ann Pollard Rowe, 243–74. Washington, D. C.: The Textile Museum.

_____. 1987a. "The Living Textiles of Tarabuco, Bolivia." In *Andean Aesthetics: Textiles of Peru and Bolivia.* Edited by Blenda Femenias, 46–59. Madison, Wisc.: University of Wisconsin-Madison, Elvehjem Museum of Art.

_____. 1987b. *Otavalo: Weaving, Costume, and the Market* Quito: Ediciones Libri Mundi.

_____. 1996 [1991]. "We Are Sons of Atahualpa and We Will Win: Traditional Dress in Otavalo and Saraguro, Ecuador." In *Textile Traditions of Mesoamerica and the Andes: An Anthology.* Edited by Margot Blum Schevill, Janet Catherine Berlo, and Edward B. Dwyer, 145–78. Austin, Tex.: University of Texas Press.

Meisch, Lynn A., and Ann Pollard Rowe. In press. Introduction to *Contemporary Indigenous Costume of Highland Ecuador.* Edited by Ann Pollard Rowe, with text by Lynn A. Meisch, Laura M. Miller, Ann Pollard Rowe, and others. Seattle, Wash.: University of Washington Press; Washington, D.C.: The Textile Museum.

Messenger, Phyllis Mauch, ed. 1989. *The Ethics of Collecting Cultural Property: Whose Culture? Whose Property?* Albuquerque, N. Mex.: University of New Mexico Press.

Miller, Laura Martin. 1996 [1991]. "The Ikat Shawl Traditions of Northern Peru and Southern Ecuador." In *Textile Traditions from Mesoamerica and the Andes: An Anthology.* Edited by Margot Blum Schevill, Janet Catherine Berlo, and Edward B. Dwyer, 337–58. Austin, Tex.: University of Texas Press.

Miracle, Andrew W., Jr., and Juan de Dios Yapita Maya. 1981. "Time and Space in Aymara." In *The Aymara Language in Its Social and Cultural Context.* Edited by M. J. Hardman, 35–56. Gainesville, Fla.: University of Florida Press.

Muñoz, Ivan. 1989. "El periodo formativo en el norte grande (1.000 a.C. a 500 d.C.). In *Culturas de Chile: Prehistoria; Desde sus origenes hasta los albores de la conquista.* Edited by J. Hidalgo L., V. Schiappacasse F., H. Niemeyer F., C. Aldunate del S., and I. Solimano R., 107–28. Santiago, Chile: Editorial Andres Bello.

Murra, John V. 1962. "Cloth and Its Function in the Inca State." *American Anthropologist* 64, no. 4: 710–28.

_____. 1982. "The Mit'a Obligations of Ethnic Groups to the Inka State." In *The Inca and Aztec States 1400–1800:* Anthropology and History. Edited by George A. Collier, Renato I. Rosaldo, and John D. Wirth, 237–62. New York and London: Academic Press.

Nardi J., Ricardo L. Saugy, and Catalina Saugy. 1982. *Cultura Mapuche en la rgentina: en recuerdo de Susan Chertudi. Buenos Aires.* Argentina: Marcos Victor Durruty.

Nuñez, Lautaro. 1989. "Hacia la produccion de alimentos y la vida sedentaria (5.000 a.C. a 900 d.C.)." In *Culturas de Chile: Prehistoria; Desde sus origenes hasta los albores de la conquista.* Edited by J. Hidalgo L., V. Schiappacasse F., H. Niemeyer F., C. Aldunate del S., and I. Solimano R., 81–105. Santiago, Chile: Editorial Andres Bello.

Oakland, Amy. 1982. "Pre-Columbian Spinning and *Lloq'e* Yarn: An Ethnographic Analogy." *Andean Perspectives Newsletter* (Institute of Latin American Studies and Department of Anthropology, University of Texas at Austin), no. 4 (Fall).

_____. 1986a. "Tiwanaku Textile Style from the South Central Andes, Bolivia and North Chile." Ph.D. diss. University of Texas, Austin.

_____. 1986b. "Tiwanaku Tapestry Tunics and Mantles from San Pedro de Atacama." In *The Junius B. Bird Conference on Andean Textiles.* Edited by Ann Pollard Rowe, 101–21. Washington, D.C.: The Textile Museum.

Price, Sally. 1989. *Primitive Art in Civilized Places.* Chicago: University of Chicago Press.

Prochaska, Rita. 1988. *Taquile: Weavers of a Magic World.* Lima, Peru: Arius.

Quispe Fernández, Bonifacia, and Tomas Hunaca Laura. 1994. "Aymara Traditions." In *All Roads Are Good: Native Voices on Life and Culture.* Edited by Terence Winch, 146–55. Washington, D.C.: Smithsonian Institution Press; National Museum of the American Indian.

Rivera, Mario. 1991. "The Prehistory of Northern Chile: A Synthesis." *Journal of World Prehistory* 5: 1–47.

Rodman, Amy Oakland. 1992a. "Textiles and Ethnicity: Tiwanaku in San Pedro de Atacama, North Chile." *Latin American Antiquity* 3, no. 4: 316–40.

_____. 1992b. "The Women of Coyo: Tradition and Innovation in Andean Prehistory, San Pedro de Atacama, North Chile (A.D. 500–900). In *Textiles in Daily Life, Proceedings of the Third Biennial Symposium of the Textile Society of America,* 61-72. Seattle, Wash.: Textile Society of America.

Rodman, Amy Oakland, and Vicki Cassman. 1995. "Andean Tapestry: Structure Informs the Surface." In *Art Journal* 54, no. 2 (Summer): 33–39.

Rodman, Amy Oakland, and Delbert True. n.d. "Caserones in Tarapacá: A Re-evaluation." Unpublished.

Rolandi de Perrot, Diana S., and Dora Jiménez de Pupareli. 1983–1985. "La tejeduría tradicional de la puna argentino-boliviana." In *Cuadernos del Instituto Nacional de Antropología* (Buenos Aires, Argentina: Instituto Nacional de Antropología) 10: 205–89.

Rowe, Ann Pollard. 1977. *Warp-Patterned Weaves of the Andes.* Washington, D.C.: The Textile Museum.

_____. 1978. "Technical Features of Inca Tapestry Tunics." *The Textile Museum Journal* 17: 5–28.

_____. 1984. *Costumes and Featherwork of the Lords of Chimor: Textiles From Peru's North Coast.* Washington, D.C.: The Textile Museum.

Rowe, John Howland. 1979. "Standardization in Inca Tapestry Tunics." In *The Junius B. Bird Pre-Columbian Textile Conference.* Edited by Ann Pollard Rowe and Elizabeth P. Benson, 239–64. Washington, D.C.: The Textile Museum; Dumbarton Oaks, Trustees for Harvard University.

Saltzman, Max. 1986. "Analysis of Dyes in Museum Textiles or, You Cannot Tell a Dye by its Color." In *Textile Conservation Symposium in Honor of Pat Reeves.* Edited by C. C. McLean and P. Connell, 27–39. Los Angeles: Los Angeles County Museum of Art.

Schevill, Margot Blum. 1986. *Costume as Communication.* Bristol, R.I.: Brown University, Haffenreffer Museum of Anthropology.

Seibold, Katharine. 1992. "Textiles and Cosmology in Choquecancha, Cuzco, Peru." In *Andean Cosmologies through Time: Persistence and Emergence.* Edited by Robert V. H. Dover, Katharine E. Seibold, and John H. McDowell, 166–201. Bloomington and Indianapolis, Ind.: Indiana University Press.

_____. 1995. "Dressing the Part: Indigenous Costume as Political and Cultural Discourse in Peru." In *Contact, Crossover, and Continuity: Proceedings of the Fourth Biennial Symposium of the Textile Society of America,* 319–30. Los Angeles, Calif.: Textile Society of America.

Siegel, William. 1991. *Historic Aymara Textiles.* Krefeld, Germany: German Textile Museum, Krefeld.

Southon, John, Amy Oakland Rodman, and Delbert True. 1995. "A Comparison of Marine and Terrestrial Radiocarbon Ages from Northern Chile." *Radiocarbon* 37, no. 2: 389–93.

Stocking, George W., Jr., ed. 1985. *Objects and Others: Essays on Museums and Material Culture.* Madison, Wisc.: University of Wisconsin Press.

Taullard, Afredo. 1949. *Tejidos y ponchos indígenas de sudamérica.* Buenos Aires, Argentina: Guillermo Kraft Limitada.

True, Delbert, and Lautaro Nuñez. 1971. "Modeled Anthropomorphic Figurines from Northern Chile." *Ñawpa Pacha* (Institute of Andean Studies, Berkeley, Calif.) 9: 65-86.

True, Delbert, and Harvey Crew. 1980. "Archaeological Investigation in Northern Chile: Tarapaca 2A." In *Prehistoric Trails of Atacama: Archaeology of Northern Chile.* Edited by C. Meighan and D. True, 59–90. Los Angeles, Calif.: University of California Press.

Ulloa, Liliana. 1974. "Analisis del Material Textil Sitios: Chinchorro, Quiani, Camarones-15, PLM 7, Faldas el Morro y Alto Ramírez, en Aspectos sobre Desarrollo Tecnológico en el Proceso de Agriculturización en Norte Pre-Hispano." *Revista Chungara* (Arica, Chile) no. 3: 96–103.

_____. 1982. "Estilos decorativos y formas textiles de poblaciones agromaritimas en el extremo norte de Chile." *Revista Chungara* (Arica, Chile) no. 8: 109–36.

Vergo, Peter, ed. 1989. *The New Museology.* London: Reaktion Books.

Vogue Knitting magazine. 1989. *Vogue Knitting: The Ultimate Knitting Book.* New York: Random House.

Vreeland, James. 1986. "Cotton Spinning and Processing on the Peruvian North Coast." In *The Junius B. Bird Conference on Andean Textiles.* Edited by Ann Pollard Rowe, 363–83. Washington, D.C.: The Textile Museum.

Wallert, Ari, and Ran Boytner. Forthcoming. "Dyes from the Tumilaca and Chiribaya Cultures, South Coast of Peru." *Journal of Archaeological Science.*

Wasserman, Tamara E., and Jonathan S. Hill. 1981. *Bolivian Indian Textiles.* New York: Dover.

Weismantel, Mary. 1988. *Food, Gender, and Poverty in the Ecuadorian Andes.* Philadelphia, Pa.: University of Pennsylvania Press.

Wilson, Lee Anne. 1996 [1991]. "Nature Versus Culture: The Image of the Uncivilized Wild-Man in Textiles from the Department of Cuzco, Peru." In *Textile Traditions of Mesoamerica and the Andes: An Anthology,* edited by Margot Blum Schevill, Janet Catherine Berlo, and Edward B. Dwyer, 205–30. Austin, Tex.: University of Texas Press.

Yorke, Roger. 1980. *Woven Images: Bolivian Weaving from the 19th and 20th Centuries.* Halifax, Nova Scotia: Dalhousie Art Gallery.

Zorn, Elayne. 1986. "Textiles in Herders' Ritual Bundles of Macusani, Peru." In *The Junius B. Bird Conference on Andean Textiles.* Edited by Ann Pollard Rowe, 289–307. Washington, D. C.: The Textile Museum.

_____. 1995. "(Re-)Fashioning Identity: Late Twentieth-Century Transformations in Dress and Society in Bolivia." In *Contact, Crossover, and Continuity: Proceedings of the Fourth Biennial Symposium of the Textile Society of America,* 343–54. Los Angeles, Calif.: Textile Society of America.

About the Authors

BARBARA ARTHUR is a fiber artist and educator who has studied weaving with Nancy Welch, Kay Sekimachi, Emily Dubois, Janice Sullivan, and Ed Franquemont. She assisted Margot Blum Schevill in cataloguing the Appleby collection.

ED FRANQUEMONT is an archaeologist, anthropologist, and weaver and fiber artist who has worked in the Andes for more than thirty years. Since 1977 he has been conducting studies of the textile traditions of contemporary Inca peoples: How weavers learn and think, what cloth and patterns mean, and the economic and social role of cloth in Andean society. Ed is currently affiliated with the Institute of Andean Studies, Berkeley, California.

LYNN A. MEISCH first traveled in Colombia, Ecuador, Peru, and Bolivia in 1973–1974, studying textiles. Numerous fellowships allowed her to continue her field research, which culminated in various books and articles on Andean textiles and a doctorate in anthropology from Stanford University. Lynn combines her love of the Andean countries and people and her interest in their textile traditions by returning each summer, frequently leading adventure-travel treks or textile tours.

AMY OAKLAND RODMAN first encountered Andean textiles during a visit to Lima and Machu Picchu in 1974. She lived in La Paz, Bolivia, from 1983 to 1989, and conducted field research on archaeological textiles in both Bolivia and Chile. Currently she is completing a monograph on a collection of pre-Columbian Peruvian coastal textiles in the Phoebe Hearst Museum of Anthropology, University of California, Berkeley. She teaches art history at California State University, Hayward, California.

MARGOT BLUM SCHEVILL was guest curator for the Appleby Andean textile project, responsible for cataloguing the collection. Among her books on ethnographic textiles are *Costume as Communication: Ethnographic Costumes and Textiles from Middle America and the Central Andes of South America* (1986) and *Maya Textiles of Guatemala* (1993). In addition, she co-edited *Textile Traditions of Mesoamerica and the Andes: An Anthology* (1996 [1991]) and contributed a chapter to *The Maya Textile Tradition* (1997). Currently she is a research associate at the Phoebe Hearst Museum of Anthropology, University of California, Berkeley, California.

INDEX

Traditional Textiles of the Andes: Life and Cloth in the Highlands
was produced by the Publications Department of the Fine Arts Museums of San Francisco.

Ann Heath Karlstrom, Director of Publications and Graphic Design
Karen Kevorkian, Managing Editor

Book design by Robin Weiss Graphic Design, San Carlos, California
Photography of objects by Joseph McDonald, Fine Arts Museums of San Francisco
Copyediting by Frances Bowles, Orinda, California
Type composed on a Macintosh Quadra in Granjon
Printed in Italy by Milanostampa, Farigliano